Exploring
the Spirituality of
the World Religions

Also available from Continuum:

Exploring the Spirituality of the World Religions

The Quest for Personal, Spiritual and Social Transformation

Duncan S. Ferguson

continuum

Continuum International Publishing Group

The Tower Building	80 Maiden Lane
11 York Road	Suite 704
London SE1 7NX	New York, NY 10038

www.continuumbooks.com

British Library Cataloguing-in-Publication Data
A catalogue record for this book is available from the British Library.

ISBN: HB: 978-1-4411-8737-6
       PB: 978-1-4411-4645-8

Library of Congress Cataloging-in-Publication Data
Ferguson, Duncan S. (Duncan Sheldon), 1937–
  Exploring the spiritualities of the world religions : the quest for
  personal, spiritual and social transformation / Duncan S. Ferguson.
       p. cm.
  Includes index.
  ISBN: 978-1-4411-8737-6
  ISBN: 978-1-4411-4645-8
  1. Religions. I. Title.

BL85.F47 2010
204–dc22
                                                    2010005015

Typeset by Newgen Imaging Systems Pvt Ltd, Chennai, India
Printed and bound in Great Britain by CPI Antony Rowe Ltd,
Chippenham, Wiltshire

*This modest volume is dedicated to my former and
current students who have taught me more
than I could ever teach them.
It is dedicated in particular to my students at Eckerd College who
endured a course with much of this material as its content.
They were patient and kind.*

Contents

Preface   ix

Part I   THE CONTENT AND APPROACH TO THE STUDY OF SPIRITUALITY

1 The Spiritual Quest   3

Part II   THE SPIRITUAL PATHWAYS ROOTED IN NATURE AND CULTURE

2 Indigenous Wisdom Traditions   23

3 Classical Expressions of Culture-Based Religions   41

4 Current Expressions of Nature/Culture Religion   59

Part III   THE SPIRITUAL PATHWAYS OF TRANSCENDENT MONISM

5 Spiritual Pathways Within Hinduism   81

6 Spiritual Pathways Within Buddhism   100

7 Spiritual Pathways Within Confucianism and Taoism   118

Part IV   THE SPIRITUAL PATHWAYS OF THE ABRAHAMIC MONOTHEISTIC RELIGIONS

8 Spiritual Pathways Within Judaism   139

9 Spiritual Pathways Within Christianity   159

10 Spiritual Pathways Within Islam   177

Part V **THE COMMON ELEMENTS OF
LIFE-GIVING SPIRITUALITIES**

11 Finding a Spiritual Pathway   207

Notes   219
Index   235

Preface

The motivation for writing this book has been with me for many years. I have had a deep interest in religion, especially in Christianity, since I was introduced to its basic beliefs and values during my high school years. It was then that I plunged into a religious quest with some innocence and discovered that my simple faith had a profound influence on my life. For the most part, my faith orientation helped me to find a way through those early years in a very constructive manner. There was some naiveté about the Bible and its history and a trace of judgment about other religious traditions that were not like mine. But overall, my faith gave coherence and integrity to my life and instilled a sense of well-being, the positive values of respect and compassion for others, and a concern for social justice in our society and world. I had found **a spiritual pathway**.

Across the years, as I studied religious thought and behavior in some depth, and as I had the opportunity to travel to various parts of the world where faith families other than Christianity were in the majority and visibly active and observable, I began to wonder if nearly all religious faith, regardless of specific beliefs and practices, might have the potential to be a positive influence in human experience. I also observed (and experienced) some practices, both within my own Christian faith and in the religious life of other traditions, that had a negative influence on me and the people within these other religious communities. It struck me that religious faith can be enormously powerful in human experience, lead to health, human flourishing, and social responsibility, but also it can lead to an orientation of fear, zealotry, and intolerance. In short, I discovered that religion can be both life-giving and life-denying. It can be a positive force for good and a negative force for that which is harmful for human life. The larger question came into my thoughts and continues with me regardless of my personal faith: Is religion an asset or a liability as the human race seeks to move forward to a more fulfilling, just, and peaceful existence? It is a question that will not go away, even though my life and career have been devoted to advancing a mature approach to religious belief and practice.

My reflections led naturally to an exploration of what beliefs and practices within a faith community tended to be positive and create a life-giving and socially responsible environment, and those beliefs and practices that tended to create an environment that had a negative impact on people and was sectarian in spirit. As I observed religious behavior in my own faith family and the religious life of other traditions, I began to make lists of life-giving beliefs and practices and life-denying beliefs and practices. I was given the opportunity in my professional life to teach courses in world religions, and I began to suggest to students that there were both healthy and unhealthy religious ideas and practices. The students engaged in these conversations with energy and insight, and I remain grateful for their honesty. In other conversations with devout practitioners and scholars in religious studies, I began to try out my hunches. In time, patterns emerged and were continually refined. What has become clear across the years of teaching and direct exposure and participation is that when people truly understand the core beliefs and practices of traditions other than their own, they are inclined to be at least tolerant. As they understand more (better), they begin to appreciate the core beliefs and practices of religions of the world and see how these beliefs and practices can lead to personal and social transformation.

Three other major trends in the religious life of the human family began to intersect with my ruminations about healthy and unhealthy religious beliefs and practices. One of those trends was the general increase in the **interest in and practice of spirituality**, a movement now several decades old and continuing, but has really been with us from the beginning of human reflection. Spirituality has been variously defined, and I tend to follow the more generic definition that it has less to do with belonging to an organized religion and more to do with the transformation of the person and society, although belonging to a religious community may be the primary way that spirituality is nurtured and sustained. Spirituality is a lived experience that is both internal ("I am being transformed") and external ("I will live in a responsible way"). In general, it has to do with our experience of the divine, and the transformation of our consciousness and our lives as the outcome of that experience. It engages our heart or our center and how it is that we purify our heart and live a life of compassion.

Although it may be a bit difficult to prove, it appears that during these past three decades or more, the world has become more religious and many of those engaged in religious renewal are in the midst of a quest for a deeper and more profound spirituality. There are diverse reasons for this tremendous energy and resurgence of religious life, but certainly one of them is that the foundations of our way of understanding the world and our place in it are changing. Most of humanity has been impacted by rapid changes in our world, and we are finding it incredibly difficult to accommodate these enormous changes. Change can be difficult, and people in the midst of change tend to be afraid and threatened. Under stress, they seek in their religious commitments and spiritual quests somewhere safe, a link with the past that provides some security. They want a place to stand in the midst of rapid change, a divinely sanctioned context to call home, an anchor in what feels like a powerful storm.

I have been personally affected by the way that religion in general and spirituality in particular have emerged as a concern for all kinds of people, and I have noticed that religion is front-page news. I was influenced in part by the thought that reached its zenith in the decades of the 1960s and 1970s which argued that we are living in a post-Christian or post-religious era, a time when we heard the phrase "God is dead" by which we meant that the concept of God was no longer germane to our understanding of the world and the unfolding of our lives. So now, I am adjusting to a new reality, and it invites me and all of us to pause and reflect.

In addition to the increased interest in the spiritual life, there has also been a strong **tendency toward fundamentalism,** and in some ways, the two movements have overlapped and been interwoven. Fundamentalism is a word honored by some who maintain a more conservative view of their religious heritage, but the term is used more commonly to describe a narrow belief system that tends to be intolerant of religious beliefs that differ from one's own; it is sectarian in spirit. It is a word often used to describe a particular form of Christianity, but the term is now used to describe the more radical, even militant side of all religious traditions. In some cases, the new and emerging spirituality has taken the form of intolerant sectarianism. Many of those in a more moderate centrist position have anxiety about the larger place these movements have in our common life, and have been especially conscious of the increase of the militant Islamic faith. But the resurgence of fundamentalism is not limited to Islam; it was present in the persecution of Christians and Muslims by Hindus in India in the late 1990s and the early part of this decade, and one author has made the case for the way that a form of Christian fundamentalism has shaped American policy in the Bush administration. What occurred on September 11, 2001 reshaped the world and made us all keenly aware of the role and place of "radical" religion in the world.

My experience, observations, and study of religious life coupled with the rise of spirituality and fundamentalism have led me to the conviction that **religious beliefs and practices and their expression in spirituality are shaping contemporary life** in quite profound ways. In fact, as understanding of other religions increases, I have become persuaded that people become more tolerant and respectful of other religious traditions. Intolerant fundamentalism tends to fade away (though not always), and spirituality as common ground becomes a resource for justice, peace, and reconciliation. The subject of *Exploring the Spirituality of the World Religions: The Quest for Personal, Spiritual, and Social Transformation* is timely and germane. The starting point is that the world is religious, and in some cases more religious than it has ever been, and that religious beliefs and practices shape the values and behavior of not only individuals, but also large groups of people in associations (al Qaeda) and nation states (the United States). Perhaps religion is the missing dimension of peace-seeking.

The book opens with an analysis of our context and what sort of spirituality is especially appropriate for our time and place in history. There will be a description of several characteristics of our time with an emphasis on the rapidity and profundity of change and its impact on the religious and spiritual pathways that are emerging. Following the description of the context will be an introduction to the nature of the spiritual quest and an attempt to provide a common universe of discourse. There will be a discussion of the meaning of religion and spirituality and the many ways that human beings seek to find and sustain a spiritual center.

The next sections begin the discussion of several of the major religious traditions of the human family. These religious traditions are separated into three categories for clarity and convenience, although such classification runs the risk of oversimplification and even distortion. The risk will be worth it if the discussion does provide more clarity and a deeper understanding. The three groups are: spiritual pathways rooted in nature and culture; spiritual pathways rooted in transcendent monism; and spiritual pathways rooted in the Abrahamic monotheistic religions of Judaism, Christianity, and Islam. The core beliefs and practices of each of these religious traditions will be described briefly, and an effort will be made to distill the **soul** or **spirit** of the religion. Then the religious traditions will be examined with regard to their life-giving or life-denying characteristics. Finally there will be an assessment of the potential of the spiritual pathways of these traditions to lead honest seekers to understand and respect other religious traditions.

The final section of the book will address the way that contemporary pilgrims might pursue a healthy and life-giving spirituality. We will affirm the positive qualities of the many spiritual pathways of the great religions of the world.

There will be study questions, a glossary, and brief bibliography at the close of each chapter.

I am grateful to many for their assistance in preparing the manuscript. I am especially grateful to Vickie Drebing for her editing and formatting.

Part I
The Content and Approach to the Study of Spirituality

This section addresses the ever-changing character of our world and places the resurgence of religious energy and the growing interest in spirituality within this frame of reference. Given the mixed character of this revival of religion world-wide, categories of assessment are introduced. There are suggested ways of finding common language and categories for this high-octane religious fervor in the hope that bridges might be built between conflicting religious groups.

> The world is becoming smaller and smaller. Nations are far more interdependent than before. Our generation has reached the threshold of a new era of human history: the birth of a global family. Whether we like it or not, all the members of our vast and varied human family have to learn to live together somehow. We need to develop a great sense of universal responsibility, on both the individual and collective level.[1]

The Spiritual Quest

Chapter Outline

Living east of Eden   3
Finding a spiritual pathway   7
An approach to spirituality   10

Living east of Eden

In John Steinbeck's *East of Eden,*[2] we read about several generations of two families, and how each generation copes with the changing circumstances and complex challenges of the farmland of California's Salinas Valley. As one generation ages, they look back on how life used to be, a time that seemed easier, safer, and more secure. As a new generation comes along, they see the new order as the way the world is, but soon they too find themselves struggling to manage new and unfamiliar trends in the world around them. There is conflict, confusion, misunderstanding, and Cain and Abel cannot find their way through the mist. Each generation finds it difficult to live east of Eden and looks back to simpler times when life seemed to be more like it was in the Garden. The tectonic plates have shifted and are shifting, and the continents are in different places.

I think of my spiritual pathway in an analogous way, having come to faith in the Eisenhower era, and now finding my way at the end the first decade of the twenty-first century. There are moments when I think my home continent has shifted and moved east of Eden. This observation is certainly true in regard to my faith journey; I know that my innocence has gone as I have eaten from the tree of knowledge, passed through the world of the critical historical study of scripture, the give and take of rigorous theological debate, and immersed myself in the thoughts and patterns of the various religions of the world. Simplistic faith is no longer an option, although simple faith remains an ideal. My mentors now seem altogether human, frail, with faults, and less than omniscient. Along the way, I lost my heroes and heroines, but gained some friends who share my human limitations. Even my faith community became problematic. I discovered that it had pockets of vested interest, even dishonesty, was led by people who were occasionally short-sighted and lacked vision, and who were not only slow to make decisions, but also didn't always make the right ones. They didn't even appreciate my criticisms. In short, it was a human community, this church that was my home. It, too, faced the seismic changes, lived on a fault line, and felt the shift of its ground moving east of its comfort zone.

To live east of Eden is to live in a **postmodern moment**,[3] a time when so much of the culture and technology of our political and intellectual landscape is fading away. The geography has changed on this new continent. The modern *zeitgeist* has been deconstructed and very little fills its place as we struggle to erect new beams and buttresses, peer through new lenses, and attempt to create new paradigms. For more than a century and perhaps as many as three centuries, we have lived and been educated in modernity, and the modern is a hard act to follow. Now we face what is to follow, a new era for which there is no compelling and descriptive name. We speak about pre-this and post-that and even define our time *via negativa* (what we are not). Philosophers speak of postfoundationalism, the trend to call into question the search since Descartes for a method that would provide indubitable truth claims to serve as the foundation for human knowledge and action. Postmodernism, rooted in the arts and humanities, has come to represent a movement that celebrates the loss of unambiguous meaning. All truth claims are tainted by historical, cultural, and personal perspectives. Now one wonders if postmodernism has run its course and perhaps even run aground with its pluralistic relativism and epistemological reductionism. There is the alternative point of view that truth comes in many forms, and that the assertion that there can be no absolute claims to truth that do not need deconstruction is overstated. What remains is an open market for ideas with few or none carrying the labels of absolute or ultimate.[4]

Such a time presents a challenge to those seeking a spiritual pathway and center because so many of the options available are linked to a modern worldview, and even more to a pre-modern worldview. As the modern worldview collapses, we feel our spiritual center threatened, nailed as it is to the framework of pre-modernity and modernity and convictions about absolute and ultimate truth.

To live east of Eden is to live in a **global age**, one in which all distances have shrunk and connections between peoples from every corner of the world are direct.[5] The dramatic shifts in our economic structures, the new map of geopolitics, and the omnipresence of information technology underline the global character of our existence. The expanding economies of China and India, the conflicts in Iraq and the Middle East, the draught and disease in Africa, and our direct communication with those in other parts of the world through cyberspace have direct implications for us. Who, in my grandparents' generation, would have guessed that our financial well-being and way of life would be so tied to the economies of Asia and the oil of the Middle East? Who would have predicted one of the world's dominant ideologies would crumble and nearly disappear with the demise of the USSR, and that the United States would ascend to the highest rung of global influence and be the one true superpower in the world (although threatened in this status)? Who would have guessed that the way we teach, learn, gather information, and communicate around the world would be so inextricably tied to digital processes? The global character of our world forces us to review our faith commitments and our spiritual pathways as we interact with others, the stranger, whose points of view and faith positions are quite different from our own and held with equal sincerity.

It follows that to live east of Eden is to live in a **pluralistic, multicultural world**, one that requires us to learn how to live with those whose culture, language, customs, beliefs, and values are very different from our own. And these strangers are our neighbors[6] and, in a very real way, all of the world's peoples are our neighbors. We are connected to them in a multitude of ways, and because of our differences, there is conflict.[7] The conflict is local, regional, national, and international, as a deep chasm separates the rich and the poor, peoples of the Northern and Southern hemispheres, and people with different understandings of the way the world should be ordered. The dominant presence of the United States in Iraq and Afghanistan, and the open conflict with militant Islam and the West illustrate how deep these conflicts are. Solutions are very elusive and religion plays a subtle, but central role in problem-solving. Our spiritual pathway must take into account the cultural diversity in which we live.

Still another reality, living east of Eden, is the presence of a range of **problems facing the earth and its inhabitants that are overwhelming in size**

and complexity.[8] The list is long, but I will mention two that are illustrious and seem to elude solutions. The first is that we live in an ecologically threatened world and the second is the reality of global warming. These realities demand a whole new understanding of our way of living in the world and a holistic view of reality.[9] The worldwide conferences held in Rio de Janeiro and Kyoto underline the critical nature of global warming and the ecological crisis. We learn from these conferences and careful scientific analysis that what is needed is not some sentimental love of nature, but a deep love of the earth.[10] We have been informed about this "inconvenient truth" by the vision and leadership of former Vice President, Al Gore.[11]

What is needed is not an artificial leveling of all distinctions between human beings and other forms of life, but the realization that our existence is one with the immensity of all that is and is in the process of becoming. An ecological perspective insists that, in the most profound ways, we are not our own. From the cells of our bodies to the finest creations of our minds, we belong to the intricate, constantly changing cosmos, an ecosystem. Relationships and interdependence, change and transformation are the categories of this new paradigm. The paradigm argues for the development of a global consciousness in relation to human solidarity and solidarity with other levels of life. The ecological model suggests an ethic toward others, both human and nonhuman, characterized by both justice and care. No longer can the universe's unruly and unrivaled child, the human being, live out of control and without thought for other lives. The task of global management and the threat to survival challenge our spiritual center in fundamental ways.[12]

Still another problem that is dodging solutions is that of poverty, and its concomitant partner, world hunger. Let me quote a passage from a recent book by Jonathan Sacks as a way of grasping the urgency of these concerns:

> The average North American consumes five times more than a Mexican, ten times more than a Chinese, 30 times more than an Indian. There are 1.3 billion people—22 % of the world's population—living below the poverty line; 841 million are malnourished; 880 million are without access to medical care. One billion lack adequate shelter; 1.3 billion who have no access to safe drinking water; 2.6 billion go without sanitation. Among the children of the world, 113 million—two-thirds of them are girls—go without schooling; 150 million are malnourished; 30,000 die each day from preventable diseases. In eighteen countries, all African, life expectancy is less than 50 years. In Sierra, Leone it is a mere 37 years. Infant mortality rates are higher than one in ten in 35 countries, mostly in Africa but including Bangladesh, Bolivia, Haiti, Laos, Nepal, Pakistan and Yemen. . . . The assets of the

world's three richest billionaires were more than the combined wealth of the 600 million inhabitants of the least-developed countries. The enormous wealth of the few contrasts starkly with the misery of the many and jars our sense of equity and justice.[13]

We must find ways to address the extraordinary and overwhelming needs of our global context and draw upon the resources of a changing economic world[14] and the motivation provided by our spiritual commitments to make changes in our world.

Finding a spiritual pathway

It is in this new world, in which one often feels lost and overwhelmed, that we must find our spiritual pathway. It is a quest that is contextual, and we engage in the quest with those who live, search, and struggle in a different context. But we all do so because we need a center for our peace and stability and a thoughtful and responsible path to follow. We join with the vast majority of humankind in seeking a life-giving and responsible way.

But such a way is not always easy to find. In some cases, the power of religion and the spiritual pathway of the individual or group can lead to compassion, understanding, tolerance, and the pursuit of peace and justice—the appropriate response to our new world. In other cases, the religious energy and spiritual pathways of individuals and groups can lead to hostility, intolerance, harsh and fierce orthodoxy—even militant terrorism, and a failure to engage in building a more just and humane world.

What, then, should be the contours of our spirituality in a postmodern, global, pluralistic, multicultural, and ecologically threatened and needy world? First, it must be a **simple** pathway. God, as the Bernstein mass so eloquently proclaims, is the simplest of all. I do not mean a simplistic faith in which there is zeal without knowledge, a literalist understanding of scripture, little historical perspective, and the passionate belief that one has all the truth and those who differ are wrong, even heretical. We must avoid the worst forms of fundamentalism that suffers from ignorance, arrogance, and intolerance. We must guard against our own intellectual, moral, and cultural pride which claims that our way is the only right way.[15]

By a simple pathway, first, I mean pure and uncluttered, not ideologically narrow and provincial. Simple faith is a deep and profound personal understanding of the divine way that seeks the truth, lives in love, and pursues justice.

It was Oliver Wendell Holmes, the former Supreme Court Justice, who said: "I would not give a fig for simplicity on this side of complexity, but I would give my life for simplicity on the other side of complexity." It is a faith akin to second naiveté, the first having vanished in the trip east of Eden. It is a pathway, having been born in the garden, toughened in the give and take of a violent and rapidly changing world, and now gone full circle to a new purity and integrity.

Second, it is an **open and thoughtful** pathway, a pathway that seeks new directions and has a base that is intellectually credible. Rooted in truth, love, and justice, it knows that it has no claim on the absolute definition and expression of truth, love, and justice. It is a way of being that is keenly aware that our understanding of the spiritual center and pathway is limited by our time and place in history, by our human limitations, by our culture, and even the language we speak. Our faith-constructs and metaphors are but approximations which participate in divine truth and enable us to truly meet God, but do not contain the whole truth about God.[16]

Further, as an open pathway, it is one **in dialogue and in transition**—a pathway that meets others. It is informed by the scripture and tradition of the faith family and by association with others who seek the will and way of God—by the community of faith. It is also informed by other cultures, traditions, and faith families. It listens to others, lots of others. It has conversation with the infinitely complex world it inhabits and grows out of the context of life. It struggles with postmodernism and the many other "isms" of our time, it acknowledges the global and multicultural context, and has compassion for earth and its inhabitants. It is sufficiently strong to doubt current constructs and develops as life unfolds and intersects with the changing world in which we live.

It is an **ethical** pathway, rooted in a spiritual center that cares for this world and all of its creatures. It is a pathway that leads to courageous love, challenging all forms of injustice, and seeking peace for all. It is a faith grounded in love freely given for the good of one's neighbor. This love, *agape*, is unlimited, unconditional, and active. At the very least, it has the following qualities:[17]

1. It is **extensive** and reaches to every nook and cranny where human suffering and need are present. It is easy to love the loveable, and it takes more effort to love those in our immediate surroundings although we often do so because we are close by and share the same culture and behavioral norms. But it is very difficult to find the motivation and energy to love those who are distant and different from us.

But love reaches out, extends itself, not unlike the good and gifted people who have made such a difference in assisting those who suffered from natural tragedies.

2. It is **intensive**, filled with compassion and caring. It is exceedingly important to do "good deeds," to challenge and change the infrastructure that discriminates against classes of people, and to support those agencies (schools, hospitals, etc.) that improve the condition of others. But it is also important to have a presence, to demonstrate by word and touch that you truly do care for those who are needy and those who suffer. They need to feel loved by our activity, yes, and also feel our presence which demonstrates the intensity of our caring.

3. It is **enduring** and lasts across time, resistance, and fatigue. Generally, there are important causes for which there is enthusiasm and energy, at least for a season. It is more difficult to sustain the effort when the spotlight has shifted and other causes have more appeal. Yes, there are reasons for causes, but love lasts as it does within a family structure. It endures across time, even if there is no one acknowledging the effort and extending gratitude. Racial justice within American society is such an issue.

4. It is **pure**, has integrity, and offers help without thought of personal gain.[18] Not infrequently our motivation is mixed as we extend ourselves in a helping way toward others. We may gain enormous satisfaction when showing love to others, not an altogether bad thing. But when the behavior is about us and our needs, and when we only engage in "loving" behavior for personal gratification, then the love ceases to be *agapic* in character, becomes a relationship of co-dependence and not a love that is solely driven by the welfare of the other.

5. It is **adequate** and appropriately meets the needs of the other. Often our inclinations to find ways to help others are accurate and on target. We are able, with a measure of empathy, to understand the need of those whom we are trying to help, and our offerings of love are healing and redemptive. But there are times when we want to impose our ways on others, ways that are controlling and manipulative. These efforts may grow out of our own needs, reflect the feelings of "should" and "ought" that are inside of us, and be strategies to change another person according to our specifications. A truly loving act provides that gift of love which is adequate and appropriate, serving the well-being of the other.

As a kind of summary, as we move to a discussion of definitions, approaches and expressions of spirituality, let me suggest the following categories to assess those spiritual dynamics that are healthy and life-giving and those that are unhealthy and life-denying for an individual and a community of faith. It is a list "in progress" as it runs the risk of being bound to my understanding of faith, rooted as it is in my culture, place and time in history, and the traditions of Protestant Christianity. It is a humble offering:

Life-giving characteristics of spiritual pathways:

1. The spiritual pathway **empowers** the person or the group to behave in constructive ways that lead to love, compassion, understanding, and acceptance.
2. The spiritual pathway **guides** the person or group to be socially responsible and
   concerned about creating a more just and humane world. It guards against being
   taken over by a political point of view.
3. The spiritual pathway is intellectually credible and **encourages** the person or group
   to be open and responsive to new ideas and challenges.
4. The spiritual pathway helps the individual or group to **flourish and integrate** the
   beliefs and practices into a life of coherence, conviction, serenity, and integrity.
5. The spiritual pathway offers guidance and practices that **sustain** the individual and
   group in times of difficulty and challenge.

Life-denying characteristics of spiritual pathways:[19]

1. The spiritual pathway is **sectarian** and closed to other religious traditions and
   points of view. It is cultic, judgmental, and exclusive.
2. The spiritual pathway is **ideological** in character and is suspicious of those whose
   religious beliefs and practices are unlike their own. It is intolerant of difference and
   "the other." It does not account for new ways of understanding reality and is not
   intellectually defensible.
3. The spiritual pathway tends to **confine and control** the individuals within the
   group and asks for blind obedience. It does not liberate, but imprisons.
4. The spiritual pathway is filled with **zealotry** about its way and is inclined to force
   its way on others, even violently. Often the ends justify the means as religious faith
   is captured by a political ideology.
5. The spiritual pathway inculcates **fear, mistrust, and intolerance** and does not
   reflect the positive values of personal transformation, compassion, justice, and
   peace.

We turn now to the nature of the spiritual quest, suggesting a common universe of discourse, exploring ways of seeking a spiritual center, and identifying
approaches to nurture and sustain our walk on a spiritual pathway.

An approach to spirituality

Recently, my wife and I had the opportunity to travel to Australia, and one of
the highlights of our time there was seeing the Sydney Harbor (Harbour). It
was as beautiful as it had been described to us. We were especially impressed

with the contours of the Harbor Bridge, the world's widest and heaviest arch bridge, linking the south and north shores. This bridge, like so many bridges in other parts of the world, serves to connect different sections of a region, allowing people easily to cross over and be in another community. The Harbor Bridge became a kind of symbol for us, as we crossed over into other cultures on our trip.

Healthy, life-giving spirituality has the capacity to be a bridge between people, enabling them to meet and understand one another even though the cultures and religious traditions may be quite different. Not long ago, I was invited to speak to a good-sized gathering (about 250 people) of the Muslim student group at a large university. An Islamic scholar and I were asked to speak about the way that Jesus is understood in the Bible and the Quran. My task, I knew, was to find some common ground so that the Muslims and Christians might have a better understanding of one another. There were many possible "bridges," but the one that seemed most helpful was to speak about Jesus as a deeply spiritual prophet, sharing with Muhammad the responsibilities of bringing the Word of God to the people. Of course there were questions, as I expected, about the Trinity and the Resurrection, and while there were differences, we did seem to find a bridge that took us across into one another's communities.

I would emphasize again that we are living in a time when people in our country and around the world are strengthening their religious commitments and searching for ways to deepen their spiritual life. These endeavors are many and varied, depending in large measure upon the context of those engaged in the quest of finding a more authentic spiritual pathway. Because these searches are so diverse and complex, it is necessary to have attitudes, language, and categories that give a common universe of discourse. We must find a way of bringing order and making sense of this global phenomenon, and a way of understanding and appreciating those who differ from us. The peace of our world depends upon it.

As we begin, it is important to note the difference between an **insider's** perspective and an **outsider's** perspective.[20] Often a bridge is needed between these two groups. As a general rule, the insider is one who has made commitments to the beliefs and practices of a religious tradition and finds a spiritual center within the context of the religion. It is also the case that the insider has an affinity with these beliefs and practices and finds the inherent worldview persuasive and life-giving. There is a special kind of sympathy for and insight about the larger frame of the religious tradition that comes to the believer. The risk, however, in being an insider is that I come to believe that my way is the only way. My faith may be life-giving and healthy, but it can cause me to turn in judgment upon those who are on a different spiritual pathway. I could have reflected a spirit of intolerance at the meeting of the Muslim student group (our concepts, and especially our metaphors were quite different), but I didn't show intolerance and was therefore able to connect with a group of thoughtful Muslim students.

The outsider is one who does not share and participate in the beliefs and practices of a particular religious way, although there may be great interest in the religious tradition and a desire to study it with sympathetic appreciation and fairness. I was the outsider the evening I spoke at the university, but it was possible for the "outsider," in this case, to still appreciate the worldview that was the foundation of the Muslim pathway and to affirm all the ways that the pathway enabled these believers to find meaning and guidance in life. It is possible, even probable, that the outsider may take the view that the religious beliefs and practices do not always seem to make sense and empower the followers to flourish. It may be that outsiders lack appropriate empathy, do not have the experience to fully appreciate the spiritual pathways of traditions that are different from their own, and are unable to understand and nuance the subtle dimensions of the religious tradition.

First, as we look within our own beliefs and practices and observe those spiritual pathways that are different from our own, we need consciously to cultivate a range skills and attitudes that will allow both genuine understanding and more accepting relationships with others.[21] The place to start, as has been mentioned, is with an attitude of **openness** rather than a spirit of intolerance and judgment. We should go into our exposure and observation of other religious traditions with a perspective that enables us to understand how the spiritual pathway works for others—rather than an outlook that says, "Their way is not my way and is therefore wrong." This is a perspective quite difficult for the monotheistic religions because of their belief that God has spoken quite distinctively within their faith tradition.

Second, this will enable us, to be **honest and fair** with all that is positive in the religious tradition and take away the tendency to oversimplify, distort, even stereotype and caricature the beliefs and practices of the tradition. It is currently very easy in the United States to judge harshly the beliefs and practices of Islam because what Americans see in the media are those extreme elements of Islam that perpetuate terrorism and violence. And, to be sure, terrorism and violence should be resisted without naiveté or an artificial political correctness. What Americans often do not fully appreciate is the way that

U.S. foreign policies, including those of Israel, are viewed in the Islamic world as containing terrorism and violence, and as policies connected in some way with Judaism and Christianity.

We do need to be better **informed** in order to be honest with and fair about the beliefs and practices of other religious traditions. It is necessary for us to study, observe, and be in conversation with those who have different religious traditions. There are many opportunities in our communities to see first-hand the ways in which other religious traditions are practiced. They are a number of good introductory books,[22] classes taught in churches and community colleges, and easy access for visits to religious groups that differ from our own—all good bridge-building opportunities.

To be open, honest, and well-informed leads us to another integral part of the bridge, the exercise of **critical judgment**. A reflective and thoughtful assessment is important for an outsider learning about other religious traditions, and also for the insider, when we examine with care the beliefs and practices of our own religious tradition. It is acceptable and helpful to express our reservations about the coherence and logic of the religious beliefs and the relative healthy or unhealthy practices within a religious tradition. We do need to be tolerant and have to learn more, but we may discover that there are elements within the religious tradition that are not defensible, even harmful to those within the community of faith. For example, for those in the biblical traditions, it is harder to justify any violation of justice and love, or to be persuaded that any means of violence and injustice will lead in the end to a more peaceful and just world.[23]

There are a number of words and concepts that we may use in everyday conversation, but which may lack precision and clarity and carry a variety of meanings. An effort at common understanding will help us with our bridge-building. "Religion" is certainly one of those words, and scholars and practitioners of religion have not always agreed on a single definition. Some link religion to a belief in God[24] (the monotheistic religions) while others suggest that it has more to do with the rituals and practices of a community that share common social norms and values such as Confucianism.[25] One recent reference book on religion, after a thoughtful review of the range of possibilities, finally settles on, "religion is a system of communal beliefs and practices relative to superhuman beings."[26] Superhuman beings, in this definition, are beings that can do things that humans cannot do. I would replace the word "divine" for superhuman beings in that the world religions originating in India (Hinduism, Buddhism, etc.) often understand the divine as universal consciousness, not as a "being." Generally, scholars of religion agree that most religious communities have at least four common elements as given below, although I will often shorthand these as "beliefs and practices."

- They have a **creed** or a set of beliefs that are affirmed and which give the members of the religious community a worldview and a way of understanding the religious life. The Apostles Creed, The Nicene Creed, and the many other creedal statements are examples within the Christian context. The Four Noble Truths is comparable within Buddhism as are the Five Pillars of Islam.
- They have a **code** or a set of ethical principles that guide the members of the religious community in their behavior. Judaism refers to the law of God expressed in the Ten Commandments as the foundation of their ethical code.
- They have **rituals** or **cultic practices** that affirm and nurture the beliefs and values of the religious community. A faithful Muslim will pray five times per day facing Mecca, and a faithful Jew will carefully celebrate the great holidays of the tradition.
- They have a **community**, organized with regular meetings, holy days, and systems of support. The Buddhists affirm their belief in the *Sangha* (community) as the way to be supported in the practice of Buddhism, and there is encouragement to live within the separated community for periods of time to study with a mentor (guru) and be supported by the practices within the community.

The word "spirituality" is nearly as difficult to define. It derives from the Hebrew word *ruach* that is usually translated as breath or spirit. In the creation story of Genesis, God breathes life into humans. This understanding points toward the word used in the New Testament, *pneuma* that means breath or wind. With both energy and vitality, the Spirit moves like the wind, unseen, but powerful. Spirituality is often used in reference to a religious tradition, a set of disciplines and practices, or a movement specific to a historical and cultural context.[27] Nearly all of the major religions of humankind speak about being devout and faithful and offer ways of nurturing the religious life.[28] Some of these pathways are quite specific such as the Sufi tradition in Islam or the mystical path within Judaism called the Kabbalah. A well prescribed path of discipline for Christians is offered by Ignatius Loyola (1491–1556) in the *Spiritual Exercises*. The Dalai Lama offers, as did the late Pope John Paul II, a worldly spirituality that invites respect for all of the religions of humankind and a commitment to social responsibility.

It is difficult to find a single definition that encompasses the many understandings of spirituality, although practitioners and scholars in religion have made a noble effort. For example, Alistair McGrath, in his introductory book on Christian spirituality, proposes a generic definition of spirituality and writes that "spirituality concerns the quest for a fulfilled and authentic religious life, involving the bringing together of the ideas distinctive of that religion and the whole experience of living on the basis of and within the scope of that religion."[29] Drawing to some extent upon his definition, I would suggest that spirituality is the effort to fully utilize the relevant elements of our religious tradition and other religious traditions as our guidance in life, leading to our development as persons growing toward wholeness (holiness), insight, joy, and responsible living.

As we practice our religion and seek a deeper and more profound spirituality, we do so in the context of **tradition**,[30] and nearly every religious family, while sharing common beliefs and practices, has several traditions, even separate branches. We speak, for example, within Buddhism of the Mahayana and Theravada traditions; and within Islam of Shias and Sunnis. Basically, by tradition, we mean the patterns of belief and practice inherent in a religious community that has been passed down from one generation to the next.

Frequently, it is the tradition within the larger family in which we find our religious guidance that leads us toward an understanding of how we should relate to the **culture** within which we live. Culture may be understood as the variety of behavioral patterns and values held by the majority of people who shape that common life of a community.[31] There are many ways that a particular religious tradition relates to the surrounding culture.[32] H. Richard Niebuhr's study of Christianity and culture, which speaks about five different ways that various traditions of Christianity relate to culture, is informative although perhaps dated in a post-Christendom era. Let me suggest, as a simplification, that religious communities have at least three primary ways of relating to the culture in which they practice their religious faith.

1. The first is a general **accommodation** to the culture, an acceptance of the behavioral norms and the inherent values of the culture. There is no serious conflict felt by the members of the religious community as they go about their daily life. From time to time, there may be opposition to particular laws or norms, but these may be addressed within the decision-making structures of the political system.
2. The second way that a religious tradition relates to the culture surrounding it is by challenging the values and practices inherent to the culture and by attempting to **transform** the culture. The assumption of this position is that the norms and values of the culture are not in agreement with the beliefs of the religious tradition and that every effort should be made to challenge them. The challenge may take the prescribed method of social change (vote, run for office, use the media, etc.)

or it may be a more serious challenge to overthrow the government structures (often by violent protest) and impose the religious beliefs and practices on the people, as in the case of the Taliban in Afghanistan.

3. The third way for a religious community to relate to the culture in which it finds itself is essentially to **retreat** or withdraw from it. There may be a conviction that the culture does not affirm the beliefs and practices of the religious tradition, and that the only way to be true to one's faith is by establishing a separate community with a way of life built around the beliefs and values of the religious tradition. The Qumran community at the time of Jesus was such a movement. A variation of this mode of relating to the culture is when a particular group of people, for example nuns or monks, may be called into a more isolated lifestyle in order to practice the faith with concentrated intentionality. Many of the great religions have this practice built into the very essence of their practice of spirituality.

The spiritual pathways of the religions of humankind, and those spiritual quests that really jettison traditional religious affiliation, do have many common elements, although they do not all contain the same elements. Understanding these commonalities provide us with ways of bridge-building and peace-making. For example, while the mixtures and language may be different, one might argue that the spiritual quests have comparable goals and disciplines. One way of speaking about these goals is by the directional metaphor of **reaching upward, opening inward, and expanding outward**.[33] We reach upward in our desire to be in harmony with the divine, or to find unity with the One, or to be integral with the universe, however we may understand our spiritual connection. In our spiritual quest, we begin to talk about, understand, and internalize this connection, and our religious traditions or more secular pathways give us language, images, and metaphors for our beliefs. We find a place to stand, to call home, and talk about, and internalize our spiritual center within our community of faith. I have known many who have found the language of Higher Power to be very helpful as they seek to overcome their addiction and form a healthier life through Alcoholics Anonymous.

As we find and sustain that harmony with the divine, we open inwardly and begin to flourish. We learn to love ourselves, find and cultivate our true identity, discover how to experience joy, and begin to have inner peace and serenity. It is never easy, and those who describe it as easy are a bit overcome by their enthusiasm. It is more of a gradual process, mixed with all the ambiguity and ambivalence of life. But in time, we do gain a spiritual center that pulls the many pieces of our inner lives (sometimes wildly out of order) together and makes us whole (holy), integrated, and focused by self-understanding and purpose. We begin to discard harmful, even destructive practices, begin to practice new patterns of life that are healthy and life-giving, and develop habits and disciplines that keep us on the growing edge.

This journey is life-long, and there is no clear and precise chronological order to human and spiritual formation,[34] but along the way we begin to expand outward. We find a community that accepts us, expands our understanding of the divine or our core beliefs, and continually helps to know who we are and our purpose in life. This community of trust and intimacy sustains us and also points us outward to others who need love and compassion. We develop a sense of ethical responsibility; begin to understand our part in building a more just and humane social order; and find tangible ways of expressing our evolving and emerging vocation to be a positive force for good in the world.

We are made keenly aware through personal observation of the religious life in our immediate circumstances and by our daily contact with the media's reports on the world situation, that religion and the culture in which it is often interwoven can be very divisive. For many, religious beliefs, values, and practices "are worth fighting for" and we observe the fighting all around us. It is also true that there are many spiritual people and religious traditions that are devoted to peace-making and healing. The models of our modern prophets (e.g., Mahatma Gandhi, Martin Luther King, Jr., Mother Teresa, the Dalai Lama) teach us about the positive energy of religion and that religion can be an important dimension in global diplomacy.[35] While the use of religious ideas and energies is delicate and difficult, it is nevertheless wise to utilize religion and the spirituality that derives from the practice of religion in the pursuit of peace, justice, and "people-making" strategies. The spirituality of the human family can be a powerful force for crossing the bridge to others.

We turn now to a discussion of specific religions and how they have and are currently functioning as a positive force for good, and in what ways they may have a negative tug on human welfare.

Discussion questions

1. In what ways is our spiritual center and pathway shaped by our context? Our culture? Our traditions?
2. How does living in a postmodern moment and a global and multicultural context make the development of a spiritual pathway more complex and difficult?

3. What makes a particular religious orientation and spirituality healthy or unhealthy?
4. In what ways should our spiritual center and pathway shape our response to the world's most pressing needs?
5. What are the major differences in perspective between those who are "outsiders" or "insiders" in reference to a religious faith?
6. What common elements exist within religions that allow for people to find common ground and enable them to talk with one other with understanding and respect?

Key terms and concepts

1. **Fundamentalism:** An orientation that affirms that there are certain basic beliefs that constitute the essence of Christian faith; more generally, the term has come to mean a religious faith that is ideological, inflexible, and intolerant of other religious beliefs and practices.
2. **Postmodern:** A description of our time in history that questions the assumptions of modernity and argues that truth claims must be taken on their own merit without reference to the existence of absolute truth; and that assumptions and concepts that claim to be absolutely accurate in their descriptions of reality are filled with cultural distortion and vested interest and need to be deconstructed.
3. **Life-giving :** Patterns in the religious life of individuals and groups that are healthy, lead to wholeness, human flourishing, and social responsibility.
4. **Life-denying:** Patterns of religious life in individuals and groups that control and manipulate, lead to fear and intolerance, and prevent human flourishing.
5. **Global:** The ways that the world is interconnected through economic structures, information technology, the spread of knowledge, and immigration patterns.
6. **Ecological paradigm:** A way of viewing the world that understands human beings as interdependent upon nature and responsible for the well-being of the earth and its inhabitants.
7. **Religion:** A set of beliefs and practices within a community that are related to the divine. Generally, these beliefs and practices include a set of beliefs, an ethical system, a form of worship, and a sustaining community.
8. **Spirituality:** The effort to incorporate the elements of our religious traditions into our lives in a way that provides guidance in life, leading to our development as a person growing toward wholeness (holiness), insight, and responsible living.
9. **Religious tradition:** The patterns of belief and practice inherent in a religious community that have been passed down from one generation to the next.
10. **Culture:** The socially transmitted behavioral patterns, values, and beliefs of a community or population.

Suggestions for reference and reading

Beversluis, Joel, ed., *Sourcebook of the World's Religions: An Interfaith Guide to Religion and Spirituality* (Novato, CA: New World Library, 2000).

Bowker, John, *World Religions: The Great Faiths Explored & Explained* (New York: D K Publishing, Inc., 2003). There are many fine introductory books in the general field of world religions; the strength of Bowker's volume is its simplicity, clarity, and extraordinary illustrations and pictures.

Doniger, Wendy, ed., *Encyclopedia of World Religions* (Springfield, MA: Merriam-Webster, Inc., 1999).

Eck, Diana L., *A New Religious America: How a "Christian Country" has Become the World's Most Religiously Diverse Nation* (San Francisco: HarperSanFrancisco, 2001).

Gore, Al, *An Inconvenient Truth: The Planetary Emergency of Global Warming and What We Can Do about It* (New York: Rodale, 2006).

Grenz, Stanley J., *A Primer on Postmodernism* (Grand Rapids, MI: William B. Eerdmans Publishing Company, 1996).

Hitchcock, Susan Tyler and Esposito, John L., *Geography of Religion: Where God Lives, Where Pilgrims Walk* (Washington, D. C.: National Geographic, 2005).

Kessler, Gary E., *Ways of Being Religious* (Mountain View, CA: Mayfield Publishing Company, 2000).

Kimball, Charles, *When Religion Becomes Evil* (San Francisco: HarperSanFrancisco, 2002).

Post, Stephen G., *Unlimited Love: Altruism, Compassion, and Service* (Philadelphia: Templeton Foundation Press, 2003).

Sachs, Jeffrey D., *The End of Poverty: Economic Possibilities for Our Time* (New York: The Penguin Press, 2005); see as well *Common Wealth: Economics for a Crowded Planet* (New York: The Penguin Press, 2008).

Sachs, Jonathan, *The Dignity of Difference: How to Avoid the Clash of Civilizations* (London: Continuum, 2002).

Smith, Huston, *The World's Religions: Our Great Wisdom Traditions* (San Francisco: HarperSanFrancisco, 1991).

Part II
The Spiritual Pathways Rooted in Nature and Culture

This section will discuss the traditions that discern and experience the divine within the natural order and structures of society and government. The spiritual pathways within these traditions understand the divine and the human connection with the divine as expressed in a plurality of religious objects and structures located within nature and society. This understanding is often expressed in personified statements of how humans relate to the world and how humans deal with the vicissitudes of life.

> There was no hope on earth, and God seemed to have forgotten us. Some said they saw the Son of God; others did not see Him. If He had come, He would do some great things as He had done before. We doubted it because we had seen neither Him nor His works. The people did not know; they did not care. They snatched at the hope. They screamed like crazy men to him for mercy. They caught at the promise they heard He had made. The white men were frightened and called for soldiers. We had begged for life, and the white men thought we wanted theirs. We heard that soldiers were coming. We did not fear. We hoped that we could tell them our troubles and get help. A white man said the soldiers meant to kill us. We did not believe it, but some were frightened and ran away to the Badlands.
>
> Red Cloud[1]

Indigenous Wisdom Traditions

Chapter Outline

A vast and complex world   23
The view of the world   25
Representative indigenous wisdom religions: Africa   28
Native American religions   31
The contributions and challenges of the spirituality
     of the indigenous wisdom traditions   35

A vast and complex world

From earliest times, it appears that the human family had religious inclinations as a means of understanding and coping with the challenges of life in their vast and complex world.[2] Given the nature of ancient human life, there was the inevitable concern with birth, subsistence, and death. With a life expectancy less than half our own, these first humans were concerned about survival in an environment that was often threatening. Food and children were essential to the survival of these first humans, and they had to navigate a context that demanded that they focus all of their energy on the hunting and gathering of food, avoiding and curing disease, protecting themselves from natural disaster, having children to provide security and ensure that there would be another generation.[3]

Part of these efforts went beyond practical endeavors for survival and included ways of dealing with fear, loss of hope, and conflict; they were spiritually vulnerable and sought ways of controlling the threats with supernatural powers and hoped for an afterlife. In their rites, partially revealed in the art in the prehistoric caves, we see evidence of the ways they sought to make contact with the powers that control life and death. For example, there is evidence that more than 500,000 years ago, in the Dragon Bone Hill caves near Beijing, human bodies were buried with the hope of an afterlife. Some of these earliest peoples challenged the harsh reality of death and began to think and dream about ways to survive beyond it. It is evident that the cyclical and dynamic interaction between life and death formed the center of prehistoric religion.[4]

Over the centuries, these religious impulses took many forms. The early humans viewed themselves as a part of the chain of nature, connected to the plants and animals and the seasonal cycles, and wondered if their fate was comparable to what they observed in nature. This concern with nature manifested itself in a preoccupation with fecundity and survival, and their art and symbols began to reflect sexuality, hunting, and the memory, even presence of, ancestors. Often the religious beliefs and practices of our prehistoric ancestors were focused on Mother Earth, the source of life, and myths and stories developed about their origin and destiny and were expressed in religious practices.

These nature-based religious beliefs and practices dramatically changed across the millennia with the rise of agriculture and the emergence of the city-state.[5] As the religious beliefs and practices evolved, the social dynamics of the culture began to be incorporated. Not only did nature create a sense of awe and religious sensitivity, but also the way humans began to come together in groups, guided by powerful leaders who helped them to manage the complexities of life and seek common goals.

As humans moved across the continents, they took with them their wonder about nature and their fascination with ways of organizing and controlling the flow of life. Integral to this reflection and practice was the belief in another world, a second "layer" that had inordinate power. This mysterious power, manifest within nature and culture, would fill them with fear, but also invite them to ponder the ways that it might be controlled for their benefit. Religious creeds and codes emerged and a variety of cultic practices and patterns of community life developed.

Some assume that these early religious beliefs and practices, generically called the nature/culture religions, have disappeared, given the rise of modern scientific and historical understanding. This assumption is partially true in some regions of the world, but it would be wrong to conclude that nature/culture religions are a phenomenon of the past. In fact, they are alive and well, and while it may be difficult to determine how many people of the world practice their religion with the belief that the divine should be understood and encountered within nature and culture, it is clear that a sizeable part of the human family holds these convictions. In China, for example, 27.5 million people may be categorized as "folk believers."[6] Further, it can be argued that there is a resurgence of religious beliefs and practices that affirm that these indigenous traditions contain extraordinary wisdom, guidance for life, and spiritual direction that transform human consciousness and lead to liberation.[7] It is safe to say that there is a trend toward the "reenchantment" of the world, with the premise that the sacred is present in nature and culture.[8] Accompanying this trend is the profound awareness within the major religious traditions of the human family that nature is no longer that against which we push, but an integral part of human existence and contains elements that are religious in character. In addition, there is an equal awareness that our religious values and commitments influence the way we organize our world and inspire us to engage in the pursuit of peace and justice.

In this chapter, we will focus our attention on those religious beliefs and practices that are rooted in this understanding of nature. In the succeeding chapter, we will turn our attention to religious traditions linked to culture, and then we will see how these indigenous nature/culture religions and their spiritual pathways take expression in the contemporary world.

The view of the world

The ancients (and moderns) whose religious beliefs and practices are discerned within nature and culture have a profound sense of the sacred. They see within nature and culture an expression of the divine, and they attempt to understand themselves and the patterns of their lives as being lived on the threshold between the layers or liminaries, between the ordinary and the divine. On this border between the preliminary and the postliminary, they sense that there are **sacred powers**, **sacred stories** that speak about this power, **sacred actions** that influence this power, and **sacred space and time** in which humans experience the power and presence of the divine.

Sacred power is expressed in a variety of ways, but most often in the form of superhuman beings who exercise or have the capacity to exercise great influence. In some cases, these beings are viewed as merely superior to humans in the exercise of power, and in other cases these sacred beings are invested with ultimate power.[9] In native religions (those that have beliefs and practices that tend to be confined to particular families, tribes, and places) there is often the practice of **animism**, a belief that the spirits and souls inhabit and animate most of the natural world. The natural world, filled with mountains, trees, lakes, rivers, and animals, and more than can be named have spirits whose power should be acknowledged, honored, and respected. They contain the vital force that might help or hinder human beings in the normal course of life. Of special concern in native traditions is the place of **ancestors** whose spirits continue on and can affect the course of life from the other side. In Asian (e.g. the *Kami* in Shinto beliefs) and African traditions especially, prayers and sacrifices to the spirit of ancestors appear as a way of influencing sacred power. In some native traditions, there is a strong belief in the power of a **totem**, usually an animal that incarnates sacred power and the spiritual essence of a group. For example, the bear and the raven appear as totems in Native American religions.

Not infrequently, sacred power is personified and given identity and personality. In many cases, these indigenous native traditions are polytheistic, with gods and goddesses representing the range of power within nature and the human experience. In some cases, pantheons are created, whole families of gods and goddesses that are able to both explain and influence the unfolding of human life. As we shall see, these patterns appear in many ancient religions such as those of Egypt and Greece.

The reality of sacred power in the indigenous native traditions is characteristically articulated and passed on to succeeding generations through legends expressed in sacred story or **myth**.[10] Characteristically, these stories employ powerful images, symbols, and metaphors that engage the imagination of the religious community. These stories, often about ancestors or the gods and goddesses of pantheons, give guidance for life decisions to members of the clans and tribes. The stories provide quite well-prescribed codes of conduct and principles of ethics and behavior, and contained in these codes are clear prohibitions or **taboos**, which, if violated, may provoke the anger of the gods. These stories also provide hope that their prayers and rites will be able to influence the divine powers to provide safety in this life and security about an afterlife. They deal with a wide range of subjects, including the nature of the divine, the origin of the cosmos and its eventual ending, the ethical example of victory over evil, of heroes and avatars, codes of conduct, the nature of divine and demonic beings, and the model of the extraordinary lives of great kings and martyrs.[11]

Even with the guidance of the sacred stories, calibrating one's life on the borderline between the sacred and the profane is not easy. The profane can easily become the dominant force in life, and the most challenging questions and problems are not answered or solved. Life can be an endless round of fear, despair, and mere survival. The religious traditions rooted in nature and culture have sought a wide variety of means to access the divine power described in the guiding myths of the religion as a way of giving meaning and hope in life.

How does one achieve unity with the divine and become empowered to overcome conflict, anxiety, and the threat of death? A primary way is through sacred actions (rituals) than can be practiced to influence divine power. There are rituals that address nature itself, including rain dances, hunting rituals, and prayers for a good harvest. There are rituals that address the transition from one state of life to another (rites of passage) such as birth, coming of age, marriage, and of course the passage to the next life. There are rituals that address physical and mental illness and increase one's capacity to cope with the vicissitudes of life. There are rituals that nurture the spiritual life and others that secure one's place in the life to come. There are rituals of propitiation that cleanse, purify, and facilitate reconciliation with the divine. Prayer, meditation, discipline of body, mind, and spirit (yoga), sacrifice, song, dance, reading of sacred literature, liturgies, and the guiding homily are common ways to hear and respond to the divine.[12] Of special importance is the role of the holy person, the **shaman**, who has the power to control the spirit world and may even be able to leave the world of the profane to travel to other worlds. Evil spirits must be controlled and the good spirits have to be "called in" to provide help with the rough edges of life. Not infrequently, the shaman supplies healing substances, herbal or hallucinatory, to heal, combat natural disasters, or attack enemies.[13]

Within the rhythm of life, as the followers of these indigenous religions practice their faith, there are sacred places where the divine is more dramatically present and sacred times when the divine is experienced, honored, and celebrated. The sacred stories often refer to a special time when the pivotal events of the cosmos occurred, the known world came into being, and that sacred events occurred in special places at particular times (redemptive events). The believer is taken out of linear time and ordinary space and is transported into the presence of the divine. It may be on a sacred mountain that one goes to celebrate the entrance of the divine into human life. Moses meets God on the mountain in the burning bush (Exod. 3.1–6), and brings down from the mountain the code for human life. We too, may find the divine in the sanctuary on the birthday of the founder of our religion with support from well crafted words, art, architecture, and music. Sacred time has a special place among the Australian Aborigines, who discover access to divine power in **dreamtime** as do many of the prophets and patriarchs in Hebrew religion (Gen. 40–41). The message of the dream may be direct and easily understood, and in other cases it comes in symbolic form and must be interpreted. At these special times and places, we may have a religious experience—enlightenment, liberation, visions, guidance, comfort, inspiration, a calling to a way of life or a particular mission—and we know that we will never be the same again.

Representative indigenous wisdom religions: Africa

These traditions, containing most of the features we have described appear in many places in the ancient and modern world. We see them in Africa, America, Australia, the Middle East, South Asia, East Asia, and Europe. Our point of entry will be to briefly explore their expression in indigenous African religion and Native American religion. Our goal is to capture the way they illustrate the family of indigenous wisdom religions, the spirit of these traditions, and suggest dimensions of the spiritual pathways we all seek. We will not describe them in detail[14] but hope that we may learn about the wisdom and character of their spiritual pathways which have the potential to be of great value to the whole human family.

We start in Africa, in part because it may in fact be the cradle of humanity. While written records are scarce, there are nevertheless several sources for the study of indigenous African religions including an oral tradition, archeologic, and linguistic evidence, continuing practice, and the art and clearly marked sacred spaces.[15] Nearly every group has parents, priests, and storytellers who maintain an oral tradition. In addition, many of the African native religions have preserved traditional art, artifacts, and dress. From these sources (and visits to the regions[16]), it is possible to gain an appreciation and some understanding of the indigenous religious traditions of Africa, though not living in the culture leaves one an outsider and observer.

These traditions are **native** in the sense of local and contextual. There are different versions of the creation story, given distinctiveness by the natural and social environment of a region. Kenya, for example, has a creation story filled with the natural surroundings of East Africa. There is a dramatic account of the origin of the first couple, Gikuyu and Mumbi, from whom the group is descended. There are rich and colorful descriptions of the created land, full of lush growth, with Gikuyu looking over the creation from Mount Kere-Nyago (Kenya), the mountain of brightness.

The Yoruba of Southwestern Nigeria have a more complex and detailed account of the creation and understand the beginning of time as a period when there were heavens above and a watery wasteland below. In summary, the pantheon of divinities (*orisha*) delegated Obatala, one of the gods of *orisha* to create the earth with some loose soil in a shell that eventually covered the watery space.[17] This first attempt failed when Obatala got drunk, and another deity (Oduduwa) was sent to finish the creation. Oduduwa formed the Yoruba people and founded the Yoruba kingdom. A third creation story comes from the Dogon people who live south of the Sahara in the cliff villages of Mali. According to this story, creation began with the supreme God, Amma, who existed alone, but who contained within himself the principles and materials to create the universe. At his sacred word, a cosmic egg containing the elements of earth, air, fire, water with fertile seeds, was caused to spin, but on this first try, the water was thrown out, causing the seeds to dry up. Again, a second attempt was made and succeeded, creating humanity which was given the responsibility of maintaining life and the structure of the world. The failed attempts at creation may be commentaries on the ambivalent nature of the human experience.

These indigenous traditions and the many others in Africa also contain descriptions of a spiritual order populated with divine beings, often structured in hierarchical order. From this pantheon flowed the vital force (*mana*) that shaped the earth and human life, a force that can be influenced so that its power can improve the condition of humanity. In some cases, this pantheon was led by a supreme divine being and creator, usually male but occasionally female (e.g. Olorun and Olokun among the Yoruba). The divine being (s) maintains equilibrium and is surrounded by other gods and lesser spirits who are connected to particular people, tribe, and sacred places such as a rock or a river. The ancestor spirits are part of this grouping and offer protection to the living persons that are related to them.

It is in nature that the indigenous African religions find their sacred spaces, places, symbols, and times. For these peoples, the universe is viewed as God's creation and is filled with the divine presence. Therefore life itself tends to function in accord with the patterns and rhythms of nature. The villages tend to be organized in a way that respect nature and enables those who live in the village to structure life around the more predictable cycles of nature such as the seasons. Natural settings become places of worship and centers of interaction with the divine and the world of spirits. The rituals of cleansing may take place in a river, and a mountain may be the dwelling place of the gods and goddesses. Fire also has sacred meaning as it gives warmth and is used for the preparation of food. It should be noted that natural objects and places are not generally worshipped, but are settings for worship and provide access to the divine and the spiritual understanding of the world.

Special persons are integral to the spiritual understanding of indigenous African religions. A leader or a holy person will help in the formation of a community and create a social order, giving a place and role for all the members of the community. There are many norms and expectations within the community, some explicit (the taboos) and others more implicit and intuitive. Especially important in nearly every community is the carefully defined relationship between men and women as they join as partners in life and share in the divine creation. It is in this arena, as in nearly every culture, that communal life is often disrupted. These traditions believe that each person has a compound character made up of material inherited from one's parents and the spiritual dimension which defines one's character and distinctive personality. There are times when humans in their weakness violate the norms of the community and create tension within it. It is frequently the religious practices that help to achieve reconciliation, restore harmony, and offer a more satisfying way of life. Essentially it is the religious structure and ethical norms that serve to hold the community together, and it is the clearly designated responsibility of a variety of individuals like the holy persons or shamans to provide guidance and support to the members of the community.

On occasion, growing out of and sanctioned by the community, prophetic figures take on particular challenges in times of crisis and change. In recent history, these prophetic figures were instrumental in providing leadership as Europeans came to Africa, posing a threat to the traditional way of life. At times, to argue for certain behavior and actions, kings would be endowed with sacred power, reflecting the interdependence of political and religious affairs.

It is important to underline that the religious communities have a pattern of sacred practices including the rites of passage, sacrifice, rituals for hunting and agriculture, modes of communication with ancestors, and artistic depictions of the deities and sacred persons. These rituals provide support, guidance, and nurture the spiritual journey of the people. It is the religious community with its beliefs and practices that provides direction for moral conduct and the structure and order of society. In a very powerful way, a person's value is measured by the meritorious character of his/her behavior and the contribution one makes to society. The primacy of society over the personal ambition of the individual is stressed in order to create a society of peace and order. There are clear expectations and norms in interpersonal relationships, and each individual is expected to follow his/her conscience and avoid wrong-doing. Evil or misconduct is understood as a violation of the spirit of the ancestors and the gods and has consequences, but ways are provided in rituals for forgiveness and purification.

As in many indigenous religions of the world, the native religious traditions in Africa have been severely challenged by the enormous changes of recent times. The influx of Western people, the missionary endeavors of Christianity and Islam, urbanization, the global character of the economy, the challenges of the environment with the accompanying limited food supply, and the conflicts among tribes and nation states have threatened the existence of these religious communities and indeed, a large percentage of the African people. The question remains whether these religious traditions may prove to be a positive resource for the creation of a more humane and just social order for the African people.

Native American religions

The religious beliefs and practices of the Native American peoples are intricately linked to nature, as are the indigenous religious traditions of Africa. These peoples, most likely immigrants from Asia, arrived in North America over several thousand years ago, from approximately 40,000 to 20,000 BCE with some of the Eskimo tribes of Alaska coming later. The calculation of precise dates varies among scholars, and there are alternative theories about the migration southward into Central and South America. Our goal is not to trace this history of immigration and migration, but to describe the way these peoples ordered their universe by using religious beliefs and practices. As with the African traditions, the religious beliefs and practices of the Native Americans[18] were native, in that they were local and contextual and embedded in a particular culture. While these people, often grouped in tribes, had distinctive creeds, codes, cultic practices, community life, and they also shared many beliefs and practices. There is a common view of the world that is discernable, and it is the "soul" of this worldview that can inform and enrich those from other times and cultures. To understand the heart of a religious tradition that is not our own is the first step to the acceptance of the "other" and the sharing of a common planet.

Once again, access for the outsider into the world of Native American religions is difficult for many reasons. As with the African religions, the culture is unique and subtle and therefore hard for the outsider to fully understand and appreciate. Further, the initiation rites for full entrance into many of the tribes involve a long and complex process, one that gives the insider a unique experience and nuanced understanding. A comprehensive understanding of Native American religions is also limited by the fact that there are few written resources; it is primarily an oral tradition. Fortunately, we are now being taught by native leaders and scholars, have access to the art and artifacts of the native religious traditions, and have been given access to most of the tribal regions and people. In part, the motivation for majority people of the people in the Americas to learn about Native American religions has been sparked by an obligation to make restitution for the mistreatment of the indigenous people of the Americas.

Most of the Native American religions have beliefs about the origin of the universe. They ask: How did the world begin? How do humans fit into the larger frame of the cosmos? Was there a divine origin of the world? How do humans connect and relate to the rest of the known world? As theories about the origins of the world developed, the Native American people saw little difference between human life and the rest of nature, the world of animals, plants, lakes, rivers, and mountains. Humans were an integral part of the natural world and needed to understand that they were intimately connected to nature and should respect nature in all of its rich diversity. Yes, in order to meet basic human needs, humans had to master parts of nature, but they did so with great reverence, even religiously, as they tried, for example to kill a buffalo or harvest a whale. The Osage of the Southern Plains region in their creation myth speak about the time when the earliest ancestors lived in the sky and sought the counsel of the sun and the moon about their origins. Nature was their teacher and their mother, and they learned that they were related to all of the life on earth, with each part having its place "under the sun."

A survey of the many creation myths suggests that these sacred stories took two primary forms: creation comes out of chaos and brings some order; and creation is the result of violence between forces of good and evil.[19] In those legends in which the world comes out of chaos, there is usually some super-human being that emerges from the chaos, discovers and shapes the earth, and brings humans, animals, and plants into existence. The story of the Crow nation (Northern Plains) follows this pattern, giving a central place to the Crow people. Old man who did everything, wandered over the earth covered with water and created the world as we know it.[20] The second type of creation story is seen in the Seneca people of the Eastern forests. They speak about how the bride of the great sky chief falls to earth and lands on the back of a turtle. She is impregnated by the wind, has twins, and as in the Biblical story of Cain and Abel, the twins have conflicting motives as they piece the world together, with one being more positive and constructive and the other more harmful and destructive. We now live in such a mixed world.

In most of the Native American religious traditions, there is a strong belief in another layer or world inhabited by numerous gods and spirits. In some cases, there is the explicit belief that these beings influence the course of human life, and that they are in many cases the intermediaries of the high God who lives in the sky. Also, the pantheon is Mother Earth, and she too gives and takes, and makes all of life and events in the natural world sacred.

As with the African indigenous religions, certain people within the Native American religions are given unusual spiritual power and status, adding to the complexity of their religious beliefs and practices. At the top of the hierarchy is usually a high God who must be honored through rituals, and who, when displeased demands propitiation and ritual action.

The numerous other spirits and powers require attention as well, and the shaman plays this key role in most of the Native American religions. The Zuni people, part of the larger Pueblo people in the Southwest of the United States, have a society run by a three-person council made up of shamans. These shamans, endowed with special spiritual power, are understood to be able to communicate with the spiritual world, explain unusual events, and even pre-dict future happenings. Surrounding and giving community life to this struc-ture are the rituals of life, sacred costumes and colors, dances that have religious significance, healing, and agricultural ceremonies.

Of note as well, because of the lore associated with it, is the **sacred pipe**, one of the universal symbols of the Native Americans. The substance and the shape of the pipe vary, but it is consistently made with great care. It takes many forms and is often decorated with animals, birds, and human faces. In the Eskimo tradition, pipes are made from bone, ivory, stone, or metal. The stems are wood and carved in a way that makes cleaning possible. Usually, the bowls for the pipes are made in the shape of arctic animals such as the seal or the whale. As the tribes gather to make decisions or as the leaders of various tribes meet to solve common problems, the pipe is smoked by the leaders, even as treaties are ratified, contracts signed, and oaths are made. The pipe is a sign of welcome and viewed as the bond between the family members and tribal leaders. The promises made, ritualized by the smoking of the pipe, are sacred in character and should never be broken.

The sacred pipe is but one of the sacred rituals practiced in Native American religions. There are many other sacred actions and ceremonies including the rites of passage usually divided into the four cycles of infancy, youth, adulthood, and old age. The marriage ceremony is given an important place in most of the tribes as the relationship between a man and woman enhances the stability of the tribe and results in children who will perpetuate the tribe and its values. Linked to the growing children in the family is the **vision quest**, viewed as one of the most important ritual practices in the Native American tribes. It is open to both males and females, but expected to be undertaken by all males. It is a challenging wilderness adventure in which the young person must utilize all of the resources of nature to survive in the quest to find one's guardian spirit. It serves the purpose of preparing young men as brave warriors and helps both young men and women to learn about the worldview of the tribe and their respective places within the tribe. Prepared by fasting, the ritual steam bath (sweat lodge), and the guidance of elders, the young person is given a challenging assignment in the wilderness that must be completed in four days. Though differing in details, the vision quest was (is) present in most Native American tribes.

In nearly all of the Native American tribes, there is a delicate and complex interweaving of religious beliefs, moral standards and ethical behavior, and the systems and structures of society. The universe is under the control of the gods and intermediary spirits and is managed in an orderly way. Native Americans honor the authority of the gods and attempt to order their personal lives and their society in a way that pleases the gods who are in charge of the universe. The ethical norms are both personal and social, and a good person lives a moral life and is socially responsible, creating an orderly, just, and peaceful society. Tribal unity, respect for leaders and elders, and care for others are values distributed differently within the moral structures of the many tribes.

In earlier times, as the Native Americans lived close to nature, life was precarious. It was made so by natural disaster, disease, famine, and warring conflicts with other tribes. Death was a constant companion, and Native Americans developed a profound awareness of the proximity of the next world. Because the Native Americans see the next world as an integral part of their reality, they came to accept death as natural and inevitable. Songs, rituals, ceremonies, and burial grounds were a part of the furniture of life, as people hoped for a continuing existence in the next world.

Just as the African indigenous people had to find ways to adjust to the influx of people from other parts of the world, so too did the Native Americans as "white people" took over their land. It is not a "pretty story" yet one that needs telling and re-telling in order to insure that all people, regardless of ethnicity and culture must be respected. An understanding of the religious beliefs and practices of "others" is integral to building a just society and a world of respect.

The contributions and challenges of the spirituality of the indigenous wisdom traditions

For the vast majority of the people, especially those who lived in an earlier time, who lived and moved and had their being in the context of their indigenous religious tradition, life *was a spiritual journey.* Their known world was fundamentally spiritual in character, and the divine was omnipresent in a rich variety of forms. The case may be made as well that even contemporary people, whose world view and way of life is connected with the indigenous wisdom traditions, understand themselves as being on a spiritual journey. But contemporary people within these traditions wrestle with the realities of a global and secular context with its array of competing outlooks and values. In a sense, they live in two worlds; they feel divided and sometimes conflicted by these competing values. As I traveled in Alaska and interacted with Alaska Natives, I sensed that these people were being asked to leap forward from a subsistence economy and a way of life intimately interwoven with nature into a world of global economics, digital communications, and national politics. Life for these people, and perhaps for the whole human family, means struggling to find a workable combination of traditional and modern, even postmodern worldviews and values—a demanding spiritual journey.[21]

There are many beliefs and practices that are life-giving within the indigenous wisdom traditions, ones that can be brought forward into the contemporary world and nurture and sustain present day pilgrims.[22] In fact, all religious traditions face this hermeneutical challenge, asking the sacred events of their history, often written about in sacred scripture or kept alive in oral tradition, to leap forward into the present for instruction and give guidance for the future. Worship in the Jewish, Christian, and Muslim communities is prototypically such an event.

Our point of entry in this task for the indigenous wisdom traditions is to suggest a few of the beliefs and practices inherent in the traditions that might have universal relevance and life-giving potential for all who are on a spiritual journey. Our suggestions will be illustrative rather than comprehensive, and will point to the finest expression of the traditions, knowing full well that every person and culture struggles to live up to its ideals. The goal is not to romanticize those in the religious communities of the indigenous wisdom traditions; in fact in practice they were and are filled with inconsistency as believers in every religion are. The goal rather is to learn from their best insights and values, honor and respect these people and their distinctive culture,[23] and restate the wisdom in ways that might be applied to our time and place. Let me suggest five dimensions of wisdom that may be life-giving and have the potential to guide our spiritual journeys.

1. The indigenous wisdom traditions have tremendous **respect for nature** and see human life as integrated with nature rather than as exploitive of nature. Their outlook, while not fully articulated in a scientific way, is fundamentally ecological in character. These people know that they belong to nature, heart and soul, and must live in harmony with it in ways that honor the patterns and order of the universe. The whole human family is learning this "inconvenient truth" that they now must live in ways that respect nature, given the overwhelming challenges of a deteriorating environment and global warming. Spirituality is profoundly ecological in character.

2. The indigenous wisdom traditions propose a way of life that is **centered** rather than fragmented and alienated. It is holistic in tone and invites a pattern of life that is congruent, focused, and ordered around accepted values and patterns of living. Is there a need to challenge the present order and speak truth to justice? Yes. Is there too much to do? Yes. Is there stress? Yes. Are there conflicts? Yes. Are there tugs and pulls in many directions? Yes. But is there a center that helps manage all of these distractions and challenges? Yes, there is a spiritual center grounded in their belief that there is a divine vital force running through all of reality. It is this insight contained in the wisdom of these traditions that must be cultivated and sustained by personal discipline and corporate spiritual practices.

3. It follows that the indigenous wisdom traditions understand the **divine as omnipresent and integral to all of human life**. To be sure, there are personified projections of the divine taking form in a variety of ways, such as the Great Spirit or High God with an array of intermediaries who live far away and seem unconnected to the daily concerns of life. But these personified divine beings represent a spiritual realm that is immediately present, and both "layers," the material and the spiritual are fundamentally one in these wisdom traditions. It is all one world, more monistic than dualistic in character and it is the "practice of the presence" of the divine that gives one guidance and leads to a life of inner peace and serenity.

4. The indigenous wisdom traditions offer a **way of knowing** that complements rational and scientific ways of knowing. Rational and scientific ways of knowing give us our understanding of the very foundation of our physical world, but they do not teach us how to love, enable us to achieve enlightenment, and lead us to harmony with God, however God may be understood. The spiritual life uses other ways of knowing such as prayer, music, meditation, reflection, discipline, and worship. The scientific understanding of the universe may lead to awe and amazement, but it is the humility before the mystery that takes us to the heart of divine mystery.

5. The indigenous wisdom traditions teach an **ethical way of life** that places value on personal character, respect for all, and responsibility and duty within the social order. Other religious and philosophical traditions do as well, but there is a persuasive and evocative understanding of the call to an ethical life in the wisdom traditions, one rooted in nature, story, and personal experience. Again, we are cautious not to romanticize native peoples; they struggled in the ways that all humans struggle to close the gap between the *is* and the *ought*. Were there those within the communities that practiced the faith of the indigenous wisdom traditions who violated the ethical norms of the tradition and is there hypocrisy in their current expressions? Of course, but the vision of the ethical way of life in these traditions is one model for those of us who struggle to live with integrity and honor our deepest beliefs and values, pulled away as we are by a selfish and materialistic culture, which teaches that happiness consists in the abundance of things possessed.

There is much in the indigenous wisdom traditions that feeds our spiritual life, but there are also elements in these traditions about which we need to think critically. There are beliefs and practices that are limited and potentially life-denying that present challenges to these peoples. Let me just hint at some of these:

1. The first is that the worldview and especially the stories contain **distortions of reality** as we know it on this side of the scientific understanding of the world.

While the sacred stories (myths) have parabolic value, there is now the need to remove the literal understanding of these stories and see them as metaphors and images of spiritual truth. As possible, within these traditions of wisdom, the emphasis should be on the wisdom and less on the actual description of the universe. The hard work of integrating religion and science must take place here as it does in many other religious traditions.

2. There is the challenge within these traditions to understand how they might **connect with other peoples and cultures** that are now living as neighbors. It is important that indigenous people advocate for their rights, pursue the continuation of their customs and cultures, insist on being treated justly and equitably by law, and be able to live *their* way of life. It is positive to want to preserve one's language and way of life, but some accommodation to the realities of their context is necessary. The world has become too small to live in isolation, and adjustments to the global context of life are necessary. It is important for indigenous people to do it for themselves in a thoughtful and careful way or majority people and more powerful cultures will impose their way.

3. It follows that it is easy for people whose way of life is challenged by others, as happens in a crowded world, **to become violent** and attack those who threaten them. In parts of Africa it is not uncommon, especially when the basic provisions of life are so limited and land is necessary to sustain the people, for traditions that have a strong warrior tradition and class to resort to violence. As happens, neighboring tribes are demonized and attacked and everyone suffers. The best of the religious teachings of wisdom traditions dictate against violence toward others, although the archetypical warrior is often viewed as heroic and a savior.

4. So too, is there the risk that those in power, such as the kings and shamans, may **turn on their own people**, exploiting them for their selfish ends and the quest for power. There are many examples of those in power, claiming for themselves inordinate power and viewing themselves as having divine sanction. They may turn on a minority group within their own society or tribe and viciously torture and kill them. Again, the religious wisdom in these traditions would clearly dictate against this kind of behavior.

5. Finally, I would mention that it is often the case that these kinds of destructive behavior have their origin in a religious ideology that is fundamentalist, **xenophobic**, sectarian, and divisive. It is the claim to have all the truth and nothing but the truth that distorts and squashes the life-giving truth that exists in the wisdom teaching. It is tragic that the present world has many of these kinds of religious movements which are so harmful and destructive. In the case of religions rooted in the indigenous wisdom traditions, there is the clear mandate to work for peace and a more just and humane world.

It is often within religions that see the divine as intimately linked to culture that these potential dangers are present, and it is to these religious traditions and their understanding of spirituality that we now turn.

Discussion questions

1. What are some ways in which the indigenous wisdom traditions differ from the monotheistic religions such as Judaism, Christianity, and Islam?
2. What are the major challenges to the survival of the indigenous wisdom religions in the current world order?
3. What would be comfortable and uncomfortable for you if you were asked to serve in the Peace Corps in a setting where the people practiced an indigenous native religion?
4. What are the essential features of the indigenous native religions that are potentially life-giving and life-denying?
5. What wisdom from these indigenous wisdom traditions might be passed on to other cultures and countries to improve the quality of life?

Key terms and concepts

1. **Ancestral spirits:** The souls of ancestors believed to continue to take an active interest in their communities, and capable of both great good and great harm if displeased.
2. **Animism:** The belief that the spirits and souls of ancestors or divinities animate and inhabit most of the natural world.
3. **Mana:** A Polynesian term, now commonly used and best translated as vital force animating all living things.
4. **Myth:** A sacred story that captures a profound moral or sacred truth.
5. **Rites of passage:** Rituals that address and enable the transition from one state of life to another.
6. **Shaman:** A person who is sanctioned by the community to exercise powers of spirit-control, divination, healing, and contacting the gods, usually exercised through rituals and in a trance state.
7. **Taboo:** A prohibition against a certain action such as eating a certain food, going to a certain place, or violating a sacred rule, enforced through fear of the anger of gods or spirits.
8. **Totem:** An animal or plant believed to have special relations to a particular tribe or subgroup.
9. **Vision quest:** The ritual quest for a guardian spirit, usually undertaken at puberty. The youth seeks the spirit by going to a remote place where it may appear to him/her in a vision.

Suggestions for reference and reading

Eliade, Mircea, *A History of Religious Ideas* (Chicago: University of Chicago Press, 1978–1985), 3 volumes.

Frazer, James, *The Golden Bough*, edited in light of recent scholarship by Theodor H. Gaster (New York: Criterion Books, 1959).

Gill, Sam D., *Native American Religions: An Introduction* (Belmont, CA: Wadsworth, 1982).

Kessler, Gary E., *Ways of Being Religious* (Mountain View, CA: Mayfield Publishing Company, 2000). See chapters 4 and 5. See as well Gary Kessler's *Studying Religion: An Introduction Through Case Studies* (New York: McGraw-Hill, 2003).

Parrinder, E. G., *African Traditional Religion* (London: S.P.C.K., 1971).

Roberts, Elizabeth & Amidon, Elias, *Earth Prayers* (San Francisco: HarperSanFrancisco, 1991).

Smith, Huston, *Forgotten Truth: The Primordial Tradition* (New York: Harper & Row, 1976).

Sullivan, Lawrence E., ed., *Native American Religions: North America* (New York: Macmillan Publishing Company, 1987, 1989).

Yates, Jr., Kyle M., General Editor, *The Religious World: Communities of Faith* (New York: Macmillan Publishing Company, 1988).

Classical Expressions of Culture-Based Religions   3

Chapter Outline

Culture-based spiritual pathways   41
Classical expressions of spiritual pathways rooted in culture   44

Culture-based spiritual pathways

We are exploring the ways that members of the human family have used to conceive the divine, achieve levels of harmony with the divine, and live lives in ways that bring a sense of being linked to the divine purpose. The outcome of this endeavor is a life of fulfillment in daily responsibilities and the interior sense of peace and joy. We have called this endeavor a quest for a spiritual pathway, and our goal is to learn about the many spiritual pathways that humans have found that give meaning and serenity. It is our deep conviction that learning about these pathways will enable us to enrich our spiritual journey and to be more tolerant and respectful of others whose views differ from our own. With this personal enrichment and understanding of others, we will be better able to contribute to the formation of a more humane, just, and peaceful world as we honor and receive with joy those who are different from us. Religion remains one of our most challenging sources of conflict and one of our richest sources for reconciliation.

We have grouped these quests for authentic spiritual pathways into three large categories of religious expression: the religions that see the divine as manifest in nature and culture; the religions that understand the divine as one transcendent reality (transcendent monism); and the Abrahamic monotheistic religions with the foundational understanding that there is one personal and sovereign God who has created all and guides the human family. Our goal in this chapter is to understand better those religions that have seen the divine as manifest or expressed in the surrounding culture.

It should be noted that these three categories for classifying religions are somewhat arbitrary and used as a way to catch the emphasis or spirit of a religious tradition. In fact, the groupings overlap and contain understandings of the divine and approaches to spirituality that share similarities with religions placed in the other categories. Although we focus on the distinguishing characteristics of a category, the groupings nevertheless have much in common.

In addition, we are making some judgments about how these spiritual pathways may be life-giving, giving the followers a way of putting the world "together," a good, purposeful, and happy life, and encouraging them to pursue the well-being of others. We have also said that some expressions of these traditions are life-denying, harmful to the followers, create a climate of fear and suspicion, and are exclusive and sectarian in character, judgmental, and in some cases, even demonizing of others. We have also maintained that our ability to make a contribution to building a more peaceful world comes through an informed and empathic understanding of the worldviews and commitments of those who are different from us, especially as we are able to grasp the more positive dimensions of the religion. Through exposure, dialogue, and study, it is possible to genuinely appreciate the spiritual pathways of others and to learn from those pathways that differ from our own.

As a way of gaining a deeper understanding of these spiritual pathways, we have suggested categories of understanding (a common universe of discourse), in order to "make sense" of these complex human patterns of belief and practice. We have spoken about how most religions have a creed or a set of beliefs; a code of conduct, and a sense of the ethical life; a cultic expression of corporate worship and ritual; and a community of support and shared life. We have spoken about how these religions are contextual and grow out of the culture, and how these religious convictions develop and take different forms across time, giving each of the major groups various traditions within the larger family. We have noted that in some cases the assumptions will be rooted in a premodern understanding of reality which uses or used categories of magic and miracle and did not have the benefit of the knowledge and insights that come from the rise of scientific and historical study. Some of these religious traditions may have attempted to accommodate to a modern understanding of reality, incorporating the insights of what some have called "the Enlightenment project," but in most cases still carry assumptions forward that are premodern. Now, the challenge for all religious thought and practice is to find ways of formulating a faith that preserves the heart of the religion while incorporating the best assumptions of the Enlightenment. It may also need to take into account the best insights of postmodernism, the view that questions that purely objective pursuits of knowledge are possible, that knowledge is discovered exclusively in the inherent reductionism of the scientific method, and affirms that all constructions of knowledge and "truth" need to be deconstructed in order to discover possible bias. In addition to these categories, we will also assess the ways that our time and place in history shape our religious understanding, looking at religions that originate and develop at a particular time, in the Middle East, Asia, Europe, Africa, or the Americas.[1]

Those religious views and practices that have understood the divine as integral to the surrounding culture have tended to assume a premodern view of the world, giving a sacred dimension to the social structures and endowing leaders and rulers with a divine identity. We will examine this religious understanding, but give due consideration to a more contemporary expression of culture-based religious outlook which is facing the shift in the way that the world is understood and attempting to adjust to modern and postmodern outlooks as well as our global context.

The religions that have primarily understood the divine within the dimensions of a particular culture have much in common with the indigenous wisdom traditions that discerned the divine within nature. The categories of their religious understanding have as a foundation, the notion of the sacred as near and ever-present, not only in nature, but in the ways that society is given structure and leadership and organized to insure that life would continue in ways that enabled people to have their physical, social, economic, and psychic/ spiritual needs met. We will see how the categories and practices based in the notion of the sacred were used in agriculture, in the formation of the city-state, and in the investment of power in religious and political leadership.

There were the sacred stories or myths that were told and retold as ways of explaining human fertility, the success of crops, the relationships and conflicts with neighboring tribes, and social groupings that were more urban in character. These myths, containing ways of understanding and behavior were acted out in sacred ritual and ceremony. Creeds containing statements of doctrinal belief and codes prescribing moral values and ethical behavior were framed. The religion had a profound social dimension as well, as it became a way of understanding group identity and providing community life.

Religious and political leaders were vested with sacred power to lead the people in religious activity that shaped their external social order and give them experiences that were internal and spiritual in character. It is this story that we must now tell as it played in the classical cultures of Egypt and Greece. The choice of these regions of the world is a way of illustrating the concept of religious understanding rooted in culture; religious traditions in Mesopotamia, Rome, Northern Europe, and China (Confucianism) would illustrate the concept as well.

Classical expressions of spiritual pathways rooted in culture

Ancient Egypt: the gift of the Nile

Ancient Egypt (*ca*. 3500–1000 BCE) had a remarkably stable history that lasted over twenty-five centuries. There is evidence of civilization (burial sites, irrigation systems, wells) that goes back as far as 4500 BCE. But a more advanced agriculture and the emergence of the city-state came primarily because of population increases in the region. The social structures became more sophisticated and two separate regions (kingdoms) were formed in the fourth millennium BCE called Upper and Lower Egypt. It was in the kingdom of Upper Egypt (southern) that we see the beginnings of a major civilization developing. In the period from about 3100–2700 BCE, called the Archaic Period, a unified kingdom formed in Memphis. The political unity was achieved under Menes who founded Egypt's first political dynasty, and this remarkable achievement may in part be attributed to the favorable geographical location, protected by the sea and desert from foreign enemies and access to the Nile that allowed for trade and the movement of goods and people. It was in this period that a system of pictorial writing was devised called hieroglyphics.

The next several historical periods are often classified in terms of its kings: the Old Kingdom (2700–2200), the Middle Kingdom (2050–1800), and the New Kingdom (1570–1165). Across these centuries, the Egyptians developed a religion of remarkable complexity and richness, one that changed and evolved over the centuries. The splendor of its temples, the power and wealth of its priests, its animal-headed gods, the divinity of the pharaoh whose identity was part sun, part falcon, and judge of all souls, and the elaborate structure of the pyramids all point to a subtle understanding of the divine and the quest for immortality. In fact because of the complexity and changing character of

Egyptian religion, it is difficult to describe it as one unified system. What is apparent is that Egyptian religion was woven into and developed with the agriculture and social structure of this land. Our goal in the brief overview of Egyptian religion is not to describe in great detail the rich variety of beliefs and practices contained within it, but to point to its primary character as a religion that is intimately connected to the culture, social order, and leadership of the region. It had the following features:

1. As in the religions rooted in nature, the religious outlook of Egypt was **tied to the sky, the water, and the land**, and in particular it was shaped by **the flow of the Nile** and what seemed like the eternal presence of the sun. Year after year, the floodwaters would rise to fertilize the fields, the sun would bring warmth, and the result was an abundant harvest. With the improvement of the techniques of agriculture, there was usually sufficient food for the people. The regularity of a good harvest also meant that the divine pharaoh could rule with order and relative peace. For the better part of 2500 years, Egyptian life remained essentially the same as the Egyptians lived under the eternal sky, sun, sand, and water.

2. The flow of the Nile and the mild climate gave the Egyptians a relatively stable structure for society, though not without the injustice of a rigid class system or freedom from slavery as, for example, in the case of the Hebrews and story of Moses. It also suggested a worldview, articulated in mythological stories that saw **history as cyclical and social structures as unchanging in character**. The stories would be told differently in various regions and times, but common themes about creation, the nature of the universe, and the structures of society held the various stories together. The Egyptians perceived the sky as the goddess Nut whose body stretched to form the heavens that included the sun, moon, and stars. Nut was supported by Shu, the god of the winds and air. Below Shu was the ocean god Nun on which the earth god Geb lay. Part of Geb was red representing the hostile desert and part of him was black representing the Nile Delta and valley. The waters of the Nile were believed to flow down to the underworld, the land of the dead. It was from this basic worldview that the different cosmologies developed in the various regions and times, in Heliopolis, Hermopolis, Memphis, and Thebes.[2]

3. The primary threats then were not the harsh character of nature that had to be appeased nor the invasion of aggressive neighbors, although both nature in terms of drought and famine and hostile neighbors were integral to Egyptian history. But there was a long period of remarkable stability in ancient Egypt, and it was the flow of the Nile and the warmth of the sun that provided the props for an ongoing mortality play. **Death** was the primary threat and the goal of religion was to provide the passageway to the next world.

4. A major event in the history of religion in Egypt was the unification of Upper (southern) and Lower (northern) Egypt in approximately 3100 BCE and with it came the primary religious belief of Egypt, that of **divine kingship**.[3] It was this dogma

that gave some order to the array of religious beliefs that characterized the religious practices of the Egyptians, and the nature of the leadership of the divine pharaoh would play a large role in determining the quality of life of the people.

5. There were **locals gods** that had great influence on the life of the people and developed into full-blown pantheon. These gods became the subject of stories or myths that explained the challenging mysteries of being human. We know the major ones by a variety of names including Atum, Ptah, Aton, Osiris, Horus, and Aman-Re (Ra). Both blessing (peace, long life, healthy children, etc.) and curse (drought, famine, disease, etc.) were explained in terms of the activity of the gods.

Hence, it was the sun and the annual flow and flooding of the Nile, the formation of a worldview expressed in mythological stories, the profound concern for an afterlife, a divine pharaoh, and an array of local gods that provided the contours of Egyptian religious life. There is no implication here that Egyptian religion was organized and simple; it in fact was diverse, lenient, and often lacking intellectual rigor. It allowed a variety of expressions, and therefore can be quite resistant to logic and order. But let us at least sample some of the ways in which these five factors interacted in the spiritual pathways of the Egyptian people over the centuries.

With the unification of Upper and Lower Egypt came the splendor for which ancient Egypt is known, as it expanded its empire, refined its agriculture, displayed advanced architecture in its structures (e.g., the pyramids), developed cities, invented a solar calendar, and produced skillful physicians and mathematicians. Religion was interwoven with this extraordinary achievement in human history. Let us illustrate:

- In the Old Kingdom (2700–2200 BCE), there was the **formation of a view of the divine that justified the new kingdom** centered in Memphis. The regional god of Memphis, Ptah, became the primary creator god, and was viewed as superior to Atum, the supreme god of the older belief system. It was the divine, imaged in a local deity, that created the world, gave sanction to power, and provided order to society. Religion and politics were mixed in ways that gave sanction to power and social structure.
- The Middle Kingdom (2050–1800 BCE), with its capitol in Thebes, gave more attention to the **regional gods**, and the common people were given the right to participate in religious practices and ceremonies which had previously been reserved for priests and royalty. Religion became democratized and supported by a large contingent of priests and the building of temples. These local gods took many forms and were often symbolized by animals, for example, Thoth as a baboon, Anubis as a jackal, and Sekhmet as a lion. A variety of religious ceremonies and practices

became a part of the daily life of the people, although the temple was not generally the worship center, but the abode of the gods. Only the priests and the servants were admitted to the innermost chambers where they attended to the needs of the gods. The primary purpose of this temple worship was to strengthen the life of the god, who in turn would sustain the life of the people.

- In the period of 1800–1570 BCE, we see the rise of the belief in Aton, linked to the Sun, and the **ways in which the gods connect with one another**, and whether there is a senior god in the pantheon. It was a central feature of the New Kingdom (1570–1165 BCE), with the change in the name of the primary divinity to Amon. One pharaoh during this period, Akhenaton (1379–1362 BCE), began to oppose the worship of Amon and demand the worship of Aton. Helped by his more famous wife, Nefertiti, Akhenaton introduced the worship of Aton imaged as the solar disc and attempted to close the temples in which other gods were worshipped. He is best known for the profound and beautiful hymns of praise to Aton. An imposed change in religious views was difficult then as now, and little is known about his fate except that he was succeeded by his son-in-law Tutankhamon (King Tut) who resisted the Atonic reforms. During the reign of Ramses II (1290–1224 BCE), there was speculation[4] about a god that stands behind and above all the regional gods, and hints of movement away from the more mythological characterization of the divine.

- Throughout Egyptian history, the most important gods were associated with nature (sun), death, and afterlife. The names of these divinities, as we have suggested, varied across time and place. The most important name for the sun-god was Re (or Ra), symbolized by the sun's disc or the falcon. In the *Book of the Dead*, we read about how Re conquered all of his opponents and became the king of the gods.

- It is in the myth of Osiris that we read about the other "layer" or the underworld in Egyptian religion. The story is centered on the cult of the dead and search for an afterlife out of which developed the elaborate funerary rites and the cult. As the somewhat complex myth of the underworld unfolds, we read that Osiris and Seth were brothers, and Isis was Osiris' sister. Osiris ruled the world, but Seth hated him and killed him using guile. Osiris is put in a coffin and sent down the Nile, but he is recovered and revived by Isis, only to be killed again by Seth and hacked into fourteen pieces which were scattered across the land. Isis finds the pieces of his body and carefully buries them. In the midst of this drama, Isis conceives a son by Osiris, named Horus, and he is hidden in the marshes from Seth. As Horus grows into maturity, he becomes recognized as the heir of Osiris. Each of the characters in the story represents a part of the **order of the world**. Osiris remains the lord of the underworld as judge and with power over vegetation, Isis becomes the king-maker and mother, and Horus becomes linked to pharaoh. Seth represents death, and as the story unfolds, Horus and Seth do battle and later are reconciled, demonstrating the intimate connection between life and death. At the accession of the new pharaoh, this myth was reenacted, with the death of Osiris, emphasizing the passing of one pharaoh and his rising again in the Other World. Osiris' son Horus stays in this world and is identified with the new pharaoh.

Ultimately, the goal of Egyptian religion, and the primary attribute of the gods, *is life*. Life is present in the sun that daily brought light and warmth. It is present in the Nile, with its annual flooding, that enabled the crops to grow. The gods oversee the great drama as the people worship and honor their gods who reside in the temples. The pharaohs are given divine power and sanction to rule, and seek afterlife as they are mummified and placed in the tombs of the great pyramids. Baffling and complex, the religion of Egypt is not unlike the Nile itself, broad and deep, changing with the seasons, dividing into many branches, yet one as it nourished the ancient land.[5] The spiritual pathways of the religious life of the people were intimately connected to their culture in ancient Egypt.

Greek religion: from myth to rational reflection

The religious ideas of the ancient world and its many civilizations, though somewhat hidden behind the current superstructure of contemporary life, are nevertheless present in today's world. This reality is especially true about the religious ideas and practices of ancient Greece.[6] They are alive in our western languages, arts, philosophy, science, and politics. While one reads with only historical curiosity about Zeus, Apollo, or Dionysus, these gods live on in many aspects of contemporary religious and cultural life.[7] The ancient ruins of the Acropolis in Athens, showing the scars of time, are a vivid reminder of the debt that the modern world owes to Greek civilization.

It is somewhat difficult to paint a clear picture of the religious beliefs and practices of Greek religion in spite of the survival of so many artifacts and texts. Part of the problem may be the abundance of material given interpretation from a range of disciplines including history, anthropology, archeology, ethnology, comparative religion, and philosophy. It is also a subject that was in motion, and a brief overview of the history of the formation of Greek civilization may be the best access into understanding the diversity of religious thought and behavior in ancient Greece.[8]

We begin our brief description of the religion of Greece with an eye on the ways which it was mingled with and influenced by the extraordinary culture that emerged. Most scholars would mark the beginning of Greek culture and thought, in the third millennium BCE, in the Minoan culture of Crete.

The Cretans were advanced for their time, made use of bronze tools and weapons, and became skillful as shipbuilders and traders. Their ships sailed to the many ports of the Mediterranean including Egypt, Asia Minor, Syria, and Sicily. By 2100 BCE, they had an elaborate royal place at Knossos, one that was rebuilt again around 1600 BCE. It was filled with wall paintings that depicted the life of the Cretans and hinted at their religious practices. We learn that the kings of Crete were also priests, and that their religious practices were patterned on the religious practices of Asia Minor. Goddesses were central to their pantheon and the Great Mother was the primary deity. Not long after 2000 BCE, the Minoan civilization began to decline as Indo-European people from the north, known as the Dorians, invaded and conquered the region. In time a second Aegean civilization known as the Mycenaean developed, and it was these people who settled in the region of Southern Greece and became the spur of change leading to the city-state civilization of Greece's golden age. Some of the features of Greek religion in the golden age go back to the Mycenaean influence, including the names of the gods (Zeus, Apollo, etc.) and rites and ceremonies which formed integral parts of the common life of family, clan, and state.

The story of the civilization of ancient Greece reaches a highpoint in the ninth century BCE with the composition of two of the greatest works of Greek literature, the *Iliad* and the *Odyssey*. These great works of art are attributed to a blind poet named Homer, whose name crowns an age (Homeric), but may be the written form of the oral recitations of wandering bards. The *Iliad* tells the story of a Greek military expedition against Troy in Asia Minor.[9] It involves kings, wives of kings, heroic warriors, and a final victory for the Greeks and the destruction of Troy. The *Odyssey* serves as a sequel to the *Iliad* and tells the story of the return of the warriors to Greece. Odysseus is the heroic character in the *Odyssey*, and he is known as much for his wisdom and reflections on life as he is for his prowess as a warrior. He wanders for ten years on the Mediterranean, aided by the goddess of wisdom, Athena, and threatened by the god of the sea, Poseidon. He returns home to political and domestic problems which he solves with the help of his son Telemachus.

These two classic compositions become a major source of information about the religion of the Homeric Age. This era is generally understood as stage 1 in the formation of Greek religion as suggested by Gilbert Murray in his classic study, *The Five Stages of Greek Religion*. A central theme of these great stories is that all of the important events were shaped, even determined, by the omnipresent gods. In order to gain their favor and succeed in a victorious cause, the heroes and heroines had to engage in sacrificial rites, pouring libations of wine on the ground, slaughtering and offering sacrificial animals, and arranging feasts to placate the gods and gain their goodwill. The local gods may have been everywhere, but all of the Greeks honored the 12 major gods who formed the divine pantheon on Mount Olympus.

All Greek gods had human forms although some combined the human with animal forms that were from an earlier time. These gods would watch the great exploits of the warriors, with some favoring the Greeks and some favoring the Trojans. On occasion, they would even engage in the battles, fight one another, and then proceed to the battleground to rescue their favorite soldier. Zeus was the father of the gods and the ruler of the universe.[10] In control of the sky and its power, Zeus would bring storms and lightning bolts to control conditions on earth. As a great lover of women, he became the progenitor of semi-divine heroes and heroines. In addition to Zeus,[11] the Pantheon was made up of:

- Hera, the jealous wife of Zeus and the goddess of women, children, and childbirth;
- Apollo, the son of Zeus and god of archery, prophecy, and music;
- Hermes, the god of highways and the marketplace;
- Poseidon, the god of the sea;
- Artemis, the goddess of the moon and hunting;
- Athena, the goddess of wisdom;
- Demeter, the goddess of vegetation and grain;
- Ares, the god of war;
- Aphrodite, the goddess of love and beauty;
- Hephaestus, the god of fire; and
- Hestia, the goddess of the hearth.

Each of these deities has a unique and fascinating story, one that personifies and captures the important elements of Greek life and the depth and subtlety of human emotion. These gods were thought to be the determining forces in the lives of the Greek people, and yet all great leaders of Greece had to deal with still another force, *moira*, a person's destiny and fate. These concepts, with the addition of the creation myths of Hesiod who lived around 750 BCE formed the base of Greek religion as it continued to develop through golden age.

Murray's stage 2 (800–400 BCE) moves us to Greek mystery religions and Greek tragic drama. The Homeric gods represented an achievement in order, symmetry, and the description of the human condition. What was missing from this construction was the ways that human beings participate in shaping their destiny. The gods do not determine everything, and humans may exercise a measure of freedom in choosing the course of their lives. This missing element was provided in part by the rise of the mystery religions, cultic associations of people who had secret knowledge about how they could influence their lives and destiny. The participants in these religions would go through five steps: (1) purification in ritual bathing; (2) instruction in the secret knowledge; (3) observing the secret and sacred objects related to the knowledge; (4) narration or dramatic reenactment of a sacred story; and (5) a crowning (or wreathing) of the initiates into full membership. There were three primary traditions of mystery religions in ancient Greece—Eleusinian, Dionysian, and Orphic—all dating from the sixth century BCE and lasting through most of Greece's history. The rites in some cases (Dionysian) were quite unusual with the presence of intoxication, the killing of animals, and sexual indulgence. In other cases (Orphic), there were restrictions on meat eating, sexual intercourse, and the requirement of adherents to wear white garments. Regardless of the different practices, the participants felt that they had a part in shaping their future.

In this period, tragic drama also became a part of Greek religion, and while often viewed as secular in character, the origins of Greek tragedy were religious in character. Many of these dramas grew out of religious ritual and nearly all of them probed the issues of human fate under the gods. The great dramatists in their own way suggested that when human beings are controlled by the motivation of pride (*hubris*); they then must face their doom (*nemesis*); and hence, they are subject to the law of fate (*moira*). Many of the leading characters in the plays experience profound tragedy because of their fatal flaw. Aeschylus (*d.* 455 BCE), Sophocles (*d.* 406 BCE), and Euripides (*d.* 406 BCE) are the most famous of the dramatists and express these themes in their work.

As a third stage, Murray suggests that the great schools of philosophy of the fourth century BCE are emergent from Greek religion, developing out of mythological stories, although philosophy takes its own course of time. In some ways, the philosophers took myth to metaphysical speculation and reasoned reflection on the nature and order of the universe, the ethical life, and the best way to order and rule a society. In these reflections, we see the development of thoughtful criticism of religion as in the case of Socrates (*d.* 399 BCE) who, as "a gadfly to Athens," argues for rational thought and logic over what he viewed as unreasonable and immoral in traditional Greek religion. Plato (*d.* 347 BCE) follows a similar course and offers an outline of a reconstructed religion in the *Republic* as he posits the realm of **ideas** that lie beyond the realm of changing appearances. In his ethical teaching, he speaks of the **good, the true, and the**

beautiful which are the greatest values. He makes mention in the *Timaeus* of a divine "architect" or demiurge of world order. Plato's student, Aristotle, had fewer themes than Plato that connected with religious thought although he, too, spoke of an "unmoved mover" that stands behind the order in the universe. Both of these great philosophers were to be used in the formation and development of thought in the monotheistic religions of Judaism, Christianity, and Islam.

Murray, with a hint of his bias against religion, speaks about a fourth period (300 BCE–400 CE) in Greek religious thought and calls it a "failure of nerve" as it yields to the irrationalism of the mystery cults, and even included the rise of Christianity as part of this failure of nerve. His stage 5 is essentially the same period of time as stage 4 and focuses on the rise of Neoplatonic mysticism and the writing of Plotinus (*d.* 270 CE). Plotinus in the *Enneads*, attempted a systematic teaching of Plato's philosophy that had a more mystical and religious tone than Plato's writing, and it came to be called Neoplatonism. Plotinus taught that there was one supreme reality, the One, with several grades of being emanating in concentric circles from the center and then returning to it. It is mystical union with the One and that becomes the object of religion.

Religion was interwoven into the life and culture of ancient Greece. Nearly every Greek through all the classes in the society, from peasants to nobility, believed the gods shaped the contours of life. If only, they believed, they could get the gods to be on their side and favor their position. The gods, epitomized by but not limited to the 12 in the pantheon, were viewed as intimately connected with the course of life. They were particularly instrumental in determining the resolution of conflict between the city-states of the Aegean, perhaps favoring one side against the other or one warrior over another. The Greeks believed that it was the gods who could determine the outcome of a war, the fate of the people, and the nature and destiny of one's life. This perspective is captured in persuasive and artistic ways in the Greek tragic dramas, and in these great dramas, we see the place of free will and choice as factors in determining the fate of the characters.

The relationship with the gods was negotiable, and sometimes it was not all that easy to determine just how to play it. The gods were not perfect, and at times were even fickle. The gods were viewed as engaged in behavior and having emotions that had human characteristics, although often more intense, more powerful, and not always more noble and admirable. It was as if the full range of human behavior and emotion were projected onto the gods. It is not surprising that the gods were often pictured or imaged in human form or in animal form if it projected greater power. There were prescribed ways to gain favor with the gods, but, as way leads upon way, the methodologies of rites, ceremonies, and sacrifices did not always achieve the desired end. These "negotiations" were tricky at best.

There were also depictions of the gods as being the source of power and enabling the faithful to be true to the highest values of the culture and to undertake with great energy and nobility the ultimate concerns and highest values of the culture. Great military leaders and warriors, as depicted by Homer, were motivated by these promises. As the religious mythology moves toward rational discourse among the philosophers, we see noble character in the life and trial of Socrates, and the call to lead from noble principles in the writing of Plato and Aristotle. These noble concerns and ends expressed in profound ways were to influence the human family for centuries.

Finally, as part of this summary, we should note that not all of the people were motivated by noble ends, or religiously engaged with the gods of the pantheon, or reflecting philosophically about the nature of the universe, the ideal state, and the ethical life. Many of the people of ancient Greece wanted a religious experience that took them out of the daily grind of life and promised immediate release and pleasure or eternal life. This was found in the mystery religions and to some extent in the mysticism of Neoplatonism.

A central goal of this volume is to assess the ways in which the many families of faith guide people in spiritual pathways that are nurturing and life-giving, and whether, as happens in some cases the spiritual ways are life-denying, based on fear, control, and exploitation. One might argue that those religious traditions that flourished in another historical era are irrelevant to our current situation and circumstances. After all, what do the religions of ancient Egypt and ancient Greece have to do with finding a spiritual pathway that enables humans to flourish in the first quarter of the twenty-first century? It is a valid and provocative question, and my limited and developing answer is twofold. The first part of the answer is the fairly obvious one that the spiritual quest of humankind has not fundamentally changed across the centuries although the context in which we follow spiritual pathways is very different. But we continue to want to find meaning in life, ethical norms that guide us, to structure society in ways that are just and fair, and find answers to the passing of time and the realities of disease and death. What we find, as we reflect on the religious ways of other people, whether past or present, is that patterns of belief and practice tend to be repeated.

A second part of the answer is whether pondering the religious ways of the past gives guidance for the present and for the future is that there are universal truths in these religious traditions that can be uncovered, ones that may be connected with what is ultimately truthful and of value. The risk, of course, is that we will too easily "write off" what on first glance appears to be superstition rooted in a premodern understanding of the world. Some of these characteristics may be of only historical interest and can and should be discounted as invalid spiritual pathways for our time. But we should be diligent in discerning what may be invaluable insights, perspectives, wisdom, and guidance for living in these extraordinary challenging moments of history. Perhaps our beliefs and practices in the early part of the current century may appear as irrelevant to pilgrims of the twenty-second century, but one might hope that they would reflect on the ways that our current beliefs and practices, all across the different religious traditions of the human family, are grappling with the global realities of our time and place.

Are there life-giving lessons for us as we better understand the religious traditions of ancient Egypt and Greece? Yes, and let me briefly illustrate. The first might be that these classical expressions of religion formed a religious outlook that was **intimately connected with the life and circumstances of the people**. In Egypt, varied and complex as they were, the beliefs and practices of Egyptian religion connected their understanding of the divine and divine pathways with the flow of the Nile as it gave life to the people in its yearly cycle of flooding. So, too, in ancient Greece, did the religious ideology connect with the experiences of the people. For example (and there are many) the pantheon of gods on Mt. Olympus were mythological expressions of the daily realities of life. Zeus controlled the weather; Hera spoke to the needs of women; and Poseidon ruled the seas in a maritime culture.

It follows that religious understanding in these two classical cultures enabled the people to **cope with the most pressing problems of life**. For the Egyptians, the religious understanding and the place of the Nile in their worldview gave them a way to understand how life can be sustained with adequate food. The challenge for the Egyptians was how to prepare for death and to secure a place in the afterlife. Again, their religion gave them hope and comfort. For the Greeks, the challenges were similar, although there was less stability and continuity in their lives. Again, it was their religious beliefs and practices that provided a way for them to understand their circumstances and find ways of coping. It was a matter of gaining the favor of the gods, whether the gods of the pantheon or those more local. With the favor of the gods, the city-state could be defended and basic subsistence needs met.

A third helpful insight that comes from these traditions has to do with the way that their religious outlook helped them to understand ways of **empowering**

leaders and achieving a stable social order. It was early in the formation of the religious ideas of the Egyptians that the king or pharaoh was viewed as having divine qualities. With all the risks of such an endowment, it nevertheless provided the king with the power to rule in a society without the social infrastructure that moderns, especially in the "first world" take for granted. For the Greeks, while the various leaders and mythological warriors were not divine, they were given divine sanction and gifts for leadership. Certainly one the great legacies of Greek culture, intertwined with their religious thought, was the ideal of democratic government.

We see in both of these classic religious traditions, another legacy, that of the movement toward **expressing their thought and articulating their ethics in more universal ways**. Across the centuries, there was a movement toward finding the deeper and more profound truth that was covered by the passing categories of the culture. In Egypt, we see the beginnings of understanding the divine as the ground that stands behind all of the other gods that are regional, tribal, or national in identity. We view it in Ramses II (1290–1224 BCE) who articulated a very early inquiry about monotheism. The great Greek philosophers, whose influence lives on in so many ways, reflected in rational and universal ways about the origins of the universe, how it functions, the nature and norms of the ethical life, and the ideal systems of governance.

A fifth contribution of these great religious traditions is the way that **religion contributed to their greatest cultural achievements**. In ancient Egypt, there were many ways that religion influenced this remarkable culture, but one that stands out is the achievement in architecture. This achievement is especially evident in the pyramids, but present elsewhere as well. For the Greeks, we might point to the great tragic dramas of Aeschylus (*Agamemnon* and *Prometheus Bound*), Sophocles (*Oedipus the King*) and Euripedes (*Bellerophon*).

But there were many life-denying features of the religious beliefs and practices of ancient Egypt and ancient Greece as well. As implied earlier, it was altogether too easy **to identify the divine with the rhythms of nature and the content of the culture**. It may be a bit unfair to judge this tendency, as those standing on this side of the rise of rationalism and scientific understanding. But it remains an important learning nevertheless, as we see the same tendency in the world today when claims of divine direction and sanction for policies mask programs that are harmful to the human family.

Along this line, we should also note that is was also too easy **for those in power to claim divine authority**. This claim neither allows for the give and take among leaders to find the best ways to solve social problems nor is there in the structures of government the checks and balances on self-seeking and unjust governance. The Egyptian kings/pharaohs did have inordinate power, and there were clear cases of unstable and autocratic rule. It is true that the Greeks attempted to establish a more democratic rule, allowing for challenges to the leadership, a gift about the nature of governance that was passed on to succeeding generations. But in many of the city-states, there were claims of divine sanction for policies and approaches that were harmful, especially to the common people. And democracy was largely connected to government in Athens and not in the other city-states of ancient Greece.

In Greece, and also in Egypt, there was a tendency **to adopt too easily the attitude of fatalism**. To be sure, there is some comfort in having a stoical approach to circumstance over which one has no control. There is solace in the philosophical understanding of tragic circumstances. But to seek consolation instead of solution in governance is itself to contribute to unfortunate circumstances. There were kings and leaders in both Egypt and Greece who failed to find solutions that contributed to the public good because they were persuaded that the dire conditions were preordained.

In fact, there were times when the religious ideology was **used to justify unethical, self-seeking, and destructive behavior**. Again, it may be unfair for those who live in these times in a democratic country to judge too harshly government action that did not take into account those without a voice and on the boundary of full rights and citizenship. We can say that "it was the way things were done in those times" with some justification, but we can also learn about how destructive religious justification can be for policies that are unjust and repressive.

Let us conclude with one final observation about the life-denying tendencies that were present in the religious outlook of both ancient Egypt and Greece. As it is with all nations, it was with ancient Egypt and the kingdoms and city-states of ancient Greece, that there was a **tendency to be ethnocentric**, to claim that one's understanding of the divine and religious pathway is the best way if not the only way. The clear risk when this occurs is that "God" may be imaged as a tribal king and warrior enabling oppressive and aggressive behavior to be sanctioned. The Egyptians were relatively tolerant of diverse views within Egypt, but were resistant to the views of those in other regions. The Greeks, too, defended their ways, sometimes with xenophobic passion. Our lesson in a global context is to learn how to treat the religious views of others with respect, while maintaining the integrity and the best expression of our own tradition.

It is apparent, as we look carefully at those religious views that see the divine expressed and manifested in nature and culture that such views are not limited to the past, but find contemporary expression in today's world. We look next to contemporary spiritual pathways that place an emphasis on finding the divine will and way within nature and culture.

Discussion questions

1. In what ways are the religious beliefs and practices of ancient Egypt interwoven with its geography and culture?
2. In what ways are the spiritual pathways of the people of ancient Greece a reflection of the cultural norms of ancient Greece?
3. Was the religion of ancient Egypt a positive or a negative force in the lives of the people?
4. The religious beliefs and practices of ancient Greece contributed positively or negatively to the lives of the people?
5. What are last legacies of the religious traditions of ancient Egypt and ancient Greece?

Key terms and concepts

1. **History as cyclical:** The Egyptian view that the annual flow of the Nile, with its flood and movement of fertile soil for agriculture, was a picture of human history that repeats in a circular fashion rather than progresses in a linear fashion.
2. **Divine kingship:** The view that kings may be at the least endowed with divine qualities, but may become divine in their identity.
3. **Pantheon**: A temple dedicated to the gods; home of the gods.
4. **Mystery religion or rite:** Initiatory rituals, usually secret, believed to assure an individual is accepted into the religion and will achieve immortality.
5. **Moira:** A person's fate or lot in life.
6. **Nemesis:** The outcome of one's failure, doom.

Suggestions for reference and reading

Armstrong, Karen, *The Great Transformation: The Beginning of Our Religious Traditions* (New York: Anchor Books, 2007).

Breasted, Henry, *The Development of Religion and Thought in Ancient Egypt* (New York: Harper & Row, 1959).

Eliade, Mircea, *A History of Religious Ideas, Vol. 1 From the Stone Age to the Eleusinian Mysteries* (Chicago: University of Chicago Press, 1978).

Frankfort, Henri, *Kingship and the Gods* (Chicago: University of Chicago Press, 1978).

Guthrie, W. K. C., *The Greeks and Their Gods* (Boston: Beacon Press, 1955).

Morenz, Siegfried, *Egyptian Religion* (New York: Cornell University Press, 1974).

Murray, Gilbert, *Five Stages of Greek Religion* (New York: Doubleday Anchor, 1955).

Current Expressions of Nature/Culture Religion

4

Chapter Outline

The reenchantment of the world   59
Modern spiritual pathways rooted in nature: from science to witchcraft 61
Modern spiritual pathways interwoven with nature and culture: Shinto 67
Assessment of these movements   73

The reenchantment of the world[1]

Living east of Eden

We turn now to an exploration of the ways that religions rooted in nature and culture find expression in the modern world. There is certainly the temptation to assume that religions that find their foundation in the patterns of nature and culture have passed from the scene, especially if these are thought to be premodern in their basic assumptions and to be based in myth, magic, and miracle. But the fact is that there is a resurgence of these religious pathways, and many of them (although not all) have at least partially accommodated to a predominately rational and scientific understanding of reality.[2]

There are many reasons for this resurgence, and at the base of nearly all these reasons is that contemporary people are living lives filled with anxiety and fear about a rapidly changing world that is facing profoundly challenging problems. In this context, many in the human family are left with feelings of being lost, filled with insecurity, and suffering from profound alienation. The world that they knew and in which they felt "at home" has disappeared. It is hard for most of us to find a secure place as we are thrust out of the garden and forced to live east of Eden. The tendency is to reach for a religious outlook that is part of our surroundings and history, one that is familiar and provides continuity with what we know, and the ways that we have traditionally found to give meaning and direction in life.

The human tendency to seek a religious outlook that brings security and stability to life, a commonly accepted fact, was turned in the nineteenth century and the early part of the twentieth century against the validity of religion. There was an emerging atheism, in part the product of the Enlightenment with its emphasis on critical reason over what was considered to be irrational faith. This Enlightenment outlook, with its inductive methodology and its rejection of traditional authority moved into the fields of biology, history, and sociology in the nineteenth century.[3] As the advances in the scientific understanding of human experience matured, it was an easy step to say that all religious beliefs and practices were nothing more than a way of coping with the difficulties and complexities of life. These religious frames of reference were viewed not so much as an accurate description of reality as they were projections and rationalizations that may bring some comfort. Karl Marx (1818–1883) for example saw religion as "the sigh of the oppressed creature . . . the opium of the people, which made this suffering bearable."[4] The God hypothesis may make suffering bearable, but it also alienates us from our true nature, disguises social realities, and gives us a "false consciousness." Other philosophers such as Ludwig Feuerbach (1804–1872) and Auguste Comte (1798–1857), with different starting points than Marx, nevertheless maintained that the belief in a deity distorted reality and led to alienation in human experience.

Charles Darwin in *The Origin of Species* (1859) suggested there was a natural evolution within nature that contradicted the biblical account of creation in Genesis. Behind his thesis was the question of whether it was necessary to hold the belief in a personal God who created the world and oversees its ongoing development. He asks, were there other explanations for the development of the natural world and the origin of the human family? Friedrich Nietzsche in the 1880s spoke about the death of God in quite dramatic ways by which he meant that there has been a painful and radical shift in the consciousness of the West which makes it very difficult to believe in a God who intervenes in human affairs.[5] Sigmund Freud (1856–1939), from still another angle, regarded belief in God as an illusion that mature human beings should set aside.[6] He argued that the idea of God was a projection of the human psyche of a father figure who could help manage life and insure justice. But now that humankind has come of age, we can put this projection aside and depend upon a scientific understanding of reality.

One thinker from this era who took seriously this persuasive questioning of the validity and life-giving qualities of religious faith, but who thoughtfully argued for a constructive view of religious commitment was William James. His book, *The Varieties of Religious Experience*[7] described the healthy and unhealthy dimensions of religious experience, maintaining that religious experience should be judged more by its "fruits" than by its origins. According to James, the value and truth of an abstract idea are determined by the idea's effects on the one who believes it. He maintained that a true idea is one that has pragmatic verification, one that "works," and one that satisfies. Therefore the truth is changeable and contextual. A true idea is one that agrees with reality in the sense of working for good in a particular setting, so it is possible to "make" ideas true by our actions and change the world in which we live.[8]

William James was not unaware that he was articulating a somewhat different understanding of truth than was traditionally accepted. He knew, for example, that a statement is true in one sense if it is logical and in another sense if it accurately describes reality. It was this latter phrase that he wanted to challenge or at least nuance. He argued that if something worked for a person or group, then it was not just true, but the truth. Conversely, he sought to draw a different kind of distinction, namely that truth is not quite the same as reality, in that realities are not so much true; they just are. Rather it should be said that beliefs are true about them. So it is not quite precise to say that truth corresponds to reality, as if facts were always the same as truths. It is better to say that our ideas about what is true can point us to reality. There will always be a need to distinguish between ideas about reality and reality itself, a quest that never ceases.

It follows for James, as he expands so admirably in *The Varieties of Religious Experience*, that there is a pragmatic quality about "religious truth," i.e. if it is redemptive, healing, and life-giving, then it is true, though the search for a better sighting of reality continues. There is a trace of James in our assessment of the life-giving or life-denying characteristics of religious practice.

Modern spiritual pathways rooted in nature: from science to witchcraft

There are many religious movements in the contemporary world that base their beliefs and practices in the natural world. In making this statement, it is important to observe that almost all of these expressions of religion are quite complex and the use of "neat and tidy" categories runs the risk of oversimplification if not some distortion. It is also true that most contemporary religious expressions are not always consistent, and many are sufficiently lenient to allow a variety of faith formations within the larger family. So to say that a religion is rooted in nature is to describe a tendency rather than to try to contain all aspects of the religious outlook in one category. In this light, we can say that the indigenous wisdom religions of Africa, Australia, and the Americas are rooted in nature and continue to nurture and guide the native peoples of these regions.[9] The same is true for Asia, if we understand the Shinto tradition of Japan as drawing upon nature for understanding and inspiration, and for Taoism in China as it too looks to nature in finding the Way. In Europe, the Celtic traditions continue to find new expression in Scot-Irish spirituality.

There are also those who find in their scientific inquiries a sense of awe and wonder that borders on religious sentiment. Albert Einstein unashamedly spoke of how nature filled him with a sense of awe as he stood before the mystery of the universe. He said: "If there is something which can be called religious, then it is the unbounded admiration for the structure of the world so far as our science can reveal it."[10] He also wrote about his understanding of cosmic religion, as opposed to a religion based on fear and human need. He underscores that knowledge of the existence of something we cannot penetrate, of the manifestations of the profoundest reason and the most radiant beauty, which are only accessible to our reason in their most elementary forms—it is this knowledge and this emotion that constitute the truly religious attitude.[11] Stuart A. Kauffman, former professor at Harvard University and the founding director of the Institute for Biocomplexity and Informatics and professor at the University of Calgary makes the case in his recent book, *Reinventing the Sacred*, that the qualities of divinity that we hold sacred—creativity, meaning, and purposeful action—are in fact properties of the universe that can be investigated scientifically.[12] A new study done by Robert Wright also suggests ways of framing a new religious outlook based on the thesis that the evolution of our traditional ideas about God or gods point to a credible transcendent point of view, and that a modern, scientific worldview leaves room for a point of view that may contain room for what may be called divine.[13] Mathematical cosmologist and author, Brian Swimme argues with religious insight that the universe evolves in spurts. At the origin of time, there was only plasma, and then this plasma gave birth to the galaxies. Similar quantum leaps have taken place in the living world. For a long time there were only single-celled organisms, and then the animals and plants sprouted forth. Another transition is underway. Human energies, having surrounded the entire world, are bit challenged by a new destiny. Homo sapiens are called to awaken with a planet-sized heart and mind whose purpose is the evocation of a vibrant Earth Community.[14]

In the movement known as Gaia (named after the Greek goddess of the earth), we see the near personification of earth, and with the personification, a profound sense of religious awe and respect for the earth. A leading spokesperson for this movement, James Lovelock, argues that the Earth is one great organism, evolving over the vast span of geological time. The Earth is truly alive, but is threatened by the greenhouse effect, acid rain, the depletion of the ozone layer, and the destruction of the tropical forests. He sounds a warning of the damage humans are doing to the health of the planet.[15] It is perhaps unfair to speak of Gaia as a "religion" although the movement has been criticized as bordering on ascribing to Gaia some attributes of divinity.

It is in the movement known as Wicca (from the Anglo-Saxon *wicce*, meaning witch or wise woman) that we see a full-fledged religion rooted in nature, one that has reverence for the earth/Gaia, advocates the empowerment of women, and shows deep concern for the ecological crisis of our time. The movement, while having a long history, resurfaced and became quite well-known through the writings of Gerald Brosseau Gardner (1884–1964), a retired British civil servant. He published the widely circulated *Witchcraft Today* in 1954. It was his view that Wicca was the modern expression of an old witchcraft mystery religion originating in the pre-Christian paganism of Europe, although the historical roots of the religion remain somewhat ambiguous. In recent years, it is the enormous popularity of the Harry Potter series that has brought the practice of Wicca and witchcraft more generally to the attention of a vast cross-section of the English speaking world.

Wicca has been variously called "the old religion," "witchcraft," "wisecraft," or just "the craft." Its followers do not fit the media stereotype of the witch; they are not spooky old hags who ride around on brooms, but are normal people from all walks of life, occupations, and educational levels. They are teenagers in school like Harry Potter and his friends. The Wiccans meet regularly in small groups known as "covens" in which they practice various forms of magic (there are some witches that prefer to practice alone). The magic is generally divided up between natural magic and high magic, both of which are usually directed (over the popular stereotype) toward healthy ends. High magic (often spelled magick) has the purpose of personal transformation through contact with the divine, whereas, natural magic has the goal to control natural forces and energies to make change in the physical world. There is the belief that this kind of magic can heal sick minds and bodies and even control the weather.

The movement is remarkably popular because of media coverage and the stories of Harry Potter and has therefore attracted many followers. People are drawn to the movement because, as in the case of Harry Potter, good triumphs over evil by the skill and magic of a young and unlikely hero. They are also drawn to the movement because it articulates a feminist spirituality, promises to give extraordinary power, and initiates its followers, as in the Greek Gnostic religions, into a select order with secret knowledge and symbols.[16]

Wicca is a movement that crosses countries and cultures, although not all people who think of themselves as witches would be Wiccans. There is no centralized organization in Wicca, no single and clear creed that all Wiccans believe, and the practices of the Wiccans can vary substantially among individuals and traditions. But there is a core of beliefs, practices, ethical norms, ritual structures, and community gatherings (code, creed, cult, and community) which are shared and that holds the movement together.

The spiritual pathways among the Wiccans are somewhat diverse and are generally classified into five groups which we will only mention in passing: Gardnerian Wicca, Alexandrian Wicca, Hereditary Craft, Traditional Craft, and Feminist Craft (close to the Gardnerians). Gardner was especially concerned with rooting his views of Wicca in the historical traditions of witchcraft and sought to make this ancient tradition available and accessible. Alex Sanders developed Gardner's ideas, then began to lead a coven near Manchester, England and sought to distinguish his views from those of Gardner by stressing ritual magic over folk paganism. Hereditary Craft and Traditional Craft adherents maintain that the beliefs and practices are passed down and carefully preserved by successive generations, with the Hereditary Craft followers stressing that the wisdom is handed down through families. The fifth movement, Feminist Craft, was given high visibility by the California witch, Starhawk (Miriam Simos) with the publication of her book, *The Spiral Dance: A Rebirth of the Ancient Religion of the Goddess* in 1979. We will trace her teaching and suggested practices below.

It might be helpful at this point to describe the core beliefs of the Wiccans although we mention again that there is great diversity in the movement. The vast majority of Wiccans would venerate both a Goddess and a God, sometimes uniting them and at other times seeing them as separate beings, but understanding the divine as embedded in nature. Those that affirm the duotheistic understanding of the divine would stress the complementary polarities of the Goddess and the God, embodying the life-force that drives nature.[17] At times, this understanding of the divine is symbolized as God being the sun and the Goddess being the moon. Traditionally, God is pictured as the Horned God who rules over the woodlands, sexuality, and hunting. The Goddess is imaged as Maiden or Mother.[18] In some cases, there are other gods and goddesses from the folklore of many cultures, and these divinities complete the pantheon and may represent the archetypes of the human psyche.[19]

Wicca is essentially an immanent religion; the divine is within nature and interwoven with human experience. The gods or goddesses occasionally take the form of animism, personified in animals, and frequently the divine is manifest in human form through the bodies of priests and priestesses who in rituals, such as Drawing down the Moon or Drawing down the Sun, display divine presence and power. When practicing this magic, in the casting of spells, and celebrating festivals, the Wiccans have an array of rituals and resources. Generally these occur within the coven, as the Wiccans assemble inside a purified magic circle. As the circle forms, there is often the invocation of the "Guardians" or direction points: East (Air), South (Fire), West (Water) and North (Earth). The use of this structure is an expression of the Wiccan worldview, with divine power coming from one or more of these elements. Usually, a fifth element is added called Spirit which presides at the top. Once the circle forms, a seasonal ritual may be undertaken, prayers to the God or Goddess offered, magic is practiced, and spells are cast.[20] Most Wiccans have a set of magical tools to use in their rituals and practice. These often include a broom, cauldron, chalice, wand, Book of Shadows (a Gardner text), an alter cloth, candles, crystals, and incense. These "tools" would be placed on the altar during ceremonies.

Wiccans do have a simple ethical code that can best be expressed as "Do as ye will, as long as ye harm none." There is certainly freedom for the adherents to act as they choose, but there is a strong sense that one needs to take responsibility for one's actions and not hurt oneself or others. There is inherent within Wiccan ethical understanding the notion of karma, often articulated in the Law of Threefold Return which teaches that the good or bad actions a person commits will return to the person with triple force. Wiccans encourage their followers to cultivate eight virtues: mirth, reverence, honor, humility, strength, beauty, power, and compassion.[21] These virtues are usually associated with the celebrations of the seasons known as the Sabbats. There are eight Sabbats called Greater Sabbats and coincide with Celtic fire festivals. The other four are called Lesser Sabbats and link with the solstices and the equinoxes.[22] For many Wiccans, the faithful participation in these ceremonies and the diligent practice of these virtues does have implications for life after death, especially in the context of reincarnation, although this belief is not universal across the Wiccan movement.

In order to get a more intimate sense of the Wiccan movement, it may be wise to focus on the writing of one of the leaders within the movement in the United States, Starhawk. Her earlier book, *The Spiral Path: A Rebirth of the Ancient Religion of the Great Goddess*, was widely read and well received. In fact, it may be the primary source about modern witchcraft, spiritual feminism and the Goddess movement, and ecofeminism. It is certainly recommended reading along with Scott Cunningham's *The Truth About Witchcraft Today* for those who want to understand the movement. It was first published in 1979 and was followed by a second edition in 1989 and a third in 1999, but there has been little change in the text. Although addressing the issues of Wicca, it should not be seen as exclusively devoted to Wicca in that it reaches out more broadly to visionary mysticism and ecstatic experience, and places a strong emphasis on the Goddess whereas Wiccans generally seek a balance between the Goddess and the God.

What Starhawk provides in this volume is a very informative introduction and guidance about practice. It includes:

- A history of the evolution of witchcraft as a religion
- An introduction to the eight solar holidays
- The basics of the faith and the Wiccan perspective on the divine
- Instructions for working with a coven
- Sample rituals including 25 chants/invocations, as well as 11 specific rituals
- Meditations and trances (61 different exercises) and
- Spellcrafting (18 examples).

In her more recent book, *The Earth Path: Grounding Your Spirit in the Rhythms of Nature*[23] Starhawk restates how the essence of Wiccan belief and practice is grounded in nature. The strength of this volume is the way that it incorporates a scientific understanding of the world within the framework of her religious understanding. Chapter 4, for example, is entitled "Creation: What Every Pagan Should Know about Evolution" and in this chapter, Starhawk provides a thoughtful introduction to the understanding of evolution. She returns again and again to the need to heal and care for the Earth.

In much of the book, she draws heavily upon her own experience and the entries she has put into her diary as she experiences the beauty and life-giving qualities of nature. There are a large number of exercises, meditations, and rituals, ones that in many cases rise above the particularities of the Wiccan movement and witchcraft and speak poignantly to feminist empowerment and ecological concerns. The heart of her teaching in this volume is the classic Circle of Life, given boundaries by air, fire, water, and earth with rituals and meditations of appreciation for these elements of the earth. Her "Blessing for Earth" is illustrative of her spirit and point of view:

> We give gratitude to the earth, to the dust of stars that congealed into the body of this planet, our home, and that still gives form and solidity to our bones and flesh. We honor the rocks, our sisters and brothers, and their long, slow cycles of transformation into life and back to seabed, mountain, stone. We give thanks to the living soil, the mother's flesh, and the billion creatures that haunt her caves and pores and chasms, to the beetles and the ants and the termites, to the soil bacteria swimming in the slick of water that clings to her mineral archways, to the worms, wriggling, eating, coupling, and transforming within her. We bless the plants, the roots and stems and boughs, the great trees reaching upward and the deep-rooted herbs pushing down, all who contribute to the cycles of birth and growth and death and decay that lead to fertility and new growth. For all that feeds and sustains life, for all that grows, runs, and flies, we give thanks. Blessed be the earth.[24]

Modern spiritual pathways interwoven with nature and culture: Shinto

It is a relatively big jump from Wicca to the Japanese-based religion of Shinto, but they exist side by side in their common commitment to expressing their religious beliefs and ideals through the immediate context of life, whether in human interaction with nature or in the goal of affirming or shaping social structures and customs. In many ways, Shinto religion expresses as clearly as any other religious tradition its understanding that the divine may be discerned within nature and/or culture.

Again, other choices might be made in selecting a representative religious tradition that identifies the divine with culture and social structures. For example, if we understand religion from the definition given by Paul Tillich as ultimate concern, we might point to the cultural and political strategies of Communist China under Mao Zedong, especially during the Great Proletarian Cultural Revolution. In an interesting way, that which Mao opposed so strongly was another religious tradition rooted in the culture of China, Confucianism. The same religious ethos was present in the leadership of Idi Amin, the President of Uganda (1971–1979) who all but claimed divinity for himself during his treacherous reign. The status of Kim Jan Il and that of his father, Kim Il Sung in North Korea has bordered on religious adoration. But it may be a stretch to see divinity in these rulers and reigns.

It is in the Japanese indigenous religion of Shinto that we also see the divine or the absolute within the phenomenal world. The divine or the absolute is not some remote principle or being beyond this world but is to be seen and experienced in and through the world of present appearance; in the world of nature and culture. Shinto clearly exemplifies what we have described as nature-culture religion.

The name Shinto is from the Chinese and contains two parts: *shen* which means "Spirit" or "God"; and *tao* which means "way": hence, Shinto may be understood as "the way of the gods."[25] An essential word to the Shinto tradition is *kami* which is probably best understood in English as "power" or "holy power." Sometimes this power is understood as personal and may even be invoked or prayed to, and at other times it is as impersonal as the power of nature, as in a river, mountain, or a storm. As implied, there are many *kami* and there is little effort within the Shinto tradition of ordering this well populated pantheon beyond the assertion of the primacy of *Amaterasu Omkami*, the *kami* worshipped by the dominant Yamato clan in ancient Japan. What is remarkable to the observer ("outsider") of Japanese society is that any extraordinary aspect of the social or natural world is seen as revealing the presence of a *kami* even in events such as community observances with parades or decorations of military graves. Certainly one aspect of Shinto is its similarity with civil religion in Western culture.[26]

Shinto myth

Shinto is an indigenous wisdom religion, sharing the characteristics of other wisdom traditions, and it is therefore built upon primordial myths which are recorded in two classic sacred writings: the *Kojiki*, "Record of Ancient Tales," and the *Nihongi* or *Nihon shoki*, "Chronicles of Japan." These documents may be dated in the early 700s CE, and together they contain the main mythological sources of Shinto. They are not easy to summarize, but it is possible to focus on six mythical episodes that continue to shape Shinto beliefs and practices.[27]

The first myth or guiding story might be called the creation myth, although it is unlike the beginnings in the Genesis in which a sovereign God calls the world into being out of nothing. It is nevertheless a way of understanding through story the evolution of the universe and its structure and dynamics.

The Kojiki speaks of the primordial chaos as like an ocean of mud out of which three kami sprang. All three are born without any reference to progenitors, and as is the case with kami, they become invisible. Other kami as well sprang forth including *Iza nagi* ("the man who invites") and *Iza nami* ("the female who invites"), and these two become the recurring sky father and earth mother. They are given orders by their heavenly colleagues to give birth to the earth. They are provided with a spear, descend to the floating bridge of heaven where they thrust the spear into the large body of salt water, and as they withdraw the spear, the tip forms the island of Onogora. There, they erect a palace and a pillar, discover their sexual differences, embrace, and from their union are born innumerable kami as well as the islands of Japan, mountains, rivers, sea, and the necessary fire kami. It is within this fire that Iza nami is burned to death and withdraws to the nether world. Reflection on this story provides the assurance that the divine creates the world and remains present within nature and culture.

The story continues in a sequel to the creation myth as Iza nagi descends to the underworld in search of his wife. He finds her and asks her to return to the world with him. She begs him not to look at her, but he does see her in her decomposed state, flees in horror at her sight, and is pursued by the hideous forces of the nether world. What is the meaning of this sequel? Like all good myth, its ambiguity may be its greatest strength, leaving room for a number of interpretations, including the loss of innocence as happened to Adam and Eve as they flee to the east of Eden.

The third episode in this ongoing story follows Iza nagi into the upper world where he paused by the sea to cleanse himself. Ablution and purification are common practices and recurring themes within Shinto. During Iza nagi's experience of ablutions, several kami are born, and one of them that washed from his left eye, Amaterasu, becomes the most important kami in the pantheon. From Iza nagi's right eye came the moon kami, *Tsukiyomi*, and from his nose was born the storm kami, *Susa-no-o* (or *Susa-no-wu*). The storm deity becomes a dominant character, and he reflects a violent and unpredictable style, and does great damage to the mountains and the rivers. He also does damage to the crops and perpetrates a range of misdeeds, serious enough that he is expelled from heaven to dwell on earth (near the Izumo shrine in western Japan).

Meanwhile, as the next part of the story unfolds, we encounter Amaterasu who is angry at her brother and has hidden herself in a cave. A number of kami attempted to lure her out of hiding and succeeded with an obscene dance that evokes her curiosity. Again, there are various interpretations of these myths that reflect the primitive imagination that tries to explain the perennial themes inherent in nature and culture. Amaterasu, understood as the Sun Goddess, became the deity of the Yamato clan, and when this clan won battles and assumed political leadership, their deity came to the front rank among the deities.

In particular, as the fifth "chapter" of the story develops, we observe Amaterasu sending her grandson Ninigi to the earth to rule the islands of Japan. Her charge to him is contained in the patriotic words which are learned by heart by many Japanese people: "The Luxuriant Land of Reed Plains is a country which our descendants are to inherit. Go, therefore, Our Imperial Grandson, and rule over it. And may Our Imperial lineage continue unbroken and prosperous, coeternal with Heaven and Earth."[28] The dates of this "founding" of the Japanese empire are placed in 660 BCE, but there are no historical records to support this claim.

A final phase of the guiding mythical story is the enshrinement of Amaterasu at Ise, a shrine that becomes connected with the imperial house. Across the centuries of Japanese history, people have made pilgrimages to Ise and honored and identified with the timeless truth of the mythological story. There are many other amplifications of these stories and other myths that make up the grand pattern of celebration of Japanese history and values, but this outline may be sufficient to capture the way that these stories inform the Japanese way of life.

Shinto history

Across the centuries, these myths and the ideas they provoked became the foundation for Japanese culture. As times and circumstances changed, the ways that these myths were understood and interpreted changed, and the way that Shinto took expression within the lives of the Japanese people also changed. In fact, Shintoism has shown itself to be remarkable in its capacity to assimilate different influences. What remains the common thread over time, however, is the linkage between religious thought with both social structures and nature's complex and unpredictable ways.

In the early period of recorded Japanese history in the eight century BCE, there is evidence that the Japanese had a strong appreciation for the beauty and power in the natural world. The archeological discoveries and the few written records indicate that they love their island home. The power of nature and the miracle of fertility were central to their thinking, and they tended to see themselves as intimately connected to nature rather than "'lords" over nature. All the dramatic events of nature evoked awe and the inclination to worship. It is from the dramatic events of nature that the idea of kami emerges and becomes an integral part of the religious life of the Japanese.

Kami, or the manifestation of holy power, are also linked to the story of the descent of the Imperial family from the supreme Sun Goddess, Amaterasu. It would appear that the linkage between government and religion developed very early in Japanese life. There were sacred leaders (shamans), usually female, that were responsible both for organizing the worship of the kami and for the ordering of human affairs. An integral part of this endeavor was the practice of ritual purity involving ablution, a theme that runs through the Shinto tradition right up to the present day. In time these connections between religion, nature, and governance were recorded in the classic documents, the *Kojiki* in 712 and the *Nibongi* in 720.

A second period of development, the Heian period (794–1185), would see the increased influence of the Chinese. The somewhat complex Confucian understanding of governance was welcomed by the Japanese and became a central part of Japanese culture. While one branch of Buddhist thought, Nara Buddhism, was already present, other forms of Buddhism began to flourish, including the Nichiren Buddhism founded by Dengyo Daishi with its influential scripture, the *Lotus Sutra*. Taoist thought also developed, and so we see in this period and through Japanese history, a linkage between Shintoism and these several other religious movements.[29]

The religious life of Japan, with its fusion of different religious traditions, developed and changed in the succeeding historical eras. The Kamakura period (1185–1333) was much more troubled than the Heian period, and those religious themes that promised serenity and a secure afterlife (Pure Land Sects and Zen Sects) became important to the people.[30] The Tokugawa (1334–1868), in part a reaction to the unsettled nature of the previous period, was characterized by a strong central government, internal peace, and a strong sense of order. Shinto essentially becomes that state religion of Japan and operates at all levels of society, with rituals in the imperial court, shrines and temples to support a priesthood, and pilgrimages to the sacred sites.[31]

The feudalism of the Tokugawa period comes to an end with the Meiji Restoration (1868), a time when Japan in many ways moves into the modern world.[32] The Emperor was restored to his position as head of state, the new capital is established in Tokyo, and a comprehensive tax system was adopted.

It was at this time the Shinto was established at the state religion and remained the dominant religion up until 1945. However, following World War II, state Shintoism, associated with the nationalistic ethic and Japan's war activities, came to an end. The result was a crisis in Shintoism and its popularity waned. Only in recent decades has Shintoism begun to regain its centrality in Japanese life.

Shinto practice in contemporary Japan

The reemergence of Shinto into the mainstream of Japanese life is perhaps best illustrated by the controversy that surrounded the death of Emperor Hirohito on January 7, 1989. The Crown Prince Akihito succeeded him immediately, but his enthronement ceremony did not occur until November, 1990. During the intervening period, the issue of state support for the enthronement ceremony had to be resolved. It was clear in the Constitution of Japan (1946) that no public money could be used for the maintenance and support of religion thus excluding funding for funeral of Hirohito and the coronation of Prince Akihito. However, the inherent strength of the tradition was to prevail and these ritual events were funded. The Daijosai ceremony, the occasion when the Emperor assumes spiritual power by spending the night in a special Shinto shrine was paid for with public funds.

In these events, and in their continuing love of nature, the Japanese speak easily about the presence of the divine, or the kami. The central texts of both the Kojiki and Nihong are foundation to this understanding of the world, and the primary duty of the people is to honor and worship the kami in their myriad forms. There are thousands of shrines in Japan where this honor and worship can be expressed by the offering of food, the performance of dance and music, and the chanting of prayers. Some homes have kami shelves, decorated with the pine springs of the scared *saski* tree, on which miniature shrines are placed and in front of which the people will acknowledge the kami with clapping, bowing, and praying.

More formally, there are many activities arranged and sponsored by the Shrine Association, and more than 80 percent of Japanese shrines are associated with this organization. They give a high priority to the Ise shrines which is the imperial household shrine, and it remains a very popular pilgrimage destination. This organization assumes that Shintoism is the national faith, and it has the responsibility, not unlike a bishop in certain Christian denominations, for the recognition of priestly rank and the appointment of priests to shrines. On certain state occasions, the president will even stand in for the Emperor.[33]

The Shinto festivals, with elements of worship, celebration, rite, and prayer, are organized around liturgical calendar. In these festivals, the faithful express gratitude to the kami, and there is a spirit of celebration and even entertainment. There is a festival for the New Year, ones that honor both boys and girls, and another called the Star Festival that is an expression of the appreciation for nature.

There is not a strong emphasis on law and ethics within the Shinto tradition as there is, for example, in Judaism and Islam. However, there is the continuing spirit of nationalism and the support of the emperor system with implied legal and ethical implications. But it remains true that given the coalescence of the religious traditions of Confucianism, Buddhism, and Shinto, the ethical teachings that emerge may be attributed more to the Confucian and Buddhist influence.[34] It is important to note that Shintoism provides a context for the people to feel connected to nature and the state, and there are ethical implications for these values and loyalties. It is also important to underline the role of women, at least historically, in the role of shaman and the administration of both public and private worship. Women are viewed as more intuitive and better able to discern the presence of the divine.

Shintoism continues to be alive and well in Japan, although there is the challenge of accommodating the teachings of Shinto with a modern scientific understanding of the world. On this point, it is also the case that Japanese young people, not unlike the young people in other parts of the world, are reacting to a scientific worldview that reduces all of reality to the empirical and denies the validity of the spiritual. One author, Ian Reader, remarks, "The processes of modernization, rationalization, scientific development and increased education thus tend to stimulate rather than diminish interest in spiritual matters and the world of the irrational."[35] A further challenge to Shintoism in Japan is the struggle to sustain a religious outlook that may too easily be associated with traditional ways and the excessive patriotism associated with the lingering memory of World War II.

Assessment of these movements

It is difficult to find a great deal of support for Wicca, although the movement does in quite distinctive ways represent contemporary religious views, based in nature and interwoven with culture, that seek personal, spiritual, and social transformation. In fact, other representative religious views that have a more positive image might have been selected as illustrative of modern expressions of nature/culture religions. Certainly Taoism would have been an easy choice, but it will be discussed later in the section on religions of transcendental monism. Einstein's sense of religious awe generated by the study of the complexity and grandeur of the universe and more thoroughly developed recently by Stuart A. Kauffman in his book, *Reinventing the Sacred: A New View of Science, Reason, and Religion* is easier for most of us to identify with and toward which to feel positive support. Who has not been deeply moved and humbled by the awesome beauty and complexity of the universe? But as yet, it would be hard to describe this inquiry as a religious movement. A case might also be made for an alternative choice of a religious expression that best represents a religion rooted in culture such as American civil religion. But the stronger case made for Wicca and Shinto in that they both have characteristics of more traditional religion. Given the choices of Wicca and Shinto, we now need to ask in what ways there are life-giving or life-denying spiritual pathways and whether there are beliefs and practices that might be incorporated into our lives to enrich our own spiritual pathways.

Is the spiritual sojourn offered by Wicca and witchcraft generally life-giving or life-denying? Those on the inside of the movement would say that it is a spiritual pathway that heals and nurtures the true follower. It does empower those committed to the movement to show compassion and be socially responsible, especially in feminist and ecological causes. In the case of leaders such as Starhawk, there is openness to a scientific understanding of the earth, one that is informed and wise about ways to heal the earth. She has also been a strong advocate for feminist causes, lending her support to marginalized and disenfranchised women and seeking their empowerment. Those within the movement would also maintain that they gain guidance, support, and strength from their communities.

But the movement is vulnerable to criticism and has been subject to severe scrutiny by those who find the very notion of witchcraft weird and "hard to swallow." The world of Harry Potter may be fascinating, but few believe that such a world really exists. The movement is private, generally closed to outsiders, and filled with secrets. It does have the aura of a Greek mystery religion, with its initiation rites and incantations. Few would take seriously the ability to caste spells and perform magic with the use of potions. It does tend to keep its members under some discipline, creates a sense of caution around and even mistrust of others, and a measure of intolerance for those with other points of view.[36] But great care needs to be taken not to be intolerant of those who seek a spiritual pathway through Wicca; the movement has been subject to harsh and unfair criticism, and the very term "witch-hunter" speaks pointedly to the deep prejudice against and stereotypes about witchcraft in our society. One is left with the question of whether there may be some underlying truth and insights that might emerge, if the strange conceptual framework and metaphorical word choice of Wicca were peeled away. Love and care for the earth and the strong support of women may be the place to start.

It is possible to find positive underlying truth and insights in the Shinto religion as well. The obvious one is the inherent love of nature and the deep appreciation for the beauty of nature. As in the other wisdom traditions of indigenous religions, we see in Shinto the sense of being an integral part of nature and one with the vast expanse of the natural world that is and is in the process of evolving. Because of this profound insight, there is a sense of being a dependent part of nature and the conviction that nature must be conserved and respected. It is an understanding that points toward an ecological perspective that affirms that humans belong to the cosmos, and that relationships, interdependence, and change are essential categories that shape values and responsibilities. This paradigm, intuited in an earlier period, but now understood within a scientific framework, strongly suggests a global solidarity with all levels of life, one that is sensitive and responsive to the serious threats of global warming and other forms of environmental deterioration.

There is also within Shintoism a deep respect for tradition and authority. Within the mythology, there is the underlying insight that Japan and Japanese ways have been determined by the divine and maintained and sustained by the divine. The kami are present everywhere, preserving order and guiding human behavior. Those kami that were instrumental in the formation of the natural order and authority within the social structures are made visible at the sacred sites, sites that are often the destination of a spiritual pilgrimage. There are some inherent risks in this outlook, the most obvious one being the way that the tradition may be understood as sanctioning excessive patriotism and aggressive militancy as in the case of World War II. Such an understanding also has the inherent risk of giving consent to an exclusive society, one that is prejudiced toward and may ill-treat non-Japanese members of the society. Among the Japanese themselves, there is great pride in living up to the high expectations in the moral code within the culture. But there is the accompanying emotion of shame in what has been described as a more "shame-based rather than guilt-based" culture; the regret and shame for failure can be debilitating. There are many who would argue that Shinto no longer has a very strong influence on the life of contemporary Japanese people, but the cultural norms within the Shinto worldview have a way of continuing as a trajectory from the past into the present, even if not consciously expressed in religious practice. Most of these norms have a positive impact on the Japanese way of life and help to create a lawful and productive society.

We turn now to the great religious traditions and spiritual pathways of transcendental monism—Hinduism, Buddhism, and those indigenous to China, Taoism, and Confucianism.

Discussion questions

1. Does religion primarily grow out of human need and projection? Is so, does this make it untrue and therefore unworthy of human commitment?
2. Is the Wiccan love of the earth a legitimate way to express ecological sensitivity and responsibility or does it go too far by personifying the earth and calling it divine?
3. Why do you think the Harry Potter books been so well-received?
4. Some have argued that politics and religion should be kept apart. Do you think so? If not, how might they be related and how will they interact?
5. What are the risks of elevating a religion to the status of a state religion, as was the case in Shinto until 1945, and the continuing tradition in Japan of understanding Shinto as essentially the state religion of Japan?

Key terms and concepts

1. **Wicca:** From the Anglo-Saxon meaning witch or wise woman, the religion of witchcraft.
2. **Amaterasu**: The Sun Goddess and imperial ancestor.
3. **Izangi/Isanami**: The male kami and the female kami who were cocreators of Japan.
4. **Kami**: The term, that might be translated as holy power and presence, which refers to a variety of sacred objects, including gods, spirits, ghosts, trees, mountains, ancestors, and superior humans such as heroes and heroines.
5. **Kojiki and Nihoni**: The founding documents from the early 700s CE of Shintoism containing the creation myth, early history of Japan, and legends about the generations of kami.

Suggestions for reference and reading

Bocking, Brian, *A Popular Dictionary of Shinto* (Richmond, VA: Curzon, 1995).

Dowd, Michal, *Thank God for Evolution: How the Marriage of Science and Religion will Transform Your Life and Our World* (New York: Plume of the Penguin Group, 2009).

Earhart, H. Byron, ed. *Religion and the Japanese Experience: Sources and Interpretations* (Belmont, CA: Wadsworth Publishing, 1997).

Kauffman, Stuart A., *Reinventing the Sacred: A New View of Science, Reason, and Religion* (New York: Basic Books, 2005).

Kessler, Gary E., *Shinto Ways of Being Religious* (New York: McGraw-Hill, 2005).

Kitagawa, Joseph, *Religion in Japanese History* (New York: Columbia University Press, 1966).

Lovelock, James, *The Revenge of Gaia: Why the Earth is Fighting Back and How We Can Save Humanity* (New York: Basic Books, 2006).

Ono, Sokyo, *Shinto: The Kami Way* (Rutland, VT: Charles E. Tuttle, 1962)

Reader, Ian, *Religion in Contemporary Japan* (Honolulu, HI: University of Hawaii Press, 1991).

Starhawk, *The Planet Earth: Grounding Your Spirit in the Rhythms of Nature* (San Francisco: HarperSanFrancisco, 2004).

Part III
The Spiritual Pathways of Transcendent Monism

This section will introduce the great religious heritage of South and East Asia and deal specifically with the religions of Hinduism, Buddhism, and the Chinese religions of Confucianism and Taoism. In these great religious traditions, the spiritual goal is to understand that the all of reality is essentially one. It differs from the view that God may be understood as one subject among many, although qualitatively and quantitatively different. The spiritual life is a quest to gain a viewpoint from beyond and find harmony with the One, however it may be understood.

> I am the ritual and the worship,
> The medicine and the mantra,
> The butter burnt
> in the fire,
> And I am the flames that consume it.
> I am the father of the universe
> And its mother, essence and goal
> Of all knowledge, the refiner, the sacred
> Om, and the threefold Vedas.
> I am the beginning and the end,
> Origin and dissolution,
> Refuge, home, true lover,
> Womb and imperishable seed.
> I am the heat of the sun,
> I hold back the rain and release it:
> I am death, and the deathless,
> And all this is or is not.[1]

Spiritual Pathways Within Hinduism

Chapter Outline

Transcendent monism and the great religions of Asia | 81
The context and early history of Hinduism | 83
Summary and conclusions | 96

Transcendent monism and the great religions of Asia

The human family has found and followed a wide variety of spiritual pathways across the centuries in the spiritual quest for personal and social transformation. From earliest times up to the present, it appears that humans have sought religious answers to life's fundamental questions. Who am I? Why am I here? How should I live my life? How should we organize and behave in order to live together and get along with neighboring states? How do we relate to nature and control it in order to sustain ourselves and perpetuate the race? How should we understand the universe? How might we read our history for guidance in the present and for direction in the future? Is there a God or gods, or at least another layer of reality that will guide us and help us find meaning and serenity? Humankind has been creative in finding answers to these most pressing questions.

Our goal is to sample the answers from the world's religions for three primary reasons:

1. We do so in order to better understand and enrich our own spiritual sojourn.
2. We do so in order to learn what specific beliefs and practices of others we might want to incorporate into our understanding and spiritual journey.

3. We do so in order to gain greater understanding, openness, and acceptance of those who differ from us, and in so doing, use our new understanding to build bridges to others and contribute to the formation of a more just and peaceful world.

We are fortunate in our generation to have good access to the beliefs and practices of these diverse experiments in understanding and living. The scholarship about the world's religions is abundant, rigorous, and accessible. The majority of the world's religions are no longer exclusively regional but global, with gatherings of adherents of these great religions in our own communities.[2] In my teaching about these great religions, I have been able to take my students to visit these "congregations" to observe, discuss, and be taught by their leaders. Generally, able representatives of these many traditions have been willing to visit the classroom and make presentations. Even those religious traditions that are more contextual and regional may be visited, and it has been an extraordinary privilege and an informative experience for me as I have traveled to many countries to interact with these religions.

What I have learned in my years of teaching and visiting in other settings of the world is that most of the people in these religious pathways are open to learn from others and eager to share their own convictions about belief and practice. On occasion, outsiders are viewed with some suspicion and excluded from the acts of worship; in other cases, members of these religions ask hard and penetrating questions. Often common ground is found in the areas of spiritual practices, shared values, and commitment to social justice, and in some cases, there is the unspoken agreement to simply go our own way. The goal in these endeavors is not to "water down" our beliefs or persuade others to change theirs, but to share them thoughtfully and listen with empathy and appreciate those who have faith traditions different from our own. It is the dialogue, the sympathetic listening, and the sensitive human caring that lead to increased levels of understanding and trust.

We are trying to understand this vast smorgasbord of religious creeds, codes, cults, and communities and have suggested ways that might give us some patterns, categories, and a common universe of discourse. In particular, we have suggested three groups of the religions of humankind: those rooted on nature and culture; those that affirm one transcendent reality; and those with a belief in monotheism (in our case those which find their roots in the story of Abraham). It is the middle group that might be called transcendent monism to which we now turn. Nearly all of these great religious faiths had their beginnings in Asia, and we turn first to those which were founded in India and will then discuss those that are more indigenous to China and Japan.

The consistent pattern of development of these great religions was first a nonliterate phase, moving on to oral traditions, and then to written scripture and history. The concern for survival and health, the perpetuation of the tribe or clan, and veneration of natural forces were central to the early phases of these traditions as was the presence of animism and shamanism. Across the centuries these religious traditions developed a sense of the omnipresent sacred, saw the emergence of rituals and ceremonies, and shared a rich mythology with stories to help "make sense" of the marvelous and sometimes dangerous world.

In both Hinduism and Buddhism, the spoken word was preserved and honored, and in time the Vedas (the Hindu scriptures) and the Tripitaka (the Buddhist scriptures) came into written form. Other practices were developed such as yoga in order to deepen the spiritual life and to some extent distinguish these movements from the shamanistic practices. Yoga implies "discipline" and emphasizes the disciplines of both body and mind, and puts special emphasis on meditation. The goal of these practitioners of yoga was to find a profound sense of peace by going deeper in their consciousness in order to achieve oneness with ultimate reality, leaving behind the pursuit of rational thought and transitory feelings.[3] The following chapters on the religions of China and Japan present a similar pattern. Initially shamanism and the concern for the sacred prevailed, mythological stories gave order to the surrounding context, and ritualistic and ceremonial practices were common. In Confucianism and Taoism in China, there was a gradual shift toward ethics and nature's way (Tao). The result in China was a culture that became more formal, socially stratified, and guided by clear rules of behavior, although the followers of Taoism resisted the Confucian emphasis on prescribed social order. In Japan, the direction was slightly different because the native religion, Shinto, was continued to be followed in the ancient ways, but it wasn't long before the Confucian, Taoist, and certainly the Buddhist points of view began to be vitally present.[4] It is this story of Asian spiritual pathways that we now want to explore, beginning with Hinduism.

The context and early history of Hinduism

Hinduism, a relatively new term of Persian origin for the primary religion of India, essentially means the "belief of the people of India."[5] It should be noted that there are other religious traditions within India; Jainism, Buddhism, and

Sikhism to name just a few, but the vast majority (approximately 85%) of the people on the Indian subcontinent understand themselves to be Hindu. Not all Hindus live in India; there are large populations in Bangladesh, Sri Lanka, Indonesia, Africa, Europe, and North America. But like Confucianism in China and Shinto in Japan, Hinduism is primarily rooted in India.

The Hindu religion developed within the Indian context, addressing the hopes, questions, and problems that were indigenous to the Indian environment. In particular, the geographical setting had two central features that were to shape the understanding of religious life.[6] The first was that India was an agricultural land, and at that time, one that was vast and fertile without the present day industrial cities. The river valleys of the north with rich soil extended for about two thousand miles from east to west and supported a large population. The Indians were peoples of the land. India, even today with its large industrial cities remains primarily a country of farming. With this agricultural base, it was natural that the people of India would use religious categories of fertility. Nature itself, in the early cosmology of the region, was seen as female, and female deities became symbols of the fertility of the earth. As the natural condition changed with the threats of drought, flooding monsoons, and infertility, cultic practices emerged as ways of controlling nature and insuring physical well-being. Water became the center of ceremonial practices.

Another geographical factor in the formation of the religions of India was its isolation. It was protected by mountains and seas on all sides and was shielded from the invasion of hostile neighbors. There were attempts to raid India because of its agricultural resources and wealth, but generally these invading forces were "co-opted" by Indian ways as soldiers married Indian women and invading forces hired Indians to manage local affairs. Even the Muslim and British dominations of India in the past millennium failed to displace the old social order of India. Only the Aryan invasion sometime between 1900 and 1600 BCE fundamentally changed the ancient Indus civilization, but the Aryan invasion contributed to the more homogeneous India of modern times. This protective isolation was to shape Indian religion.

It was not so much the dramatic events of its history that shaped its religious outlook, as for example it was for Judaism, but the interior challenge of finding peace and harmony. At the heart of their developing religious orientation was the deep human struggle to find personal serenity and overcome the sense of being in bondage to human impulses. The responsibility for resolving these internal tensions was not defeating external enemies, but facing the conflicts within in order to achieve a measure of tranquility and happiness.

Techniques of self-examination and self-control, being loyal to the moral teaching, and practicing meditation and yoga would lead to inner peace, and it is this quest that became the core of the religious teaching.[7]

The religious beliefs and practices in India prior to the Aryan invasion are not fully accessible, but we do know that there was an advanced civilization that existed. The ruins at Mohenjo-Daro and Harappa, in modern day Pakistan, reveal a quite remarkable culture with sophisticated cities, transportation, and the use of water systems for households and agriculture. But we have few written sources (and the language code has not been fully solved) about religious practice, only clay and stone images and the remarkable order of the civilization that is visible from the ancient ruins. It is clear that the use of water was related to the sacred as a means of purification. It is also obvious that male animals, and especially the seal, imaged religious beliefs and sentiments. There appears to be a comparable religious impulse related to plants that suggest that fertility is a central concern. These features carry over to the religious outlook of India merging with the culture of the Aryans following the invasion. Early Hinduism may be understood as a fusion of the older religious heritage of the civilization of the Indus Valley and the new sources brought by the religious tradition of the Aryan invaders.

The accents and patterns of Hinduism

Hinduism is an exceedingly complex religion that has evolved over centuries with its beginnings lost in the mist of prehistory. In fact, Hindus believe that their religion has existed forever, and the task of the follower is to discover what is already there, inherent in the nature of reality. Developing as it did, the Hindu way tends to resist precise order and systematic description; any such approach to "contain" it might miss its subtlety and extraordinary insight into the human experience. It is not easy to look back at certain historical prophets nor important historical events in order place it on a clear timeline; it does not have the timelines of the birth and life of a founder or a single great prophet, nor the belief in the intervention of personal and transcendent God who shapes Indian history. But it does have **accents and patterns** that unfold from the sages and circumstances that formed in certain historical eras, and the modern day Hindu will draw upon these accents and patterns in finding a spiritual pathway.[8]

The first accent that leads to a pattern for a spiritual pathway is the accent of the **worship of the gods** who have power over nature and the vicissitudes of human life. A primary source for the reflection upon the way to relate to the gods came in the oral traditions and in time in the written books called the *Vedas*, a Sanskrit word suggesting wisdom. By 800 BCE, this material had taken the form of collections that were preserved and used by priests who had the responsibility of the performance of rituals. The *Rigveda* was the liturgical book of recitations and hymns used in worship. The *Samaveda* was used for the musical aspects of the sacrificial rituals, and the *Yajurveda* guided the one who arranged for the details of the ceremony. A fourth collection, called the *Atharvaveda*, came later and was a collection of poetry used in pastoral care for the common people, and from time to time with the ruling classes.

Within these collections was an inherent worldview that would come to guide the Hindu people in their spiritual sojourn. The collections contained a description of the gods (*devas*) of the Aryan pantheon who had power over the world and could guide and heal persons. Within the polytheistic pantheon, two gods in particular standout, Indra and Varuna. They were seen as superior because they were believed to have power over activities that are human and social, not exclusively events in the natural realm, as most of the other gods in the pantheon did. The Vedic literature also had a primitive view of human nature that described the body, but more importantly, it suggested an inner essence and animating principle called *atman*, a concept that would be central to latter forms of Hinduism. There was also a cosmology that postulated that the universe had three levels, one the earthly realm, the second realm of the atmosphere, and the third realm of mystery and eternal light where virtuous persons could find refuge when their earthly lives came to an end. In addition, there was a force in the universe, called *Rte*, which gave order and maintained harmony in the natural and human realms.

The challenge of the human journey was (and is) to find a way of success-fully navigating through and around destructive nonhuman forces, forces that threaten the external and internal domains of life. Like other religions, this early phase of what was to become "Hinduism" addressed its adherents' most worrisome insecurities and anxieties. The gods were viewed as having the power to help with the threat of natural disease and disaster. The gods were viewed as having the power to help with the threat of others, the harmful and destructive tendencies of a society without adequate infrastructure to insure security and justice. The gods were viewed as having the power to help with hostile foreign invasions and the destruction caused by conflict and war. Extensive ceremonies and rites in the family and in public settings developed for the people to worship the gods or God in a way that they hoped would gain favor with the gods and enable them to overcome the threats to life.

A second accent in the era of classical Hinduism was that of **right living and social order**, patterns of personal behavior and social structure that would help to form the spiritual pathways of modern Hinduism.[9] In the sixth century BCE, Indian society began a period of great transformation. The Aryans had cleared large sections of land of its natural growth and plowed the land, making it available for agriculture. Local chieftains who ruled over smaller and sparsely populated regions were replaced by kings with fortified cities and regional kingdoms. The people became dependent upon the fields for their livelihood, were subject to military and social control, and new political and economic structures became the norm. This was the new context in which classical Hinduism came into a form that continues to the present day.

A new literature was developed, called the *Sutras* (thread) and these verses and sentences on a range of subjects became the textbooks used in the Brahman schools. The earliest of these compositions was called the *Strauta Sutras* and contained instructions for performing the Vedic rites. Another sutra, called *Grihya Sutras* focused on domestic rites, enabling families without the assistance of a priest to conduct worship in the home. Perhaps the most important of these sutras was the *Dharmasutras* (*dharma* translates as "pattern for right living"), which gave attention to moral living as integral to Hindu religious duty. Many other writings were composed and circulated giving guidance for and suggesting that one's religious obligations were not just the performance of rites, but living an ethical life in accord with sacred moral codes. Gradually, these compositions were recast into verse (*dharmasastras*), and they replaced the earlier writings. One of these writings, translated into English as *The Laws of Manu* are attributed to a sage named Manu. These *dharmasastras* described the ideal pattern of life in detail, with language that is clear and firm, and prescribed patterns of behavior that should not change.

Coupled with the dharma was the evolving belief in the caste system, and together the pattern of right living and the caste system gave order to behavior and social structures. The caste system was based on the belief that people are born (from the Sanskrit *jatis*, meaning births) into occupational groups that are arranged in an ascending order depending upon the status of each group's traditional work. The origin of the class system was in part due to historical circumstances related to the Aryans' challenge of arranging the stratification and control of a large serf population. The *Rigveda* does suggest a four-class theory which may reflect the Aryan need for social order, and *The Laws of Manu* spells out the system in more detail. At the top of the pyramid is the *Brahmin* class whose responsibility is to perform sacrifices, to study and teach the Vedas, and to guard the rules of dharma. The *kshatriyas* or the warriors come next and carry the responsibility to be the protectors of society. The *vaisya* caste is to engage in commerce and farming, providing for the needs of society. The *sudras* are at the bottom and engage in handicrafts and the manual occupations. This class has certain restrictions regarding the accumulation of wealth and is not allowed to participate in the Vedic ceremonies. At the very bottom, although not considered a caste, are the serfs (often called outcastes) who do the menial work and are not allowed to participate in the normal flow of life. Their work is viewed as impure and it includes the cleaning and preparation side of fishing and hunting, executions, handling corpses, and managing human waste.

There is one other guideline for the ordering of life and social structure, and it is based on age and gender. Males in the three upper classes are expected to move through four stages of life. There is first of all the **student stage** for young males who apply to and are accepted by a teacher. They submit to the teacher's guidance and undertake the study of the Vedas. Upon the completion of their study, they enter a second period of life called the **householder stage**. The young man marries, has children, and earns a living to support his family. In this state, there are clear prescriptions of the duties of the husband. A third stage which is best described as the **retired person** comes much later in life, and the man is expected to leave his family and pursue the religious life as a hermit in the retreat context of the forest. A final stage is the pursuit of **the ascetic life**, although this pursuit may begin at any point in life. In reality few men actually move to either of these final stages. In modern India, these patterns or stages of life no longer have the binding character they may once have had, but they do continue to suggest a developmental pattern in adult life, as seen for example, in the life of Mohandas Gandhi.

Integral to the accents and patterns of moral behavior and social order is the profound belief in Hinduism that human beings are reborn again and again (*samsara*) to lives determined by the moral quality of the way one lives. This doctrine, called *karma* gave a rational explanation for why one is born into a class and determines the pattern of one's life. It functions as a motivation for living a life of high moral quality and as a means of insuring that people accept the class into which they are born and the duties associated with the inherited class. The doctrine of karma continues as a central feature of the spiritual pathways of contemporary Hinduism.

A third accent and pattern of traditional and modern Hinduism is **the way of knowledge**.[10] It is a particular kind of knowledge (*jnanamarga*) that is sought, not the usual sort of knowledge that enables one to undertake the daily tasks of life. Rather it is the knowledge that gives one understanding about human existence and the way of finding release from the bondage that is integral to earthly life. The quest of the Hindu seeker, sage, and priest is to transcend the knowledge of the natural order and focus on the mystical knowledge that empowers the seeker to gain mastery over the more profound problems of life. What is unfolding in this new pattern is a movement away from viewing the gods as personal beings who granted favors. What is emerging is a more fundamental question related to finding the reality underlying the universe, a single essence behind the diversity in the world. It is also a turn away from the esoteric and magical powers of the rites and ceremonies toward a cosmic power that would provide the solution to overcoming life's most desperate problems, a knowledge that could be pursued through meditation.

This kind of knowledge came to full expression in the literature called the *Upanishads*, a term meaning secret teaching. There were many compositions that were referred to in general as Upanishads, but only 13 of these are accepted by Hindus as the *sruti*, having the status and authority of revealed scripture. This literature became foundational in the development of modern Hinduism; nearly all of the philosophical reflections and meditative practices have their foundation in the Upanishads. There is the strong belief that they were "given" in a manner similar to that of the Vedas and in essence became part of the Vedas. There are no known authors, and the literature began to appear in about 600 BCE and reached its final form in about 200 BCE.

The accumulation and formation of the literature was the product of the teaching of upper class Aryans who themselves were drawn into the mystic quest for serenity. There would be settings in which these teachers, wandering from setting to setting, would debate and proclaim their insights, and often these teachings became a part of an oral tradition that was carefully preserved by its telling and retelling. The major theme of their teaching was focused on the word "*Brahman*" which was believed to be the inherent power in all that exists and the power that controls the world. The Brahman is the source from which all things spring that which holds everything together, and the divine essence inherent in all that exists. Brahman is not viewed as a personal God who intervenes in the lives of humans, but the "energy" that animates all of reality. It was logical that the next step was to view Brahman (the divine) within the self (atman), and the goal of human life was becoming divine.

The concern at the heart of the Upanishads, with only the occasional philosophical reflection, was mystical in character. The particular concern had to do with the harsh reality of death, and the even more worrisome reality of a series of lives and deaths in circumstances devoid of meaning and peace. They viewed themselves as trapped in this endless round (*samsara*) and longed for deliverance (*moksha*), the ultimate liberation from karma. What was needed was to find the bridge between the human soul and the immortal Spirit (Brahman), a pathway that drew upon former religious practices but was more focused on individual meditation. The initial problem centered on the fact that Brahman or Spirit cannot be detected by our five senses, only through mystical union. Nor can our mind or the states of consciousness (waking, dreaming, or deep sleep) take us there. In fact they may veil or disguise ultimate reality. It is our essence, consciousness or soul (atman) that links us with Brahman or the universal Spirit and enables us to achieve Oneness, free from the round of karma and endless cycles of life.

This fundamental insight became the ground of this new pattern in unfolding Hinduism, and it is called *Vedanta*.[11] The Vedanta asserts that there is an underlying unity of all reality (transcendent monism), even though we are often confused by the seemingly diverse array of material objects and conflicting structures in the universe. It was the great teacher, Sankara, living about 800 CE, who was able to acknowledge the diversity in the world, and at the same time see the oneness that stands behind it all. He taught that all human beings are surrounded by diversity and experience the pains of change, including profound psychic needs, disease, and the fear of death. He asks, how then can humans understand themselves to be fundamentally one with the universal and immortal Brahman? He answers the question by arguing that there are four levels of human knowledge:

1. The first is verbal knowledge, the lowest level of knowledge in that words are only partial descriptions of reality and are often filled with contradictions and misinformation. They cannot be fully trusted as descriptions of reality.
2. This leads to a second level of knowledge, coming from the senses, which he calls deluded experience. Our senses may help us in limited ways, but they do not provide accurate knowledge. We are deceived often by sight, for example, as we view things from a distance.

3. Implied in the second level is the third, and that is empirical knowledge. We do see real birds, trees, lakes, and mountains. But this knowledge does not address our deepest psychic needs.

4. It is the fourth level, the supreme (*paramarthika*) experience that does not come from the senses or the intellect, but through the consciousness of atman alone. In fact, we must put a hold on our senses and intellect and concentrate on our inner-most self. Then we will be able to reach a unique state of consciousness called *samadhi*. This universal consciousness, timeless and beyond all fears and suffering, is who we really are.

We achieve samadhi in several ways. First we must find ways to resist the view of the world that suggests that ultimate reality is many rather than one, the view that truth is divided as our senses tell us in experience. There is a force, called *maya* that operates on our psyche to delude us and make us think we are separate from Brahman. In order to attain the highest form of knowl-edge, we must exercise diligence and discipline and develop sensitivity to the deceiving character of maya. This may require, as a second means of achieving samadhi that we renounce our normal life and follow the disciplined way of contemplation and monasticism. There are several ways of pursuing the life of renunciation, but common to them all is the affirmation of five moral requirements: (1) noninjury (*ahimsa*) or nonviolence toward all living beings; (2) truthfulness (*satya*); (3) honesty (*asteya*); (4) chastity (*brahmacharya*); and (5) freedom from greed (*aparigraha*). Even those unable to follow the way of monasticism may prepare themselves by practicing the five mental virtues that prepare one for the eight stages of yoga. The five mental virtues are: (1) purity in the sense of cleanliness of body and diet; (2) contentment; (3) austerity in the sense of self-denial and endurance; (4) study of religious texts; (5) and meditation on the divine reality.

Common to the practices of both the monastics and lay persons is the prac-tice of yoga, a discipline that implies yoking, joining, or uniting. It is the practice of yoga that helps bring about the conscious union of one's soul to the world soul and becomes a central feature of Vedanta in particular and Hinduism more generally.[12] There are different forms and versions of yoga, but nearly all of them place an emphasis upon the appropriate site and the body posture for beginning the practice. The simple posture of legs crossed with hands folded is common and has the goal of helping the yogis to forget the body so that a higher level of identity may be achieved. Another feature or stage of yoga is the control of breathing, a means of drawing nearer to one's soul and achieving higher levels of calmness. Next, there is the focused concentration of keeping the senses from being distracted from external objects. There is the additional step of concentrating on a particular object, perhaps an image of the divine, which may lead to a deeper meditation on other symbols of religious faith. The process may be advanced with utterances of belief and even repetitive utterances of the syllable, *om*. In time, there is the hope that the yogi will be able to put aside the needs of the self and achieve the oneness of samadhi, the full experiential awareness of union with the divine.

Another accent and pattern, which joins the others, is **the way of devotion**. The different accents, with the patterns of practice, are not exclusive of the others and are often integrated and expressed within the life of a devout Hindu. The way of devotion differs from the others in its affirmation of a personal God of the universe that gives hope for liberation. There is more than one theistic tradition in Hinduism and two have been central in guiding Hindus in the ways to understand and relate to the one God. The first major tradition is a belief in Vishnu and the second is the belief in Shiva, and these two traditions have been an integral part of Hinduism for two thousand years. The traditions have been very popular and represent the faith of the majority of Hindu people.

These spiritual pathways represent a partial disenchantment with the ascetic and more disciplined pathways of the Vedic tradition and are attempts to make the religious experience more important in one's every day life. They do not require the renunciation of normal life or the rigorous and demanding discipline of the religious sage. They also affirm that it is not enough to focus exclusively on the escape from the cycle of lives; there must be a way of salvation that can be experienced in the current life. Further, the gods of the Veda have only limited power, usually over the natural realm, and even the superior gods like Indra and Varuna were believed to control only a portion of the universe. Increasingly there were speculations about a cosmic god (Brahman) with control over the entire universe, not unlike the transcendent God of monotheism. The Vedas certainly point to such a divine being in describing Brahman as creator and the underlying essence of the entire universe, and it was the belief in Brahman that became the basis for the way of devotion to a cosmic God.

We will look first at the pattern in the worship of Shiva, who is mentioned in Vedas as a force present in nature, and typically connected with thunder and powerful rainstorms. He is described in anthropomorphic terms, as one whose back is red and neck blue and who dwells apart from the other deities in the mountains. He has and uses weapons, including the thunderbolt, and is inclined to cause both illness and heal it. Those drawn to the worship of Shiva were those who knew the harshness of life and needed the favor of the God who had the power over destructive forces. In time the followers of Shiva began to see the language about this God as metaphorical and became more hopeful in their outlook. It is interesting to observe that in this form of Hinduism the divine conception contains elements of evil and offers a creative approach to the classical problem of evil which is inherent in the affirmation of an all good and all powerful God. The images of this tradition represent fertility (primarily male, but also female) and point to Shiva's generative power. By the year 400 CE, there were many groups that worshipped Shiva as the supreme God, especially in the South, in the Tamil region.

A closely related religious outlook developed out of the worship of Shiva, placing more emphasis on the female character of God. The Goddess Shakti is viewed as one of the wives of Shiva. She is the force that controls all that happens in the natural world. She is called by many names, one of which is Durga who is honored in many religious festivals as the goddess with many arms. A closely related form of religion called Tantrism arose in the early formation of Hinduism out of the same expression of goddess worship.[13] The goal of Tantrism is moksha allowing for erotic ritual practices as a means of liberation.

Again we see that one of the central features of Hinduism is the use of image and personification, making the gods easier to understand and relate to. As we will discuss below, the challenge in understanding the heartbeat of Hinduism is to see the language as metaphorical and pointing beyond itself to a more profound reality.

A second monotheistic tradition that follows a more devotional way is the movement that worships Vishnu. Vishnu, too, is mentioned in the Vedas, and he is interpreted as more kind and associated with the sun that brings light and growth. Vishnu is present in plants, provides food, and protects unborn babies. The mythological stories that surround him are filled with acts of kindness and protection, and promises of immortality. The worshippers of Vishnu were those who valued the welfare of all people in their society and looked to Vishnu for guidance and assistance in both personal and social transformation. In times of crisis, it is believed that Vishnu would enter the world in bodily form; these are called *avatars* or descents. The most important of the avatars are Rama and Krishna. Rama is the hero of the Ramayana, a great epic popular among all classes in India and Southeast Asia. Rama is a prince of the ancient city of Ayodhya, but because of betrayal, he was removed from his father's court. His brother and faithful wife Sita accompany Rama as he goes to live a simple life in the forest. Unfortunately, Sita is taken by the demon Ravana and carried away to a place in Lanka. Assisted by an army of monkeys, and the great monkey Hanuman, Rama wages war against Ravana and prevails. He receives Sita back and finally presides over a long reign of peace. Rama, becomes the incarnation of Vishnu, the supreme human ideal—gentle, brave, and devoted. Sita becomes the model of a devoted Hindu wife.

Another monotheistic tradition developed as the followers of Shiva and Vishnu and their beliefs began to be recognized by Brahmins who served as priests to the nobility. It was not a far reach for these priests to combine the monotheism of the more popular religions with their doctrine of Brahman, derived from the Upanishads, and postulate the unification of the world in Brahman. A new literature began to develop in the second and first century BCE, called the *Bhagavad Gita*, and it was received with so much favor that it was incorporated into the warrior stories in the Indian epic called the *Mahabharata*. The *Bhagavad Gita* with its 18 cantos of Sanskrit verses was included in the sixth book of the Mahabharata, but maintained a kind of separate existence and was read in isolation form the larger epic. One principle reason for its acclaim was the fact that it addresses a critical social problem of the time, the widespread abandonment of social responsibilities by young men who were leaving normal society for the religious life. The *Bhagavad Gita* introduces a personal Lord, Krishna, and while not opposed to the impersonal and underlying principle of reality, Brahman, the author raises Krishna to a supreme status. It is Krishna who teaches in the story that the pathway of renunciation of normal life and the abandonment of society is not for all, and that the best path is to stay and fulfill one's responsibilities in the world.

The story opens with a young and devout person who is contemplating his caste duties and finds deep internal resistance to what may be required of him. Arjuna, the discouraged and guilt-ridden hero, is a warrior who is required to fight against a prince, Duryodhana, who has committed great wrongs. As Arjuna ponders his responsibilities, he realizes that he must kill those for whom he has deep affection, relatives, and respected teachers, who reside in region of the evil prince Kaurava. Arjuna, reflecting on the horror of his assignment, gives up his chariot and weapons and says that it would be better to live by begging as a monk rather than to commit such horrible deeds. In despair, he asks for guidance from the driver of the chariot who is Krishna in disguise. Arjuna is counseled to fulfill his duty and not abandon his worldly work, even with its risks of endless retributions. Krishna argues that there is shame for Arjuna in leaving his calling, but more importantly, says Krishna, it is possible to perform one's work in the right spirit that will relieve him from the judgment of karma and allow for liberation rather than bondage (karma-yoga). No karma will be created by the performance of one's duties in a selfless way. What Arjuna must do is employ the disciplines of the spiritual way and practice meditation and yoga to gain victory over desire. The end of this discipline is not just achieving oneness with Brahman, but the personal transformation that gives rise to compassion for all creatures and a capacity for a lifetime of work, free from the infringement of ego and desire. These traits become the marks of our union with God. In the last canto, after an enlightening vision of Krishna, Arjuna pledges to Krishna: "I will act according to your command."[14] The story becomes the classic account of the struggle of many Hindus, that of balancing the demands of everyday responsibilities with the call to live a holy life.

Understanding these accents and patterns that developed over the centuries in Hinduism point to, but do not fully explain and describe contemporary Hinduism. This great religion has continued to develop, taking surprising twists and turns as it entered the modern era and continues to guide people around the world. India, the primary home of Hinduism, did have to accommodate the invasion and control of the Muslim Mogul Empire, a condition that existed for five centuries. Even more familiar to those of us in the West was the British presence. The British brought to India whole new economic patterns and institutions that dramatically increased the number of Indians engaged in trade and commerce. The British also promoted education, based in the English language and British in character. With it, of course, came the collision of traditional Indian ways and values with the world transforming trends of the nineteenth and early twentieth centuries, many of them Western in tone and character.[15]

The Indian response was remarkable. There were profound changes in personal life and social structure. Many religious societies were formed,[16] and there was the rise of strong Hindu religious nationalism. Great Indian scholars and sages began to address the spiritual crisis of the age, and their writings had great influence well beyond the borders of India.[17] Perhaps the best known Indian of the modern era, whose life in many ways epitomized the great teachings of Hinduism was Mohandas Gandhi (1869–1948). He was not a Brahmin, but born into the merchant class and became a lawyer. Nor was he a religious scholar, yet his religious teaching has touched in some degree nearly all present-day Hindus, who speak reverentially about him as Mahatma (The Great Soul). He put his deep religious convictions into practice and was the primary force in the Indian achievement of independence. He was influenced by many great religious writings, but in particular, the *Bhagavad Gita*. He was not interested in theological debate so much as the simple, yet profound truths of the teachings. He was fond of saying, for example, "God is truth." By this he meant that God is the basis for order and law and the force that is the foundation of moral righteousness in the world. He was open to other religions and their teaching, but counseled that each religion speaks wisdom to the people of its own culture. Gandhi believed that his spiritual pathway was to give leadership to social transformation. He demonstrated extraordinary courage in leading India to independence and his attempt to preserve its unity. He is especially well known for his use of two strategies for reform: *ahimsa*, the commitment to not taking life and respecting all of life; and *satyagraha*, nonviolent resistance and civil disobedience, the major strategy in his leadership of India to independence.[18]

Summary and conclusions

Our goal is not to attempt an exhaustive study of the history and development of Hinduism, but to focus on the accents and patterns that guide its followers in pursuing a spiritual way of life. What are the primary beliefs and practices of Hinduism that lead contemporary Hindus in a vital spiritual pathway? We will use our categories of creed, code, cult (worship and ceremonies), and community in our attempt to summarize the "spirit" of Hinduism.

Creed: What are the fundamental beliefs of Hinduism?

1. They believe strongly in the divine, with many affirming that there is one Supreme God called by many names, others postulating the divine essence of the universe (Brahman), and still others worshipping a local deity.
2. They believe that humans have an immortal soul that is reincarnated many times in order to achieve higher levels of spirituality, and ultimately to pass into eternity from the round of births.
3. They believe that this round of births is determined by karma, that what we do impacts and shapes our future lives. It is possible to gain liberation from this cycle and achieve *moksha*.
4. They believe that there is sacred scripture, called the Vedas, to guide them in their spiritual sojourn.
5. They believe in living the moral life, with an emphasis on compassion for all living things and adherence to living and speaking the truth in thought and deed.

Code: What are the primary ethical virtues (*Yamas*) in leading a moral life?

1. Practice noninjury and be careful not to harm others in thought or deed. Live peacefully with God's creation, honoring all that lives. Here we see, what may appear as a quaint custom to many in the West, the respect for animals such as the cow, the elephant, or the monkey.
2. Adhere to truthfulness by refraining from lying and betraying promises. Speak only that which is true and kind, helpful, and necessary.
3. Do not steal, covet, or fail to repay a debt.
4. Practice divine conduct, living celibate when single and being faithful in marriage.
5. Exercise patience in all circumstances.
6. Be steadfast in overcoming the challenges of life.
7. Practice compassion toward all beings.
8. Maintain honesty in all relationships and interactions with others.
9. Be moderate in appetite, following a simple and vegetarian (preferred) diet.
10. Uphold the principle of purity in mind, body, and speech.

Cult: In what ways (*Niyama*) do we worship and celebrate our religious traditions?

1. Allow feelings of and show remorse for failing to be true to all of the virtues.
2. Nurture contentment, joy, and serenity through the personal disciplines of prayer, yoga, and meditation.
3. Be generous with others, giving a tenth of one's income to the Temple.
4. Cultivate a true faith, being guided by a *guru*, temple worship, the great teachings, and sacred pilgrimages, e.g. to Banaras.
5. Cultivate devotion through daily worship, using a household shrine and meditation.
6. Eagerly hear and study the scriptures.
7. Develop a strong spiritual will and intellect with the guidance of a guru.
8. Embrace religious vows, rules, and observances and never waiver from them.
9. Chant your holy mantra daily, reciting the sacred sound or phrase provided by your guru.
10. Practice austerity, serious disciplines, penance, and sacrifice.

Community:

1. Seek out the help of other, and especially that of a guru, and be willing to offer an apology for failure and seek the forgiveness and guidance of others.
2. Attend regular services of worship and fully participate in the activities of the temple. Share the common experience of the practice of yoga and participation in a pilgrimage.
3. Help support the temple's activities and benevolent ministries.

Is the religion of Hinduism, in all of its diversity and complexity a religion that is life-giving to its followers, and does it have, as all human organizations have, characteristics that may be life-denying? Let us look first at those features of Hinduism that are positive and nurturing:

1. Hinduism has a comprehensive worldview that gives people a frame of reference to understand the world, give meaning to life, and guidance for living.
2. Hinduism attempts to address life's most challenging problems and answer life's most perplexing questions.
3. Hinduism provides guidance to its followers in pursuing the spiritual life.
4. Hinduism offers clear ethical guidance to its adherents.
5. Hinduism is generally open to diversity within its own religion and to the faith traditions of others.

There are some dimensions of Hinduism that may be problematic, especially for those who stand outside of the tradition.

1. It may be too easy to assume that its images, diverse gods, and shrines are literal expressions of the divine rather than pointers to the divine.
2. It may live, in many cases inadvertently, too easily with a caste system that dehumanizes fellow human beings.
3. It may in fact lead people, often unintentionally, to a kind of passivity about terrible life conditions rather than urge them to resist forms of injustice.
4. Some of the religious beliefs and practices may be too bound to place, region, and culture, making them confusing and unacceptable to outsiders.
5. There are the rare cases of xenophobic, zealous, and exclusive manifestations of Hinduism.

All in all, Hinduism is one of the truly great religions of the human family, providing nurture, order, and guidance across the centuries to millions of people.

Discussion questions

1. In what ways does Hinduism allow for diverse beliefs and practices?
2. Are there risks in describing the divine in such anthropomorphic ways?
3. Does the religion of Hinduism have the capability of appealing to people of non-Indian cultures?

4. Has Hinduism been primarily a positive or a negative fore in shaping the life of India?

5. What are the features of Hinduism that you would like to incorporate into your spiritual pathway?

Key terms and concepts

1. **Atman:** The soul or essence of one's self.
2. **Brahman:** The universal being, understood to be not personal but the source and energy of the universe.
3. **Brahmin:** The priestly class.
4. **Dharma:** The cosmic order, which if adhered to, works for righteousness.
5. **Karma:** Cosmic and personal law of cause and effect by which one's thoughts and deeds determines what happens in this life and in lives to come.
6. **Moksha:** Spiritual liberation.
7. **Upanishads:** The last and most philosophical of the Vedas, centering upon the theme that Atman is Brahman, and that one's true self is the universal divine reality.
8. **Vedas:** The ancient Hindu scriptures.
9. **Yoga:** The discipline of achieving union; the path of union with the divine.

Suggestions for reference and reading

Doniger, Wendy, *The Hindus: An Alternative History* (New York: The Penguin Press, 2009).

Eck, Diana L., *Encountering God: A Spiritual Journey from Bozeman to Banaras* (Boston: Beacon Press, 1993).

Feuerstein, Georg, *The Deeper Dimension of Yoga* (Boston: Shambhala, 2003).

Hodgkinson, Brian, *The Essence of Vedanta* (Edison, New Jersey: Chartwell Books, Inc., 2006).

Kitagawa, Joseph, ed., *The Religious Traditions of Asia* (New York: Macmillan Publishing Company: 1989) part of *The Encyclopedia of Religion* edited by Mircea Eliade.

Mitchell, Stephen, translator, *Bhagavad Gita: A New Translation* (New York: Three Rivers Press, 2000).

Narayanan, Vasudha, *Hinduism: Origins, Beliefs, Practices, Holy Texts, Sacred Places* (New York: Oxford University Press, 2004).

Renard, John, *101 Questions and Answers on Hinduism* (New York: Gramercy Books, 1999).

Spiritual Pathways Within Buddhism

Chapter Outline

Enlightenment and compassion   100
The founder   101
Buddhist branches and teaching   104
Spiritual practices   109
The compassionate life   112
The contributions and challenges of Buddhist spirituality   114

Enlightenment and compassion

Buddhism grows out of a comparable context as the developing religion in India that was to become known as Hinduism. As is the case with the early life of nearly every religious movement, there are circumstances in the environment that cause people to raise and seek answers to life's perplexing problems. In most cases these probing quests are religious in character and tone and tend to draw upon the prevailing worldview and thought forms of the setting. The questions have a universal quality about them. Whether in the seventh century BCE or the twenty-first century CE, people ask about inner peace and happiness. Are you and most people whom you know happy and content? Have you or the people whom you know ever experienced deep pain and suffering, perhaps from the loss of a loved one or because of a disease? What causes suffering and is there a way to overcome suffering or at least cope with it?

It was these questions that were in the hearts and minds of many people in India 2500 years ago, and they were the ones that "would not let go" of the mind and heart of a young prince named Siddhartha Gautama. This young prince left his comfortable surroundings and devoted his life to finding answers to these questions. As he found them and began to teach them, he became known as the *Buddha*, that is, someone who has gained **enlightenment**. Today, the number of people who follow his teaching in the many forms of Buddhism total about 340,000,000, and live primarily in Asia, although Buddhism has truly become a global religion.[1] These people earnestly follow the teaching the Siddhartha Gautama in the hope that they might be enlightened and learn how to live lives of serenity and compassion.

Over the 2,500 years as a religious movement, Buddhism has developed a bewildering array of beliefs, practices, rituals, and sects or branches.[2] Our primary purpose is not to weave together these many threads of art, philosophy, sect, cult, priests, saints, demons, gods and goddesses, and cultures, but to try once again to capture the spirit of the marvelous movement which has come to be known as Buddhism. Our hope would be to discern from the variety of detail the primary spiritual pathways that lay hidden in a comprehensive social context and which have the capacity to lead the sincere pilgrim to a life devoted to personal, spiritual, and social transformation. Buddhism, not unlike Hinduism, is a total social environment and way of life and requires careful study in order to fully understand the soul of the religion. The best place to begin our inquiry is with the life and historical context of the founder.

The founder

Buddhism, as with most of the world's great religions, is founded on the teachings of an individual who discovers and teaches about a spiritual center and a spiritual pathway. As it is with many of the great religious leaders of the human family, it is not all that easy to access accounts of their life and teachings, especially texts and artifacts from the time in which they lived. So it is with Siddhartha Gautama. However, there is a basic conviction among Buddhist scholars that the central core of teaching in the Buddhist scriptures reflects the original message of the Buddha himself. There is reason to believe that his teachings were well persevered for nearly two centuries in oral form, and then written in both the Pali and Sanskrit versions. But such accounts not only reflect the teachings of Buddha, but inevitably the outlook and needs of the community of religious followers at the time of writing as well. The teachings were originally written on palm leaves and collected in baskets (*pitaka*). As the manuscripts emerged, these were put into three categories and placed in the baskets. Buddhist scripture is therefore called (in Pali) The Three Baskets (*Tripitaka*), The Discipline Basket (*Vinaya Pitaka*), The Discourse Basket (*Sutta Pitaka*), and the Further and Special Teaching Basket (*Abhidhamma Pitaka*). It is the Discourse Basket that is the most important resource in that it contains the teaching on doctrinal and ethical matters and does so in the form of a discourse by the Buddha. The authenticity and accuracy of these documents are debated and variously interpreted by scholars and devout Buddhists, but for the sincere follower, it is possible to trust that these writings reflect the teachings of the Buddha.

Siddhartha Gautama (sometimes spelled Gotama) was born around 563 BCE[3] in the region of the Ganges river in north-eastern India.[4] The religious outlook of the region in which he was born was centered on the myths, gods, and sacrifices described in the Vedas. There was the priestly caste, the Brahmins, who studied the Vedas, performed the cultic practices, and lived in accord with the priestly code of duties or *dharmas*. The Brahmins were an integral part of the upper class and enjoyed some of the worldly benefits of their wealth and power. As these conditions were observed, some began to wonder if these benefits granted to the priestly class were spiritually corrupting and whether the Brahmins were able to provide true spiritual leadership.

A group of wandering priests and philosophers, not altogether in agreement with the Brahmins, called *Samanas*, began to question the teaching and lifestyle of the Brahmins. They began to teach the sacredness of all life, nonviolence, and the pointlessness, even cruelty of many of the cultic practices including the bloody sacrifices. One of these groups, known to us as Jains, taught nonviolence and the practice of an ascetic life as the way to find liberation from karma. Prince Siddhartha learned from the samanas of his days and appreciated the emphasis on nonviolence. However, in time he found that the ascetic life does not lead to enlightenment and peace, nor do individuals have personal souls that pass from one life to another until released from the rounds of reincarnation (although Buddha did believe in rebirth and karmic continuity).[5]

Siddhartha came from a wealthy and royal family with a long tribal lineage known as Sakayas. His father was a regional king or tribal leader and provided every luxury possible to his family. The young prince was handsome and gifted and appeared to have all that one could possibly want in life, including a lovely wife and a beautiful child.

The story is told that Siddhartha, in his twenties, began to be discontent with his way of life, and his discontent was exacerbated by what has been called in the legend of "The Four Passing Sights." While not protected from worldly pleasure, he was removed from the way of life that surrounded the palace. One day, however, he was to see the first of these sights, an old man, decrepit and bent, and Siddhartha was to learn the harsh realities of old age. On riding out of the palace, he encountered the second and third sight, a person racked with disease, and later a corpse. Finally, on a fourth venture out of the palace, he saw a monk with a shaved head, a person who had withdrawn from the cares of the world and who had a serene look on his face. These sights made him question whether fulfillment was possible in his protected life of wealth and comfort. He had learned that age, disease, and death were inescapable, even in a protected environment. These "sights" were to transform his life and force him to ask whether there was a realm in which these harsh realities of life do not exist and in which the ever-present psychic suffering of humankind can be overcome.

At 29, Siddhartha made his break with his princely life (his Great Going Forth), said goodbye to his wife and son, slipped out of the palace, and rode toward the forest to seek enlightenment. He devoted the next six years to solitude, fasting, and poverty (The Great Renunciation). He sought the advice of Hindu teachers about wisdom and the practice of *raja yoga* (consciousness changing), joined a group of ascetics, and then after some disillusionment with the ascetic life, he turned to thoughtful concentration and mystic reflection. One evening, under a tree known as the Bo (Bodhi or enlightenment) tree in northeast India, he sat and vowed not to get up until he achieved enlightenment. As the morning came, after a night reviewing the many temptations and options of life, he achieved "awakening" and the bliss of finding oneness with true being.

Following this experience of enlightenment, he thought of moving on from the world of disease, old age, and death into the state of *nirvana* (state beyond sorrow and liberation from suffering and the causes of suffering), but instead decided to devote his life to teaching what he had learned. He would spend the next forty-five years walking the hot and dusty pathways of India, teaching his life-giving message and organizing an order of monks to assist him. Like all great teachers of a new way of understanding, he had some resistance, but faithfully, with a patterned life that sustained him, he continued and led an exemplary life of compassion, had great influence, and provided extraordinary teaching and counseling. His teaching is not primarily speculative, but focused on the transformation of consciousness and the practice of virtues which characterized his own personal sanctity. For example, he lived and taught that the liberated person should have the following qualities:

1. *Metta*: friendliness or loving kindness
2. *Kauna*: compassion
3. *Mudita*: gentleness
4. *Upekkha*: equanimity

He died at age 80 in approximately 483 BCE, and fortunately, we have his legacy.

Buddhist branches and teaching

Across the centuries, Buddhism has developed much like the other religious traditions of humankind. There are many patterns of belief and practice and branches with subgroups that support them and occasionally diverge from them. While our goal is not to trace the twists and turns of the growth and development of Buddhism or its current complexities in belief, practice, and organization, there may be some wisdom in mentioning the three major branches of Buddhism.[6] These branches do not include all who follow the Buddhist way, but they represent the vast majority of Buddhists. One group believed that the Buddhist way should be available to all, and they became known as *Mahayana*, the "Big Raft" or "Great Vehicle" that carried everyone. This group, most widely adhered to in China, Korea, Vietnam, and Japan emerged in the first century CE as a more liberal and innovative interpretation of Buddha's teaching. They believe that Gautama is an earthly manifestation of a transcendent celestial Buddha and affirm the accessibility and importance of many different manifestations of Buddha. The spiritual pathway to follow is not that of becoming a perfected saint (*arhat*) who has arrived at nirvana, in some ways a selfish goal, but a *bodhisattva*, a person who has postponed nirvana in order to work for the well-being of all sentient beings. Compassion becomes the chief virtue in this tradition.

Inevitably, another group, stricter in its disciplined way, was called *Hinayana* or "Little Raft" or "Lesser Vehicle," and this branch has preferred to be called *Theravada*, the Way of the Elders. The Theravada form of Buddhism, practiced in South and Southeast Asia, claims to adhere most closely to the original doctrines and practices of the original Buddha. They follow closely the Pali canon that has roots in ancient Indian Buddhism. Their spiritual pathway does lead them toward perfected sainthood or *arhat*, and they often practice within a religious order.

A third major branch of Buddhism, called Vajrayana Buddhism or Tibetan Buddhism has been given high visibility and popularity because of the extraordinary example and leadership of the Dalai Lama. This movement evolved from the seventh century CE in Tibet. It incorporates the monastic disciplines of Theravada and utilizes the symbolic ritual practices of *Vajrayana* (esoteric Buddhism). It is distinctive in its emphasis on the "reincarnating lamas" and merges spiritual and temporal authority in the office and person of the Dalai Lama.

Within these strands are several subgroups, for example the movement known as Pure Land Buddhism (*Mahayana*) that is more devotional in character. It puts an emphasis on escaping the cycle of death and rebirth (*samsara*), and creating an environment in which all conditions are favorable for attaining enlightenment or paradise (Pure Land). In addition, there is the Zen tradition which emphasizes the practice of meditation as a means of awakening, a tradition that we will say more about in the next chapter in reference to Taoism.[7] Another subgroup, not always fully accepted in the larger family, is Nichiren Buddhism linked to the teachings of a Buddhist monk who lived in Japan in the thirteenth century. He based his teaching on the *Lotus Sutra*[8] and encouraged discipline, meditation, and chanting as a means of cultivating the spiritual life.

The differences between the three major groups within Buddhism revolve around several issues. I will mention four that are closely related and interwoven:

1. There is the relative difference and emphasis placed on individual initiative or empowering grace, with those viewing the Buddha as an expression of the divine (Mahayana) putting more emphasis on grace. All of the traditions would put emphasis on human responsibility for the cultivation of the spiritual life.
2. There is the question about whether the "historical" Buddha has a divine nature as a manifestation of the celestial Buddha with a continuing series of manifestations. The Mahayana tradition would say that all true disciples of the Buddha should seek to find the Buddha nature within them. Those who disagree would place an emphasis on the purely human Buddha. The Theravada tradition would teach that following the example of the great human teacher, Buddha, is the essence of being spiritual.
3. There is the question whether it is better to live one's life in an intentional community (*sangha*) or in the normal circumstances of the society. The Theravada

tradition would say that it is in the religious order that the full cultivation of the spiritual way is possible.

4. At the root of these questions is whether the Buddha himself is more of a teacher or a savior.[9] Perhaps he is both, depending on how one understands the terms.

It is interesting to observe that these questions surround the quest for understanding Jesus as well as Buddha.

While these differences are substantial, the three groups and the many subgroups still share a common set of beliefs and practices. It is true that Buddhism within the *Mahayana* stream has clear characteristics of a religion, but the question is often asked whether Buddhism in its original form is really a religion or merely an ethical and reflective way of life. There is no final answer to this question, although it is often raised because Buddha taught a spiritual way that was relatively free from authority, ritual, theological speculation, normative tradition, empowering grace, and a clear sense of the divine,[10] characteristics normally associated with organized religion.

What he did teach, and what has come down to us as the core of Buddhism (the *dharma*) shared by nearly all Buddhists, is the "Four Noble Truths" and the "Eightfold Path" as a way of incorporating the noble truths into one's life.[11] The text of this teaching is contained in the *Vinaya Pitaka* (the Discipline Basket). The introduction to this most important passage and teaching underlines a "Middle Path" that avoids extremes on either side: the extreme of the life of sensual pleasures and the extreme of mortification and asceticism. The Middle Path is more than just a compromise between the two positions or an effort to achieve unity, but a distinctive spiritual pathway. It is the Middle Path which brings insight and knowledge and leads to tranquility and enlightenment.

The Four Noble Truths may be stated in the following way:[12]

1. **Life is filled with suffering** (*dukkha*), and human sorrow is universal. The Pali word *dukkha*, nearly always translated as suffering also carries with it the connotation of dissatisfaction because life is not what you want it to be. Being old and decrepit and being filled with pain and disease are clearly what we think of as suffering, but the term also includes a mental or psychological dimension. For example, it may mean that you have what you dislike constantly with you, or that you lose what you want, and you do not get what you desire. Most human beings suffer more over issues of love and hatred than they do living with the presence of physical illness. One might ask why the Buddha would start with this "truth" in that it is not a positive way to start, and the answer is that he wanted people to give up their denial about the harshness of life and face up to reality. The spiritual pathway begins with a clear focus on reality.

2. The second truth is that suffering and sorrow are caused by **attachment and craving** (*tanha*), our insatiable desire to have and possess. There is the desire for the pleasure of the senses, for possessions, and to hoard these possessions believing they will bring satisfaction. This constant passion to have possessions whether it is material things, property, reputation, power, controlling relationships or anything leads inevitably to dissatisfaction because what we long for does not meet our deepest needs. We find, once we possess what we desire, that we have placed unrealistic expectations on the object of our desire, and we are left with frustration and emptiness (suffering), and wanting more. We live in ignorance and sorrow. It is at this point that the construct of karma-samsara is especially germane. The second truth implies that our craving is to be bound to an endless cycle of rebirths, the life caught in samsara, and to live in an aimless way, tossed like a cork on the waves of the sea. But there is another way that frees one from the law of karma, the law of consequences for our behavior, even if we are born to a better state because of our noble actions. This fundamental truth points us to the third noble truth.

3. Noble truth three is that there can be an **end to suffering**. Buddha teaches that we must let go of our desire for possessions and root out our need for attachments. When we do, our suffering will cease. The distinction within Buddhism is made between having wealth, possessions, reputation, power, and good relationships, and our unhealthy and inordinate desire to possess it all and have more. It is not so much about our preferences and possessions as it is about our attitude toward them. We must learn to accept what we have rather than constantly crave more. It is even acceptable to be rich if we use our wealth compassionately to help others and participate in creating a more just world. Even those who live a virtuous life may be guilty of craving the reward of their accumulated merits. It is when we are free of desire, even the desire to overcome punishment for bad deeds, that we gain peace of mind. We must practice the law of righteousness (*dharma*) for its own sake. It is giving up and abandoning all greed; it is release and detachment from all greed. It is in that state that we are liberated from mental anguish and experience nirvana. In practicing dharma, we cross the shore from samsara to nirvana. We begin to experience joy and inner peace, sorrowlessness, security, purity, and sublimity.

4. The fourth noble truth has to do with the ways in which we achieve our cessation from suffering and move toward the path of transformation, spiritual liberation, and enlightenment. This way is called the **eight-fold path**.

The eight-fold path is often illustrated by the eight-spoke wheel of the dharma.[13] The eight spokes are:

1. The first is maintaining the **right view**, having right understanding, or seeing things as they are.[14] We must give up our tendency to deny the harsh realities of

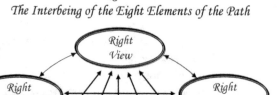

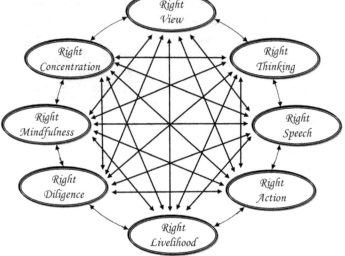

life and accept that suffering exists. Life is transient, painful, and we have no true self.[15] We must cultivate enlightened awareness and self-knowledge. In time, with the right view, we gain wisdom that gives us sanity, integrity, centeredness, and equanimity.

2. The second is **right intention** or thought. This step invites us to use our minds and our will to free ourselves from ignorance, delusion, and selfishness which only cause harm to ourselves and others. We need to think wholesome thoughts of detachment and good will. We should practice loving-kindness, empathy, and compassion toward all of creation. We find our spiritual way by developing the mind and the heart.

3. The third step is **Right speech** in our pathway toward wisdom and enlightenment. Our words do have a powerful effect on others and shape our inner lives as well. We need to avoid false witness, harsh words, gossip, and lies. So we dedicate ourselves to finding the right words that convey the truth, bring beauty to life, and love to others.

4. The fourth, we are asked as we follow this pathway to do the right thing; we practice **right action** and learn the art of living in a positive and constructive way. We avoid actions that cause harm to others and commit ourselves to help and protect others and all creatures. We refrain from killing, stealing, and wrong sexual behavior, and practice universal benevolence.

5. The fifth follows that we pursue the pathway to a better life by engaging in **right livelihood**. Our work, the way we earn a living, reflects our commitments and values.

We learn how to love our world through our work and avoid vocations that are harmful to others and to the earth. We bring our spiritual center to our daily work and understand our work, even if it is routine, as a way of making the earth a better habitat for all. It is so easy to be disillusioned with our work, to experience boredom or burnout, and to be constantly looking for the perfect assignment. We may never find it, but in the meantime, we make our work a true vocation or calling to the life of the spirit.[16]

6. As we walk this path, we must make the **right effort** to nurture our spiritual life. There are times when we neglect our spirituality and the disciplines required to sustain it. But we must strive to keep our mind free from evil thoughts and fill it with thoughts of detachment and friendliness. "Inner work" is so important to the life of peace and service, and only with the right effort will we find the passion for seeking wisdom and enlightenment. It is by thoughtful reflection (mindfulness), meditation (*samadhi*), and awareness practices that we will find spiritual awakening and transformation.

7. The seventh step on the pathway is **right mindfulness**, paying close attention to the present, what is currently happening, and being aware of our surroundings. Being overly preoccupied with our past or future, or lack of concentration on our current task, takes us away from the moment and the real world in which we live. Right mindfulness is the true guard against defensive living, behavior that is not congruent with our true values, and which does not have purity and integrity. When we neglect right mindfulness or attentiveness, negative forces may overcome us, and we can easily lose our way.[17] The Buddha is reported to have said: "The secret of health for both mind and body is not to mourn for the past, worry about the future, or anticipate troubles, but to live in the present moment wisely and earnestly."

8. So, to live a life that is authentic, we must have **right concentration**. In order to develop insight into our lives and our world, we must focus our minds and channel them toward the goal of wisdom and enlightenment. We must train our mind to restfulness and insight by periods of meditation. It requires that we harness our energy, apply mental discipline, and give appropriate attention to achieving the goal of living the authentic spiritual life. We draw in particular upon the "spokes" of right effort and right mindfulness in order to achieve our aim to be an enlightened and compassionate person.

Spiritual practices

There are, within these teachings and in other teachings, a number of foundational principles that form the basis for the pursuit of a deeper spiritual life in Buddhism, and in fact, there are so many that it is beyond our scope to attempt to discuss them all. But focusing on the core teachings will help us as we look more closely at the ways in which one finds a spiritual center and pathway within Buddhism. The first is that we all have the **potential to be enlightened**, fulfilled, free, and find a life of meaning (aware of course of the differences of interpretation within the traditions of Buddhism). One way about which this potential is spoken is that each of us can awaken the Buddha principle within. To say it directly, we all have the capacity to become Buddhas. We can all follow the way of the Bodhisattva (one who aspires to enlightenment), and it is especially relevant to contemporary times which cause so much anxiety and stress, and which take their toll on the peace and well-being of all of us.[18] Buddhism is not a religion of the past, but one that speaks to the hopes and fears of all contemporary people regardless of ethnicity, nationality, and culture.

A second fundamental tenet in the Buddhist tradition is the belief in **karma**, the workings of cause and effect in our lives. We do reap what we sow, and our virtuous actions lead to happiness and our negative actions, however small, lead to suffering. In nontheistic Buddhism, there is no God who keeps score and rewards good and evil. Rather the law of karma is built into the universe. It is like a law in physics, that for every action, there is a reaction. It is a statement about the interconnectedness and interdependence of all things.[19] The law of karma means that we can have faith in our ability to affect our own lives and the lives of others for good. As we do good deeds, we accumulate merit that affects our destiny.

Our destiny is linked to the cycle of death and rebirth called **samsara**. Our karma determines whether we will live a fulfilled life here and be reborn (or reincarnated) in some form that is positive.[20] The Buddhist traditions have varying ways to describe the forms of reincarnation and speak about multiple existences rather than an unchanging, substantial soul. A variety of psychosocial elements and states or aggregates (5 *skandhas*), composed of body, sensations, perceptions, impulses, and consciousness, ceases to exist at death, and the birth of a new self becomes possible.

Ultimately, we can achieve *nirvana*, the state beyond sorrow and liberation from suffering, but we also must acknowledge the reality of samsara, the cycle of uncontrolled birth, death, and rebirth rooted in ignorance and full of suffering and unfulfilled existence—life lived in an unenlightened way. By choosing to become a monk or at least dedication to practicing the disciplines and meditation, one can stop the wheel of birth, death, and rebirth and achieve nirvana, the elimination of samsara, uncontrollable desires, and suffering.

As a final note about foundational beliefs, we would return to what we have already implied, and that the final destiny of the pilgrim Buddhist

(*Bodhisattva*), and indeed all of us, is to achieve nirvana, a stage differently understood than the Christian concept of heaven in which our identity is preserved throughout eternity in the presence of God. An *arhat*, one who has achieved nirvana, enters "the world of no-birth and no-death, no permanence and no impermanence, no self and no nonself. Nirvana is the complete silencing of concepts,"[21] a clear break with the notion of an eternal self that is believed in many strands of Hinduism (atman).

How then does one find a spiritual center and a spiritual pathway within Buddhism? Many ways, but meditation is central to them all within the context of the Three Jewels of Refuge: "I take refuge in the Buddha (the teacher), the Dharma (teaching), and the Sangha (the community). Thich Nhat Hanh, in addressing this question, suggests several patterns laid out in good order.[22] For example, he describes the following concepts and pathways:

- The Two Truths: how relative or worldly truth gives us access to absolute truth
- The Three Dharma Seals: impermanence, nonself (or no-self), and nirvana
- The Three Doors of Liberation (or Concentration): emptiness, singleness, and aimlessness (no set program, agenda, or preoccupation)
- The Three Bodies of Buddha: the source of enlightenment and happiness, the body of bliss or enjoyment, and the earthly embodiment of the Buddha in Siddhartha.
- The Three Jewels (see above)
- The Four Immeasurable Minds: love, compassion, joy, and equanimity
- The Five Aggregates (see above)
- The Five Powers: faith, energy, mindfulness, concentration, and insight
- The Six Paramitas: giving, mindfulness training, inclusiveness, diligence, meditation, and wisdom
- The Seven Factors of Awakening: mindfulness, investigation, diligence, joy, ease, concentration, and letting go
- The Twelve Links of Interdependent Co-Arising: a description of the inner workings of past, present, and future within the human spirit
- And Touch the Buddha Within: letting the Buddha spirit emerge on one's life.

It is a helpful pattern for spiritual formation within the Buddhist tradition, and we will draw upon it as we attempt a synopsis of the Buddhist ways. Within Buddhism, the whole of life may be thought of as spiritual in character depending upon one's attitude and perspective. One thinks in particular of the Japanese custom of making beautiful flower arrangements as a spiritual practice. But the core of Buddhist spiritual practice is to live a life that is in touch with and reflective about reality and the place of one's inner and outer being within reality. It is to recognize the situation in which you find yourself, your attitude and outlook about life, and to discipline yourself through a reflective process to be more centered and focused. As one becomes more congruent and authentic through turning the mind into an ally in life,[23] one is able to experience the fullness of life and have the following qualities within one's life:

- appreciating the present moment
- knowing one's distinctiveness
- caring about friendships
- finding calm and serenity
- feeling inner harmony
- being more efficient with daily tasks, and
- expressing compassion toward others, and sensing a clear purpose in life.[24]

Mindfulness does not come easily or naturally, but must be cultivated. An integral part of this cultivation is developing awareness—of the body, of feelings, of thoughts, and of mental states. A good place to begin is to be conscious of one's breathing, then moving on to one's physical sensations, opening to one's feelings, and then focusing on the contents of the mind. One can do this in a quiet space, sitting in a meditative posture, and also with appropriate concentration within the rush and patterns of daily living. In time, one develops the capacity of focused and deep concentration, and there are practices called *jhanas* that strengthen one's powers of concentration and the ability to gain insight. The Zen tradition has emphasized focused concentration as a means of unlocking spiritual riddles known as *koans* and using them to awaken one's true nature. Ultimately, the Buddhist pilgrim is on a spiritual journey to be at peace, to gain wisdom, and to live responsibly in the world. Through right mindfulness and the practice of meditation, one gains peace, happiness, and wisdom.[25] Wisdom comes not only from reflection and meditation, but also from careful listening to the teachings of Buddha, reflecting upon it, and applying it to one's life.

The compassionate life[26]

To gain inner peace, insight into the complexities of life, and wisdom for living are great blessings and may be thought of as noble ends in themselves. But the spirituality of the Buddhist way is more than just inner peace; it has a profoundly ethical character and asks its followers to live responsibly in the world, even if living in (and often especially living in) intentional communities.[27]

There are many examples of leaders in the Buddhist tradition who have lived and are living in ways that benefit the whole human family. Certainly the life of Thich Nhat Hanh, the Vietnamese Buddhist monk, author, and peacemaker who was nominated by Martin Luther King, Jr. for the Nobel Peace Prize, who lives in France in the monastic community known as Plum Village, comes to mind. In North America, one thinks of Pema Chodron, an American Buddhist nun who is an author, a counselor, and who is active in the peace and just causes. But the example for the whole world is the Dalai Lama who has wisely and carefully led his Tibetan people in the quest to preserve their identity and homeland.[28] In doing so, he has modeled an ethic for this millennium.[29]

Pema Chodron speaks about the ethical life of the Buddhist in terms of the Three Disciplines—not causing harm, gathering virtue, and benefiting others.[30] The first of these, not causing harm, is called by the Dalai Lama "The Supreme Emotion"[31] which he translates from the Tibetan to mean "the inability to bear the sight of another's suffering." He speaks about these emotions as profound empathy for others and says that they are basic to human feeling. He acknowledges how easy it is for us to cause harm in both word and action, then to deny it, and walk past the one whom we caused to experience suffering or who suffers for any reason. The challenge to the authoritarian government in Myanmar by Buddhist monks is a contemporary expression of the belief in "not causing harm."

The way to avoid causing harm to others or ignoring their pain is to "gather virtue" by the cultivation of wisdom and empathy. With the basic practices of the spiritual life through meditation and concentration, one can become a person who has control of one's anger, is not aggressive, and has the qualities of modesty and humility. We can learn how to practice "mindful speech" with others, a way of listening and speaking that is calm, understand the feelings of others, and speak words of comfort. Our own suffering can give us the capacity to identify with others. Within the Mahayana tradition, these virtues are sometimes listed as the "six perfections:" generosity (giving), moral discipline (ethics), patience, effort, meditative concentration, and wisdom. The Theravada perfections include these listed, and then the following are added: renunciation, truthfulness, loving-kindness, and equanimity.

The third discipline of the way of the Bodhisattva is to live a life that benefits others. At no point are these seen as an easy accomplishment, especially to live the life of love consistently.[32] At the heart of living a life that benefits others is the expression of compassion, the capacity to identify with and feel the suffering of others. It is an inner awareness of shared suffering that leads to a sense of caring, a commitment to ease the suffering of others, and engagement in responsible action to improve the lives of others. In the expression of compassion, while seldom pure, one must be guarded against the temptation to disguise one's own attachments and needs behind a fig leaf of words about love and compassion. Words are empty without loving actions.[33]

The contributions and challenges of Buddhist spirituality

Buddhism has provided a spiritual center and spiritual pathway for people not only in Asia, but also around the world. It has become, in fact, a world religion because of its universal appeal and in part because of globalization. It has been life-giving to millions for several reasons:

1. It offers a life, when followed with discipline and mindfulness, of inner peace and serenity. Perhaps life has always been stressful and full of anxiety, but contemporary life seems especially demanding and challenging, creating mental and emotional anguish. The Buddhist way speaks directly to those who seek equanimity. Many of the Buddhist practices that lead to serenity may be incorporated into the life of those who are not Buddhist and remain committed to their religious tradition or to a more secular and ethical way of life and so Buddhism becomes a gift to the whole human family.

2. It is also profoundly ethical in character, calling on its followers to live moral lives, help those in need, and identify with those who suffer. Individual Buddhists are asked to live in a way that benefits others. Here again, the ethical teachings, with the core teaching of compassion, can guide all pilgrims who seek to love their neighbor and create a more peaceful and humane world.

3. For the most part, the Buddhist way is not speculative and theoretical, but practical and provides guidance for everyday living. Many of its practices are available to everyone, not unlike the practices of meditation within Hinduism. People of other religions may remain true to their traditions and yet utilize many of the practices taught in Buddhism. The teachings within the "eightfold path" are universal in character.

4. Buddhism, therefore, tends to be universal in its appeal and accepts others from different religious traditions. To be frank, there are those within Buddhism who are not open to the ways of others, or even to those within Buddhism that come from other traditions. But in general, it offers to receive others into its own community of faith, and at the same time affirms the religious pathways of other religions and honors the great wisdom teachers of the human family.[34]

5. Buddhism plays a role in building a more just and peaceful world. Many of its leaders have participated in causes that seek a more just and peaceful world. The Dalai Lama's leadership of the Tibetan people and his noble spirit in dealing with the Chinese in his quest to preserve the faith and culture of the Tibetan people is but one example.

The various parts of the larger Buddhist family face the challenges of nearly any religion that seeks to be a part of many countries and cultures. There is the ever-present caution and fear when faced with the "other." Inevitably, there are the all-too-human tendencies to yield to fear, become overly zealous about one's one way, to harshly judge the way of others, and to become exclusive. So among the challenges are:

1. Different branches within Buddhism have the tendency to become sectarian in spirit, and exclude not only those from other religions, but those groups within Buddhism with whom they differ. Buddhism is not free from internal conflicts, which in themselves, could lead to more profound understanding, but has had a tendency to divide.
2. There are also movements within Buddhism that tend to be "other-worldly" and lead to a withdrawal from society and responsibilities within society. A good case can certainly be made for living the monastic life of simplicity and purity, but such a life is most helpful when it then applies its learning for the good of others.
3. It follows that there are tendencies within Buddhism to be so exclusively preoccupied with one's own internal life of spiritual formation. The quest may become self-centered and focused almost exclusively on the internal life of the seeker, a state of self-absorption. The Buddha chose to be a bodhisattva for the good of all, and his model is normative for Buddhist spirituality.
4. There are some intellectual challenges for those who shape Buddhist thought and teaching, as there are for religious thinkers and teachers in all of the religions of humankind. For example, one might raise questions about the universal character of the karma-samsara-reincarnation construct in reference to the contemporary understanding of human evolution, and seek to find ways to integrate the two strands of thought. The central teaching of "no-self" does raise questions for the followers of many religious traditions that believe in an eternal soul.
5. There are the usual challenges of helping people from other parts of the world, outside of Asia in particular, to understand the teachings of Buddhism. There is the temptation to caricature that which we do not fully understand, for example, there are those who may think that the emphasis on suffering may be too negative and an inaccurate description of human life. But in the context of Buddhism, it is viewed as an acknowledgement of the harsh realities of life. Many Buddhist practices and teachings about gods and goddesses and demons, and the sectarian and cultic

worship forms seem strange, antiquated, and superstitious to outsiders. Again, it is the way of religion to use images that point beyond themselves to a deeper truth. Others may misread the Buddhist teaching that the world of appearances is an illusion when in fact; within Buddhist teaching, it is a calling to find the truth behind superficial appearances.

One of the great gifts of the world becoming smaller is that we now have good access to the customs, cultures, and beliefs of others. One of those great gifts to which we now have access is the wisdom contained in Buddhist teaching, wisdom that can enrich the lives of all who immerse themselves in it.

Discussion questions

1. Do you think, as the Buddhists teach, that life has within it a large element of suffering?
2. If so, what are the causes of suffering, and how is it possible to overcome suffering?
3. In what ways does Buddhism offer pathways to inner peace and serenity?
4. What constitutes the moral and ethical life within Buddhism?
5. In what ways is Buddhism compatible with other religions? What are some similarities and differences?

Key terms and concepts[35]

1. **Bodhisattva:** One who aspires to attain enlightenment in order to relieve others from suffering.
2. **Buddha:** The "awakened one," fully enlightened being.
3. **Dharma:** The spiritual teachings of Buddhism.
4. **Karma:** The cause and effect of virtuous or nonvirtuous actions.
5. **Nirvana:** The final state of being free from suffering.
6. **Samsara:** The cycle of death and rebirth rooted in a life of ignorance.
7. **Sangha:** The spiritual community.

Suggestions for reference and reading

Armstrong, Karen, *Buddha* (New York: Penguin Book, 2004).

Chodron, Pema, edited by Berliner, Helen, *No Time to Lose: A Timely Guide to the Way of the Bodhisattva* (Boston: Shambhala, 2005).

His Holiness the Dalai Lama, *The Compassionate Life* (Boston: Wisdom Publications, 2003).

Das, Lam Surya, *Awakening The Buddha Within* (New York: Broadway Books, 1997).

Hanh, Thich Nhat, *The Heart of the Buddha's Teaching: Transforming Suffering into Peace, Joy, and Liberation* (New York: Broadway Books, 1998).

Hanh, Thich Nhat, *Teachings on Love* (Berkeley, CA: Parallax Press, 1998).

Thurman, Robert, *Inner Revolution: Life, Liberty, and the Pursuit of Real Happiness* (New York: Riverhead Books, 1998).

7 Spiritual Pathways Within Confucianism and Taoism

Chapter Outline

Spirituality and transformation   118
The development and teachings of Confucianism   119
Nature's way: the spirit of Taoism   127
Contemporary expressions of Taoism ideas   132
The continuing value and recurring challenges of Chinese religion   133

Spirituality and transformation

We have suggested from the beginning of our inquiry that the human family has manifested a longing for spiritual pathways that would improve their lives. In nearly every time and place, humans have sought religious answers to life's most pressing questions. Often those engaged in this endeavor looked to their surroundings for these answers. In many cases, nature seemed inherently to have clues, if not answers, given its power and order. In other cases, the leaders of a tribe, clan, city-state, or nation represented and often claimed that they were divine or had access to divine power and direction. On the Indian sub-continent, the religious quest took still another form as people sought a deeper and more profound reality, beyond all appearances and social structures, believing that being united with a principle or power that holds the world together and gives it meaning will lead to eternal rest.

Across the span of human history, religions developed around the globe, taking a breathtaking variety of forms. We have looked at some of these religious formations and see in them, behind the details of historical development, culture, beliefs, and practices, a quest for personal, spiritual, and social transformation. There is an attempt to understand and cope with suffering and death, to have a sense that life has a purpose, and to find guidelines for how to live in the midst of all of life's challenges and changes. There is an intense desire for a life that is free from the suffering that comes with hunger, disease, and aging, and a condition of the mind in which one has a sense of liberation, joy, and serenity. There is also a prescribed way to connect with another transcendent layer of reality that has power, or gods and goddesses that can grant a better life and eternal rest.

We have argued that the spiritual quest *is* about personal and social transformation. Individuals want to move from a consciousness of fear, anxiety, and insecurity, to an interior state of insight, joy, and peace. They also want their circumstances in life to improve and have sought a different social order, one that meets their basic needs of hunger and health, one that provides some security and one that gives pattern and order to their social lives. Often, the religion that embodied these attempts at personal and spiritual transformation contained suggestions and commands to participate in creating a new social order, and what emerges is an outlook in which religion and society mix, dance, and tangle.

In this chapter, we will be looking at two of the world's great religions, both unfolding in China, which offer spiritual pathways that offer personal and social transformation. One of them, Confucianism, teaches a way of social transformation, in part dependent upon personal transformation. The other, Taoism, points more specifically to a way of personal transformation that has an impact on the social order. We will turn first to Confucianism, a religion that is practiced by fewer people in China today than it may have prior to the developments of the twentieth century and the communist revolution but still may have as many as 7,000,000 followers worldwide.[1] But even in decline, it is one that in influence, if not in daily practice, continues to shape the contours of Chinese society.

The development and teachings of Confucianism

Like all of the great religions of the world, Confucianism finds its way in a context and takes form in reference to the natural and social order of its surroundings.

Confucius (551–479 BCE) came onto a scene in which there was already an array of religious beliefs and practices. It had many features that were attempts to find answers to life's most pressing questions. Let me mention four as a way of catching the religious spirit of this moment in the vast span of civilization in China.[2]

The first was an attempt to understand death and find ways of honoring those who had passed away. From earliest times, the Chinese way was to **focus on ancestors**, and there is evidence in the archeological remains as far back as the Shang Dynasty (1750–1027 BCE), that there is a concern for the dead. Objects that the dead might need in an afterlife have been found in the excavated graves. Not unlike what we saw in ancient Egyptian practice, we see that royal and wealthy families had better prepared their ancestors for what these families thought might be needed in the afterlife. Dead royalty were provided with weapons and the sacrificed bodies of those who serve the monarchs. A few of the graves of common people had ordinary vessels or a weapon such as a knife. The primary purpose of these burials was of course to honor the ancestors, but a secondary purpose may have been to satisfy the dead relative so that he or she would not want to return to interfere with the ongoing affairs of family life. It was time to move on. Another dimension of these burials was the belief that these ancestors need proper care because those who receive proper burial and continual offerings become good spirits and those that don't receive the attention become ghosts that may cause harm to the family. Modified forms of these practices continue to the present day.

A second feature of early Chinese religion was the notion of a *Lord Above and the concept of heaven*. It was believed that there is a royal ancestor who reigns over the other ancestors and who, as a good spirit, could influence the course of life on earth, providing such blessings as rain for the crops, a good harvest, and victory in battle. In time, following the Shang Dynasty, the concept of a personal ruler above that was linked to the Shang Dynasty, merged into a more generic view of heaven (*T'ien*), a word that can simply mean sky or nature. But in the context of the afterlife, *T'ien* comes to have a strong ethical overtone and refers to the way a supreme power governs the world and human affairs. This power sees and hears all, affirms virtue and rewards it, and punishes those who violate ethical norms. A ruler is said to have the "Mandate of Heaven" when the kingdom prospered and to lose this mandate when there are crop failures or losses and trouble in the kingdom.

A third feature of religion in ancient China was strong **connection to the earth and the ways of enhancing fertility**. It is not easy to date the conscious presence of this belief in ancient China, but it is present in the Chou Dynasty in the eleventh century BCE. The gods of Earth and Grain (*she chi*) have the power to influence the fertility of the soil and provide good crops for the people. A mound of earth was placed at the edge of each village where local officials would provide offerings in order to insure the fertility of the soil and to increase human fertility. Gradually the gods of earth and grain coalesced into the worship of the Earth God. The sun and the rain came down from Heaven and were received by the Earth which would nurture the seeds and insure good crops. In time, this duality of heaven and earth began to be thought of as a basic principle underlying the operation of the universe and all of life. It was called *yang* and *yin*, and these forces were seen as complementary, with the *yang* above being bright, assertive, and masculine, and the *yin* below being dim, receptive, and feminine. There was no sense that one was superior to the other, and there is a strong belief that both are necessary and that a small part of each is in the other.[3]

There developed out of these three strong beliefs that were foundational in ancient Chinese religion a **number of devotional practices such as divination** which became a fourth feature of ancient Chinese religion. Offerings were made to ancestors and to Heaven above and Earth below. Food was given and ceremonies were performed with great dignity as attempt was made to please the powers that influence human life. Divination, the effort to divine or foresee the will of the gods or spirits, played a very important role in the ceremonies. Even today, the *Book of Changes* (*I Ching*) is used as a form of divination, as 64 numbered hexagrams of six lines each are sorted and interpreted in a way that gives clues about the future. Heaven and Earth, *yang* and *yin*, are present, and it was believed (and still is) that one can predict, measure, and relate to the course of events and make decisions about them.

What develops for the Chinese people is a patterned set of beliefs that help them to understand the world and know one's place and behavior in it. It might be summarized in five categories, ones that were incorporated in the formation of Confucianism and Taoism, each in their own way, and which continue to influence Chinese life today.[4] They are held together by the concept of harmony (*he*) and may be stated as follows:

1. The entire universe is alive and conscious, and human beings and all parts of the surrounding universe are one as sentient beings; there are not radical distinctions, but an affirmation of the unity and connectedness of all that exists.
2. There is a prescribed and "natural" place and set of behaviors for all parts of the universe, a natural way (*Tao*) for everything.[5]
3. When this occurs, there is cosmic harmony, and peace and order are achieved.

4. Human beings have a special responsibility in achieving and maintaining this harmony. They must work toward its achievement, and when it is absent, knowing that some form of human failure, perhaps ignorance or willfulness, has caused it, they must correct it.
5. Both the survival and well-being of humankind depends on achieving and maintaining harmony.

These principles of harmony have been traditionally understood in China in two primary ways, depending on the assumptions made regarding the powers and forces that shape human life. The first view, older and expressed in what is often called popular religion, generally understands these powers and forces as personal, as spirits that can be influenced just as humans are influenced with gifts, offerings, and flattery. The second view of harmony is to understand the universe as filled with impersonal forces, with natural laws, energy, and powers that shape the course of events. This view, akin to the modern scientific understanding of the world, suggests that in order to survive and thrive, one had to be aware of the nature's way. It was believed that the aim of life has less to do with pleasing personal spirits and more to do with understanding the laws of change in nature and society. This affirmation became central to both Confucian and Taoist thought.

As we move more directly into the beliefs and practices of Confucianism, we should note that Chinese religion does not tend to be exclusive and that the Chinese often speak about the "three teachings" and incorporate insights from Confucianism, Taoism, and Buddhism into their spiritual pathways. There are differences of understanding and emphasis, but often a Chinese person will blend the three and draw upon a particular insight or guideline from anyone of the three as it meets a particular need. This tapestry also has a fourth element that has been designated as "popular religion," and it refers to a range of practices (e.g. funeral rituals, consultation with fortune-tellers, health and medical routines, offerings to ancestors, using mediums, exorcism, and New Year's rites) and to the religion of the masses or lower classes as distinguished from the religion of the educated elite.

We start our discussion of Confucianism with an introduction to the historical person Confucius or K'ung Fu-tzu or Master K'ung, a quest not unlike that of founders of other great religions.[6] It is as difficult to know the details of his life and teachings as it is that of Buddha or Jesus, especially since the oldest source, the *Analects*, was compiled a century after the great teacher's death. Legends are abundant about his life, but with some care and discernment, it is possible to piece together an outline. It is probable that he came from a household that was not wealthy; he married and had children at an early age. He gave himself to intense studying, later held public office for about a year, and then became a traveling teacher. He was not altogether successful as a civil servant, and even had some difficulty in getting rulers to take his teaching about an ideal society seriously. Not unlike Jesus, he became most successful in regard to his mission after his death. Even his teaching about manners, morals, law, philosophy, and theology would have to wait for the work of Mencius (*c.*371–289) for structure and order. There is no doubt, however, that he had a great and long-lasting influence on Chinese life. As in his life, so in history, he was and became the great teacher.

If the *Analects* are an accurate reflection of his life, we get a sense of his development and religious ideas from the following passage:

> At fifteen I set my heart on learning [to be a sage].
> At thirty I became firm.
> At forty I had no more doubts.
> At fifty I understood Heaven's Will.
> At sixty my ears were attuned [to this Will].
> At seventy I could follow my heart's desires,
> without overstepping the line. (*Analects* 2.4)

It is clear from this passage that Confucius was eager to understand and follow the guidance of Heaven. He did not understand Heaven so much as the residence of a personal deity, but more as a higher power, as order and law, setting aside the more popular religious ideas of his time. He valued the past, but placed emphasis on ethical teaching and the ordering of society for his generation and time. In particular, he was concerned about the social anarchy that he saw all around him. There was the collapse of the Chou Dynasty and its ordering power and the rise of smaller units or fiefdoms that were in constant battle with one another. Earlier there may have been some rules of warfare based on chivalry with codes of honor and fairness, but by the time of Confucius, the patterns of chivalry had collapsed, and the full horrors of war were ever-present with large populations being slaughtered. The key question for Confucius was: How can we keep from destroying one another and find some form of social cohesion?

There were alternative points of view in attempting to deal with the crisis of social disintegration. The Realists, for example, said that the answer is strong resistance to asocial acts. They argued that humans are driven by self-interest, and it is not possible to change behavior with reasoned teaching. Only brute force will work. Another school of thought, called Mohism named after its founder Mo Tzu, maintained that the answer was not laws with teeth in them, but its opposite, universal love (*chien ai*). Mo Tzu said that love was not sentimental and unrealistic as a means to social stability, but a powerful force for good and social order. Confucius, drawing upon the philosophical and religious ideas of his time and using the norms of custom and tradition, taught to the crisis of the circumstances of his surroundings.

While the *Analects* are the best record of his teachings, there were several other documents known as the Five Classics that preserve the heart and tradition of his teaching. There are different judgments by scholars regarding the authorship and historical development of these documents, but they do give us a picture of the development of Confucian thought. There are:

1. The *Book of Changes*, already mentioned, which guides the reader in understanding the future
2. The *Book of History* which is a collection of speeches from royalty and chief ministers with commentary on the principles of government
3. The *Book of Poetry* which is a collection of over 300 songs
4. The *Classic of Rites* which includes a section called *Ceremonials* to guide the nobility about appropriate etiquette and the *Book of Rites* which includes a section on ritual and government regulations and treatises on education, music, and philosophy
5. The *Spring-Autumn Annals* which is an account of the decline of K'ung's native state.[7]

Confucius rejected the suggestions of the rival schools of thought about achieving social cohesion and argued that the Realists' answer was harsh and external, not really changing the inner character of the persons. He also maintained that the Mohist view of love was noble, but utopian. What he turns to is the **cumulative tradition of the culture**, and argues that it is the primary means of shaping inclinations and attitudes. In is in the "DNA" of each person in the culture, and to lift it out and direct it in an intentional way is a means of achieving social order. It would be second nature to citizens, and it just needs to be made into a system and be taught and applied in a deliberate way.[8]

There is an acceptable and traditional way of relating to others and at the heart of the teaching of Confucius is the emphasis on **the moral character of human relationships**. He taught that human relationships should be filled with regard for the other person often expressed in reciprocity and neighborliness. There is the well-known quote from the *Analects*, often called the reverse Golden Rule, "... not to do to others what you would not have them do to you."

(*Analects* 15.23) Confucius identifies five relationships in life and prescribes appropriate behavior for each. These include father-son, elder and younger brother, and friend with friend, husband-wife, and ruler-minister and subjects. Each of the relationships, including the ruler-minister and friend with friend has characteristics of the family, and therefore society may be understood as family. Each one is mutual, reciprocal, and respectful of age and seniority:

- There is kindness in the father, filial piety (*hsiao*) in the son.
- There is gentility in the elder brother, humility and respect in the younger brother.
- There is humane consideration in elders, deference in juniors.
- There is righteous behavior in the husband, obedience in the wife.
- There is benevolence in rulers, loyalty in ministers and subjects.

In each of these relationships, ideally there is the presence of *jen* or *ren* and *li*, the former having to do with the inner motivation of the person and the latter having to do with social propriety and ritual.[9] An ideal relationship has both; it has the inner resources of goodness, benevolence, and love, and the external form of respect and appropriate behavior. The qualities of family relationships provide the basis and model for social relationship and the structures of society.

Confucius is keenly aware that not all people will be loving and respectful and strongly urges that schooling, religious practice, and social structures reflect these values. Education should lead to a third ideal, in addition to *jen* and *li*. It is the ideal of *chun tzu* which might be translated as the superior or mature person. He speaks about different kinds of people in the society. There is the sage who embodies and teaches wisdom, one who embodies *chun tzu*. There is the noble or gentleman who strives to do what is right and to become a superior, mature person. There is another category of person, the *xiao-ren* or small-spirited person who acts without reference to morality.

What is needed says Confucius is to take these qualities of *jen*, *li*, and *chun tzu* and apply them beyond individual relationships to the ordering of society. There is another principle, *te*, which is best understood as the virtuous power to order society. Confucius teaches that *te* is best understood as the power of the virtuous example of the ruler, one who because of his way of life has earned the consent of the people to rule. If the people sense that the ruler has their interests and the common good as his goals, then there will be respect and adherence to principles and practices that make for a good social environment. Fundamental to the inculcation of these values is the **ritual practice**, the acting out and tangible expression of communal beliefs. Confucianism is not only an ethical religion but also a ritual religion.[10] It is the concept of *li* that anchors the doctrinal and the ritual prescriptions for proper behavior in family and society.

There is a fifth principle built into the teaching of Confucius, and that is *wen*, "the arts of peace" as contrasted with the "arts of war." Music, art, poetry, and great learning are essential to the well-being of society. They, too, must be taught and cultivated in order for the society to thrive. This dimension has implications for building respect and rapport between citizens, but also has implications for diplomacy. The state that has the fullest development of the arts, the finest philosophical foundations, and high moral character will be admired and recognized as an excellent model and worthy of positive exchange and linkage.

A final dimension of the spiritual pathway of Confucianism is the notion of heaven, and the Heavenly Mandate. When the values of *jen, li, chun tzu, te,* and *wen* are present, then there is the likelihood of the regularity of seasons, a good harvest, the correct balance of *yin* and *yang*, and peace. The ruler will lead with the approval of heaven and royal ancestors, and there will be harmony in society. This was the grand vision of Confucius, and while he was not fully appreciated by his contemporaries nor the leaders whom he tried to persuade, his ideas seeped into the nooks and crannies of Chinese life and culture and continue to have an influence in modern China, despite the challenge of the Confucian way by the communist revolution and the Cultural Revolution (1966–1976). Confucianism was and continues to be the "civil religion" of China.[11]

A final question we might ask about Confucianism is whether it is really a religion or whether it is more a way of ethics. The debate will continue, but Confucianism and Neo-Confucianism do have many of the characteristics of a spiritual pathway. There is a strong belief in heaven, another level of reality, sometimes personal in the sense of the spirits of ancestors, and sometimes impersonal in the sense of principle and natural way (*Tao*). There are temples with rituals, ceremonies, offerings, and sacrifices. There is a clearly prescribed code of conduct that runs from individual relations all the way to diplomatic linkages with other nations. The values inherent in the Confucianism do bring the people together in community and provide a sense of belonging and larger purpose. In fact, what is often referred to as Neo-Confucianism is the attempt to recover the legacy of mind and heart, the spirit or soul of Confucianism. It is not an attempt to return to all the particularities of Confucian thought, but as a response to Taoism and Buddhist thought, it offered a way to cultivate a spiritual way, a path to sageliness. It guides people who seek a spiritual pathway.

Nature's way: the spirit of Taoism

Taoism (along with Chinese Buddhism), has provided an excellent balance to the prevailing norms of Confucianism. Confucianism had and continues to have ways of touching the inner spirit of the individuals, but it has also expressed itself as more prescriptive of external patterns of behavior and the etiquette of rituals and ceremonies. Taoism has been and continues to be clearly focused on personal transformation and living as a distinctive individual in harmony with the natural way. Taoism was certainly tolerated across Chinese history, although it was "counter-culture" in spirit and it did push against the external patterns and ways of Confucianism.

Taoist thought has been traditionally associated with a person who may have been an elder contemporary of Confucius, Lao Tzu, who is said to have been born in 604 BCE. Not much is known about Lao Tzu, including his actual name; Lao Tzu is an honorary title meaning something akin to "Grand Old Master." There are many legends about him, but that pattern that emerges from these is that he served as a "librarian" and maintained the archives in his native state. There are some suggestions about his life and character that have been drawn from the writing, *Tao Te Ching* (The Way and Its Power), associated with him. From reading it, one might conclude that he was a person of great wisdom and had a deep understanding of the subtle dimensions of human life, nature, and social order. Scholars view this writing as most likely a collection of sayings that have been assembled from several sources, but also point to an editor and teacher who may have influenced the shape of the book. Not knowing much about the actual life of Lao Tzu has not been troubling to followers of the Way; it is the Way that is of primary importance.

What is the *Tao* or the Way? As the book itself suggests, one should be cautious about providing a quick and easy answer to this question. It begins, "The *Tao* that can be followed is not the eternal *Tao*. The name that can be named is not the eternal name."[12] As the proverbial wisdom from *Tao Te Ching* teaches: "Those who know don't say, and those who say don't know." (*Tao Te Ching*, ch. 56) The followers of Taoism are pilgrims, open and learning. But these followers have gone in several directions, and we can learn from their pathways and describe them as they have experienced them.[13] The word *Tao*, meaning the path or the way, has been understood in at least three different ways. The first is that *Tao* is the **way of ultimate reality**, that which holds the universe together, and that which cannot be fully described because it is beyond us and remains a mystery. We know that it exists and that it is the greatest and most fundamental reality of all, but it remains elusive, a mystery that beckons us, but that we cannot fully understand.

The second meaning of the *Tao* has to do with its manifestation in the midst of all of life. It is the **way of the universe**, the transcendent that has become immanent and which is the rhythm and power of the universe, the cohering principle behind all of nature and life. It is full of grace, giving order and beauty, and nudging the universe forward in generous and purposeful ways. It may be described as the "Mother of the World" that acts gently and gracefully, providing abundance and purpose.

Still a third meaning of the word, *Tao*, is that it is the **ideal way of human life** as humans connect with and discern the pattern of the *Tao*. The *Tao Te Ching* is filled with how union with the *Tao* is achieved and the kind of life that comes from this union. It suggests a spiritual pathway, one that is less prescriptive than Confucianism and more intuitive, one that is found rather than taught or read about, and one that is lived from the soul rather than one that adheres to society's norms and expectations. The followers of the Taoist way have utilized these foundational insights, and the gracious empowerment that comes from them, and have developed them in several directions, three of which we might highlight.[14]

The first might be called **philosophical Taoism** which is a more reflective and individually expressed and less organized as a social movement. It is a position that is more easily understood and adopted by those who may be outside of a particular cultural expression of Taoism. The goal of those who take this position is to preserve their internal power (*te*) and to learn more about it as a means of living wisely and well. It is a way of not getting sidetracked into needless conflicts and useless activities, but to focus on one's internal resources or gift of the Tao. It is to fully realize within one's personal life the pattern of *wu wei* which is literally translated as "no action" but refers to how the ideal human should learn to act, and specifically to act naturally, without force or artificial constraint. It does not deny the noble art of getting things done, but stresses the nobler art of leaving things undone. It suggests that the wisdom of life consists in the elimination of nonessentials.

A second direction of followers of Taoism have taken is **the way of cultivation**, the way of augmenting the power of the Tao.[15] Those within this tradition wanted to cultivate and increase the power of the Tao within their lives. It was and continues to be a spiritual pathway, not unlike those of other religious traditions in that it develops a pattern of practices that increase their vital energy (*ch'i*). For example, attention was given to diet as a means of increasing their vital energy and a variety of medicinal herbs are used, not so much for healing as for releasing the inherent power within. Forms of exercise were utilized, including the practices of dance, yoga, martial arts and even sexual practices. Basic to all of these efforts was the practice of meditation, a distinctive form not unlike *raja yoga* that seeks to block out life's distractions and empty the mind so that the *Tao* might flow freely into the mind and heart of the practitioner. It was a quest for inwardness that will overcome all self-seeking and cultivate purity in thought and body. It was the way to emotional calm that results in effortlessness, responsiveness, and liberation from anxiety and other distracting emotions.

A third direction of Taoism is **much more religious** in character and tone and developed among the people to respond to life's questions and challenges. Not everyone would turn to the reflective life and be philosophical about managing the given *Tao* within one's life. Nor would everyone look to a variety of disciplined and esoteric practices to enhance the quantity of the *Tao* within. Disease and death were still present, and the crops might fail. It was natural to turn to those popular traditions and practices that included soothsayers, shamans, fortune-tellers, and faith healers. This tradition developed in the second century CE, and many of the features of popular religion that were present in the culture at that time were integrated into Taoism. There were (and continue to be) gods, priests, temples, rituals, and ceremonies. The rituals, which may appear culture bound, magical, and superstitious to the outsider, were used to tap into the greater power, the *Tao*, which could make life better.

Across the centuries, the boundaries between these three "schools" of Taoism were generally porous, and it was easy to cross from one to the other and to find the common ground that was at the foundation of all three. All three sought (and seek) to enhance the *Tao's* inherent power, the *te*, and they did so in different ways across the continuum of the three traditions. These schools of thought continue to interact with one another in China, Taiwan, and other parts of the world today. It is possible to use careful reflection to arrive at a deeper knowledge. This knowledge will become transformational through mystical meditation. The transformation may be enhanced by the magic of ritual and ceremony to arrive at the belief that all will be well, even with the negative forces of life at work.

It is a matter of incorporating the flow of the *Tao* by perfecting the life of *wu wei*, and there are different ways to achieve this goal. But in all of them, it is a matter of both doing and being. The inspiration of *wu wei* leads to the "action" of putting our egos aside and yielding to the greater power that flows through us. It is to live authentically and spontaneously, without pretence and artificiality, and to consistently maintain this balance. It is to live like flowing water, carrying objects that float, passing around that which blocks the flow such as a rock, and even smoothing the sharp and hard surfaces over time. "Nothing in the world is softer than water, yet nothing is better at overcoming the hard and the strong. This is because nothing can alter it." (*Tao Te Ching*, ch. 17) The water works without working, and often stands still. It is in this affirmation of the natural way and simplicity that Taoism differs from Confucianism. It is not external form, show, ceremony, and the meticulous observance of propriety that add to the value of life, but the simple, natural, and congruent way that makes life good.

There are many other values in Taoist thought, some of which are also analogous to the flow of water. One is that it discourages self-assertiveness and a competitive spirit. It does not encourage a life that tries "to get ahead" by becoming aggressive and assertive; in so doing one just creates tension and conflict. The ideal is to be humble and selfless, allowing life to take its natural course. To be free of pride and not be ego-driven is to be able to relate to others in caring ways. So too with nature; we should not see it as something to conquer, but as friend and teacher, and follow its ways, even as we do not "conquer" the mountain, but climb and respect it as a friend. Some of the great art of China comes out of the Taoism frame of reference, and it reflects the beauty and way of nature. It follows that the Taoist pattern would be to honor others and not be proud of one's own accomplishments. Let the accomplishments in life have value in themselves and be expressive of the *Tao*. The Way is not to seek adulation, popularity, power, and fame, but to be a door through which others can pass, a window through which light can shine, and an instrument through which beauty can be expressed.

In regard to government and social order, Taoist thought is somewhat "Jeffersonian" in the affirmation that the least governance is the best governance. People should lead a simple life, respect and care for others, and let society take shape in natural ways. "If you used the Tao as a principle for ruling, you would not dominate the people by military force . . . If you know what you are doing you will do what is necessary and stop there." (*Tao Te Ching*, ch. 30). Government and military power may be necessary for order and peace, but the less it does to interfere in the lives of people, the better it is.

In regard to ethics, the Taoist teaching tends to be situational and relative, although not without pervading values. Taoism understood the ethical life in reference to the traditional understanding of the opposites of *yin* and *yang* that define the moral life. It is the *yin* and *yang* in balance and allowing them to complement and even invade each other that leads to guidance for behavior. It is a matter of seeing the whole and then placing the particular situation in the context of the whole. Seeing the whole means that good and evil do not always contradict each other, but may be opposite sides of the larger frame of reference. There may be a way that appears to be wrong at first, but in time, with perspective, it turns out to be the better way. There may be a "silver lining" in complex and difficult circumstances, even as in the case of death as one can learn to appreciate the good life that has been lived. The *yin* and *yang* are often placed in conjunction with the *I Ching* with its various patterns and elements in order to read and decipher to best way to act or proceed.[16]

In many ways, the ethical norms of Taoism are inherent in the understanding of the universe. It is a somewhat complex pattern, but essentially the earth is defined as central and neutral, with four other elements of wood, fire, water, and metal making up the substance of the earth. Each of the elements of wood, fire, water, and metal correspond to the four directions and the four seasons, and each is linked to *yin* and *yang* and assigned a color and even an animal as a symbol. It becomes possible, with this outline, to give pattern to all the manifestations of nature and to human functions and activities. All is in relationship with the other, and human activity is a reflection of the universe. When all is calm and peaceful, the elements of *yin* and *yang* begin to move, and the energy in the system begins to change and transform until a new order emerges. The acceptance of the inevitability of this process gives one a sense of peace in the midst of change, and the reassurance that what has happened is part of a larger frame of reference. The requirement is to be at rest within the movement and flow, to live in harmony with the *Tao*. In consulting the *I Ching*, one can find ways of understanding the changes of the surrounding environment.

There are images and practices, such as *T'ai Chi* (the so-called "black fish-white fish" design that expresses the interrelationship of apparent opposites) that can aid us in finding our way and achieving a sense of balance and perspective in the midst of change, even in what appears to be disorder. *T'ai Chi* in both symbol and practice represents the balance of *yin* and *yang* in the universe. The symbol of the division of the circle with the colors of black and white is a pictorial form and gentle reminder of Taoist principles. The *yin* is the dark, cold, female, and passive side of life shown in the black area, and the *yang* is the light, warm, male, and active side of life as shown in the white area. This basic duality represents all of life, and everything moves in reference to natural cycles—hours, days, weeks, months, seasons, and years. The Taoist view is that we find our way and accept our way in this cosmic order.

We do have some choice, and it is possible for us to improve our environment in order to better our life situation. For example, we can adjust our personal space in such a way that the subtle movement between the two polarities of *yin* and *yang* creates positive energy. This adjustment or correct placement is called *Feng Shui* (translated as wind and water) and its goal is to put one in tune with one's environment and to bring balance to the external energies (thought of now in terms of electromagnetic fields). The concept is often associated with creating a harmonious home or productive work space.

Contemporary expressions of Taoism ideas

The mention of *Feng Shui* does lead to a discussion of the ways that Taoist ideas and practices have come West and been introduced into our common life and even popular culture. The popularity of the book by Benjamin Hoff, *The Tao of Pooh*,[17] suggests that the life of Pooh is the ideal Taoist way of life. "Eeyore may fret, Piglet hesitate, Rabbit calculate, and Owl pontificate, but Pooh just is, accepts life, and 'goes with the flow.'" A more scholarly treatment of the Taoist understanding of the universe is represented by Fritjof Capra's *The Tao of Physics* in which the case is made that there are parallels between Eastern mysticism and modern science.[18] Taoist practices have been introduced into the health science in the form of the physical expression of tai chi, the use of acupuncture, and the prescription of traditional herbal therapies. Even the Taoist political theories calling for smaller government with less control have been given new life in American politics. The respect for nature in Taoist thought matches with the need for ecological sensitivity. It is in pop culture that the occasional Taoist emphasis appears, although it is not often called Taoism. It is present in the Star Wars films with mention of the "force" and the guidance of "doing without doing" (*wu-wei*) in the effortless way that

Luke Skywalker turns aside every stroke of the enemy. Even more important than these culture expressions is the presence in many parts of the world beyond China of those who are sincere in following the Taoist pattern of belief and practice.

The continuing value and recurring challenges of Chinese religion

Both Confucianism and Taoism with some integration with Chinese Buddhism, represent the religions of China. Other religious traditions, including Christianity and Islam, are certainly present within China, but perhaps do not represent the distinctly Chinese way in quite the same fashion. The three "Asian" religions are fully expressive and representative of transcendent monism, and continue to have great value, not only in China, but also for people in other parts of the world. Let us look first at those beliefs and practices that are life-giving to so many.

1. The Confucian way continues to be a model of respect for others and the practice of civility in governance. Respect is taught within the family; it is respect that applies within the family structure for spouse, sibling, and elder. In that the family is thought of as the microcosm of society, these same values, often taking the form of neighborliness, hospitality, and reciprocity are practiced beyond the family structure and present in all the transactions of the local region, city, and state. Are these values of respect always practiced? No, of course not, but civility and respect remain the guiding way for the vast majority of Chinese society. The spiritual pathway is primarily the ethical way, internalizing and practicing the values of regard and respect for others and caring for their needs.

2. In Confucian thought, there is also permission for the people to change the government and its leaders if the judgment is made that they have lost the "mandate of heaven." As a general rule, the mandate is thought to be lost when the country is facing extreme difficulties such as a poor economy, the failure to care for the basic needs of the people such as health and education, and the threat of international conflict. To be sure, the Communist Revolution has altered this traditional Confucian understanding, but it remains beneath the surface as "subtle and unspoken permission," even with the strong central control of the Communist government.

3. There is a keen sense of the interrelatedness of the human family with nature in the teachings of Taoism. This ancient teaching has current relevance as nature is viewed as being the source of well-being and a partner in life. Earth is home, and

it embraces us. Human beings are not "in charge" of the earth, but an intricate part of the ways of nature. We find our way in reference to nature's way. It is not a far reach to move from appreciation for the way, order, and beauty in nature to ecological sensitivity and the careful and sophisticated management to the earth, using every resource of human collaboration, modern science, and technology to conserve and preserve the earth.

4. There is a strong emphasis on respecting the individual person in both religious traditions. In Confucianism, the emphasis tends to be mutual respect, with patterns of etiquette and civility built into the social structures. Each individual is respected within their given role in the social order. In Taoism, the emphasis is more on the individual's internal life, discovering one's authentic self, living congruently with that identity, and expressing oneself in spontaneous rather than prescribed ways. Do we grow, develop, and mature primarily in terms of our relationships and sense of belonging in a social structure, or do we blossom and become our "true selves" by finding ourselves and living congruently with this discovered identity? Perhaps both are necessary, and it may be that these two traditions feed into the growth and development of the Chinese people.

5. Along this same line of thought, it might be argued that the teaching of Taoism teaches a spiritual pathway that is more focused on personal peace and serenity, living in harmony with nature, others, and the world. It might also be argued that the Confucian teaching regarding a spiritual pathway is more focused on the ethical life and the quest for a stable social order. Again, it might be that both themes are needed in massive, complex, and changing society like China.

Each of these two religious traditions within Chinese life has been challenged by change, modernity, and a government system that has resisted all forms of religion. Let us look as some of these challenges.

1. The most obvious challenge to the Confucian way has come because the Confucian way is judged to be a force for the status quo. In its early development and even across Chinese history, it may have been a means of achieving social order when chaos and destruction were always just around the corner. But in the modern era, the Communist government judged the Confucian way as being a class system, unresponsive to the needs of the peasant and working classes. The Confucian way may be inherently conservative as it teaches one to live within the inherited role of family and class. It may have given and preserved privilege for the few. Contemporary Chinese people, given the emergence of a new culture, the realities of modernization, globalization, and its government's ideology, will not easily accept a given social status and a hierarchical social structure.

2. As a spiritual pathway, Confucianism, even with the teachings of Neo-Confucianism, may not be able to touch the internal life of an individual who seeks personal and

spiritual transformation. It may have become more an ethical pattern of life and a civil religion than one that guides the pilgrim searcher in the quest for meaning, purpose, and serenity. It may not have the alluring power to call the follower to deep commitment, conviction, and spiritual practices that nurture the soul.

3. The Taoist tradition may be too inherently passive about government intervention in preserving security, developing the economy, and meeting the needs for health and education. It is important to acknowledge that the Taoist tradition is eager to collaborate with others in ecological concerns and encourage ways of achieving a more just and peaceful society and world, but at its heart, the tradition may be more focused on personal transformation.

4. The Taoist tradition in its more philosophical expression tends to be less inviting to those who want the accoutrements of a spiritual way that offers a variety of practices that touch the inner spirit. The *Tao* is more of a concept, and a somewhat theoretical and elusive one, which may be intimidating for the average person. Even that part of the tradition that offers the many ways of cultivating the spiritual life tends to have a slightly esoteric character, attracting those who seek an alternative way rather than one in the mainstream of the culture.

5. Both religions, as do most religions, face the challenge of being traditional ways in a culture and world that is new and increasingly secular with materialistic values. The dramatic changes in Chinese life, with a new and dynamic economy and a central place in the world order, do not on the surface at least invite a return to what may be considered a "traditional spiritual pathway."

At this point, we shift our attention form religions which understand reality as essential one with clear access for human beings to be in harmony with the divine, and those that postulate a personal God who is qualitatively and quantitatively separate and distinct. We turn first to Judaism.

Discussion questions

1. Is a truly life-giving religion primarily focused on personal transformation? Social transformation? Or both?
2. Is Confucianism essentially an ethical way of life and a way of ordering society or is it and can it be an authentic spiritual pathway?
3. In what ways do both Confucianism and Taoism lead adherents to personal and social transformation?
4. In what ways might both religions, founded so long ago, be brought forward into the contemporary world for those seeking a life-giving spiritual pathway?
5. What strikes you about both Confucianism and Taoism as having the ring of truth or not being inviting and persuasive for those seeking an authentic spiritual way?

Key terms and concepts

1. **ChunTzu**: A princely or noble gentleman.
2. **Divination**: An effort to divine or see the will of the gods or spirits.
3. **Harmony (he)**: The natural order of the universe in which peace and order are achieved.
4. **Hsiao**: Filial piety, including devotion to elders of the family, particularly the father, and veneration of elders.
5. **Jen**: Confucian virtue of being truly human or humane.
6. **Li**: Confucian virtue of propriety, appropriate rites and ceremonies.
7. **Tao**: Way or path; way of life in harmony with infinite reality.
8. **Te**: Virtue or power to advance virtue.
9. **T'ien**: Heaven in the sense of ultimate reality or dwelling of ancestral spirits.
10. **Wi-Wei**: Use of one's natural capacity without striving.
11. **Yang and Yin**: Interactive and complementary cosmic forces of light and dark, male and female.

Suggestions for reference and reading

Ball, Pamela, *The Essence of Tao* (Edison, NJ: Chartwell Books, 2004).

Chai Ch'u and Chai, Winberg, *Confucianism* (Woodury, NY: Barron's Educational Series, 1973).

Ching, Julia, *Chinese Religions* (Maryknoll, NY: Orbis Books, 1993).

Confucius, *The Wisdom of Confucius* (New York: Citadel Press, 2001). This is a collection of writings attributed to Confucius, including selections from the *Analects*.

Lao Tze, *Tao Te Ching* (New York: Barnes and Noble Classics, 2005).

Thompson, Mel, *Eastern Philosophy* (Chicago, IL: Contemporary Books of the McGraw-Hill Companies, 1999).

Part IV
The Spiritual Pathways of the Abrahamic Monotheistic Religions

This section addresses the spiritual pathways of the three great monotheistic religions that originated in the Near East. It frames these religions in the context of the biblical story of Abraham and their common heritage as "religions of the book." These chapters will acknowledge the complexity and many-sided character of these monotheistic religions, and then will describe those elements that constitute their core beliefs and practices. There is an assessment of the ways that the spiritual pathways within these religions lead to human flourishing or to that which is less than life-giving, and in some cases even xenophobic intolerance and zealotry.

> The great patriarch of the Hebrew Bible is also the spiritual forefather of the New Testament and the grand holy architect of the Koran. Abraham is the shared ancestor of Judaism, Christianity, and Islam.[1]

Spiritual Pathways Within Judaism

8

Chapter Outline

Monotheistic religions rooted in the story of Abraham   139

The narrative of Judaism   140

Jewish history, beliefs, and practices   147

Jewish beliefs, practices, and spiritual pathways   153

Monotheistic religions rooted in the story of Abraham

The great religions in the grouping that we have called transcendent monism postulate the oneness and unity of all of reality. There is another level beyond the level of "things" and appearances (*maya*), and beyond what appears to be reality in the everyday experience of human beings. However this transcendent level is not a separate being, but unified with and integral to all that exists. This other "layer" is immanent as well as transcendent, the cohering principle, sometimes personified, that gives order and meaning to all of reality. One view of this position is called pantheism which is the belief that all is divine (God) or the divine is all, merging all things to the divine and denying personality to the "Other." A modification of pantheism, to allow some personal qualities to the divine is called panentheism. In the great religious traditions of Asia, the word monism is used to describe the belief in these traditions that only one being or ultimate reality exists. Or to say it in the negative, monism is sometimes called in India nonduality (*advaita*), the doctrine of the fundamental identity of the supreme divinity (*Brahman*) with the human soul (*Atman*). Modifications of this same view, although expressed and nuanced differently, appear in the notion of *nirvana* in Buddhism, heaven (*T'ien*) in Confucianism, and the *Tao* in Taoism.

As we turn to the Abrahamic monotheistic religions of Judaism, Christianity, and Islam, we encounter an alternative point of view. In these great religions, there is a clear belief in a personal transcendent God, a belief that has its origins in the life and story of Abraham (Ibrahim). There are other religious traditions that are monotheistic, believing in one transcendent God, named in many ways as creator, father or mother, Great Spirit, and upholder of the universal moral law, etc. Often connected with the sky, sun or thunder, this divine being is usually spoken of as male, although in many of these traditions, there is an awareness that these descriptions are metaphorical and point to a being that cannot be contained in human language. In Persia, Ahura Mazda was supreme in Zoroaster's reform of religion, in Japan's Shinto tradition, the sun goddess Amaterasu is supreme, and in Hindu thought, there are followers of Vishnu or Shiva who call one of the other of them Supreme. In Sikhism, there is a belief in a supreme God and a rejection of avatars that were more common in Hindu thought.

The Sikh understanding of God as "the Creator, the Compassionate, the Self-Existent" is more akin to the belief about God in Judaism, Christianity, and Islam. What makes the three monotheistic religions rooted in the biblical story of Abraham a "family" is that they affirm that the transcendent God (Yahweh, Allah) is sovereign, and intimately related to the earth, the human family, and the unfolding of human history. We will trace the beliefs and practices of these three "Religions of the Book," seeing in what ways they are similar, how they differ, and the spiritual pathways they offer to their followers. We will begin with Judaism, the fountainhead of these great religions.

The narrative of Judaism

We begin with the historical narrative of the Hebrew people because it is this narrative that gives them their religious faith, and it is out of this narrative that the many spiritual pathways of Judaism are found and followed. As with Christianity and Islam, the "story" is the heartbeat of the beliefs and practices of what becomes over hundreds of years of development the religion we call Judaism. We first encounter the ancient Hebrews in the history as a nomadic people inhabiting the Arabian Peninsula. They were tribal, lived on the edge of the surrounding desert, and their culture was not unlike other tribes of the

Stone Age. They wandered across the region, seeking pasture for their animals, water for their containers, and fruit to enrich their diet. Their religious practices at this point were not distinctive, but much like that of other primitive peoples. They shared with their tribal neighbors the belief in mana that was present in certain sacred objects, such as the growth on stones and trees. They honored certain natural stone configurations in the form of pillars, believing that they contained life-giving power, and saw a range of divinities (*elohim*) in their natural surroundings. Different tribes had particular divinities that were or could be helpful in day-to-day concerns.

Gradually these tribes began moving northward into Mesopotamia, and it was out of this context that we are introduced in the Biblical narrative to Abraham(Gen. 12–24). We learn from this story that Abraham moved from Ur in Chaldea to Haran northeast of Syria, and then south to Palestine and on to Egypt. There are differing views of the religion of Abraham at this point in his life, but it is likely that he believed in a god (God) called *El-Shaddai* which translates as "the divinity of the mountains." It is the account of this belief that evolves into the monotheism of the religions that look to him as the source of their faith tradition. It is the story of Abraham and the covenant between him and God (Gen.17.1–8; 22.15–18) that is one of the foundational stories that make up the larger narrative of the Jewish people. It is Abraham's faith in his God, his sense of being called by God to go to another place ("going without knowing" Gen.12.1), and, as the story is told, his belief that his descendents would be many and blessed. This story is central to the Jewish faith, and it is also of vital importance to Christianity and Islam. There is a belief within Islam that one of his children, Ishmael, the son of the maidservant of Abraham's wife, Hagar, would become a prophet and be the father of the Arabs. In the Christian tradition, Abraham is the great patriarch and the pioneer of trust in God. (See e.g. Romans 4.1–5)

As we begin to learn about this narrative, we are dependent upon the Biblical account and its accuracy in tracing Abraham's travels, the way of life of those with whom he traveled, and how to interpret his beliefs and practices. There are those who would read the Biblical account and believe in its full accuracy and others who would introduce a more critical historical methodology in order to be as accurate as possible about discerning the actual events and beliefs of Abraham, Sarah his wife, and his many descendents. A good case can be made for a careful look at the history in order to decipher how the books of the Bible did come into being and the role of redactors editing older material and reshaping to fit the needs and beliefs of these followers of Yahweh.

It is clear that the Hebrew Bible did develop across centuries; it did not come fully written by clearly identified authors at certain moments in history. In that the history that it records is central to the religions of Judaism, Christianity, and Islam, it is essential to say a brief word about the nature and evolution of the Bible. The Hebrew Bible is generally divided into three sections. There is the Law or Torah contained in the first five books, called the Pentateuch. There is the section known as the Prophets, which includes the books of Joshua, Judges, Samuel, Kings, Isaiah, Jeremiah, Ezekiel, and the ten Minor Prophets. The final section is known as the Writings and includes Psalms, Job, Song of Solomon, Ruth, Lamentations, Ecclesiastes, Esther, Daniel, Ezra-Nehemiah, and Chronicles. The final form of these sacred writings (Canon) was set in the early part of the second century CE. Evidently, Jesus understood the Bible to be the Law and the Prophets. (See e.g. Mt. 5.17)

It was the great epochs of ancient Jewish (Hebrew) history that gave the Hebrew Bible its themes and structure. There is the account of Abraham which we have already introduced. It is preceded by the prehistoric accounts of creation and stories filled with insight about the human condition such as Cain and Abel, Noah, and the Tower of Babel. Following the story of Abraham are accounts of his descendents, and then the story of Moses and the Exodus. Moses and his experience with the Egyptians probably took place in the early part of the thirteenth century BCE (or perhaps earlier), and then follows the story of the monarchy founded in the late eleventh century BCE. The great prophets Amos, Hosea, Micah, and Isaiah lived in the eighth century, the reformation under Josiah came at 621 BCE, with the Exile occurring from 585–538 BCE. Other books of the Hebrew Bible developed later to describe the twists and turns of the semisovereign Jewish state that existed to Roman times.

Earlier parts of the Hebrew Bible took shape over a period of hundreds of years, with the majority reaching the state in which we now read them following the Exile. Most likely, the earliest writings, expressing the teachings and lives of Amos, Hosea, Micah, and Isaiah were composed in the eighth century BCE, with the Pentateuch and Joshua reaching their present state in the fourth century BCE. Oral traditions date back to a much earlier time, and at least four different strands of these traditions have been identified: "J" (called by this letter because the narratives in Genesis, Exodus, and Numbers refer to God as Jehovah or Yahweh); "E" (which identifies that narratives that refer to God as Elohim); "P" (the priestly redaction because the writer focuses on the interest of the organized priesthood); and "D" (the material from Deuteronomy).

The narrative as guide in the present

I include this brief introduction to the formation of the Hebrew Bible to underline the antiquity of the writings and the complexities of Biblical scholarship which attempts to discern the best reading of these documents. We have the Hebrew Bible (and later the New Testament) as it comes to us, and it is read and interpreted, despite uncertainties of authorship, timelines, and historical events, in a way that enables the narrative to guide the Jewish people in the present and give hope for the future. Let's examine these extraordinary stories and see how they come forward on a trajectory to guide the faithful on their spiritual pathways.

We have spoken about the foundational character of the story of Abraham. But it is the story of Moses that provides "the determining shape to Israelite religion which it has retained, not without difficulty, through succeeding centuries. It this sense Moses could genuinely be proclaimed the founder of Judaism."[2] The story of Moses, following the informative accounts of Abraham and his descendents, places him as the adopted Hebrew son of an Egyptian princess, and because of his circumstances, he is given experience and a good education that prepare him for his life work. He is spared the suffering of his people who were in slavery to the Egyptians, but observes their plight. As a young man, he rebels against the suffering of his people and is forced to flee to Midian, a region north of the Red Sea. There he settles, marries, and helps his father-in-law, a priest of the Kenite tribe. But one day, while tending his flock of sheep, he encounters God in the burning bush and is commanded to return to Egypt to liberate the Israelites.[3] Moses returns to Egypt, confronts the Pharaoh, and during the ongoing confrontation, there is the Passover, an account of how the plagues sent by God on the Egyptians pass over the Israelites. Moses proceeds to lead his enslaved people across the Red (or Reed) Sea. When he reaches Mt. Horeb (or Sinai), Moses once again is challenged, this time by his own people. It is in the midst of this challenge that he is said to be an intermediary that delivers a **covenant** between Yahweh and the people of Israel, a covenant that has a moral ingredient expressed in the Ten Commandments.

In this story we see the prototype of Jewish belief, that God intervenes on behalf of these people, sets them free, establishes a pact with them, and gives them an ethical code after which to pattern their behavior. It is Yahweh's initiative to save and to guide with the expectation that the people will live in faithfulness and obedience. It is difficult to determine whether Abraham and his descendents truly believed in a single transcendent God of all, or whether their belief was in a more regional divinity. It is likely that in the account of Moses, in the Exodus and the experience at Mt. Sinai, that it becomes clear that Israel should worship one God to the exclusion of others. Monotheism continues to develop from this history and narrative, as other gods pale by comparison as the one supreme Creator is understood to rule over the entire world.

The next major epoch in the Biblical account of the Israelites is their entrance into "the promised land," the land of Canaan, which is viewed as the consummation of the Exodus. Moses does not live to see it, but passes the mantel of leadership on to Joshua who leads the tribes across the Jordon into Canaan. The conquest of Canaan brings its own set of problems, many of them religious in nature. They encounter, as they turn from their nomadic ways into farmers, the local fertility gods and local Baals, which were bound up with agricultural life. While loyal to Yahweh, many of the Israelites also turn to the local gods linked to fertility and in particular to the goddess Ishtar. In this period, the issue of pure loyalty (faithfulness) to the one God who is said to be "jealous" (radical monotheism) surfaces. So too does the issue of governance as the tribes and their judges, many of whom had their problems (e.g. Samson), settle into their new life in Canaan.

In time, there is a movement toward a stronger central government that culminates in a monarchy. There is the extraordinary story of David (I & II Samuel) who has many gifts, but is all too human in his failures. He becomes a great warrior, is proclaimed the king, and this small region of Palestine becomes an autonomous and unified nation among the other nations in Middle East. David in the Biblical narrative, which becomes the guide to the Jewish people and informs Christianity and to a less extent Islam, becomes a symbolic leader. His reign is viewed as the great era of the Jewish people, a reign that one day may be restored to give the Jewish people their rightful place among the nations of the world. He restores the place of the Ark of the Covenant, a container that is said to carry the two stone tablets on which were inscribed the Ten Commandments and represented the covenant. He probably begins the building of the Temple for worship, a structure that is thought to be the sacred place of God's presence. Christians in their understanding of genealogy trace the lineage of Jesus back to David. (Mat.1.6) His personal life, mixed as it was, becomes a marvelous way to illustrate the ways to live and not to live, and the consequences of good and bad choices.

The monarchy continues with the reign of Solomon, David's son, who lives in the tenth century BCE. His reign is as mixed as his father's and represents the continuing struggle to remain true to the ideals of the evolving Israelite religion. Solomon does construct a magnificent temple for the worship of Yahweh in Jerusalem to provide a place for the Ark of the Covenant. But he also builds shrines for other gods, perhaps because of the influence of his many foreign wives. But in the end, in part because of the influence of the story of Moses and the increased influence of the prophets, the worship of and loyalty to Yahweh continues to be the dominant mode of religion of the Israelite people.

The next great epoch or movement which shapes the religion of Judaism is the role of the prophets who "speak truth to power." They live in a time when there are social, political, and diplomatic struggles in the kingdom, including the division of the kingdom. It is into this setting that the prophetic movement surfaces in a unique and powerful way. There are antecedents to the great prophets of Israel in the variety of religious manifestations in the ancient Near East. There were people (*nebiim*) in the various tribal cults who speak in ecstatic utterance, who claim to be able to point to if not predict the future, and on occasion call the people including the monarchs into accountability. They banded together, often danced in ecstasy, and were integral to the liturgy of temples including the offering of sacrificial rites. But in many ways the Hebrew prophets, while they may have had similarities to the cultic prophets, were pointed and profound in the call for change, not just a normal part of the religious milieu of the region. They truly altered the course of the history of Israel. Their attention was directed to the great God, Yahweh, and to this God they gave their sole allegiance. The Biblical prophets saw themselves as intermediaries between Yahweh and the people of Israel including their leaders. They spoke boldly and dramatically for the well-being of the people, often "demanded" the leadership to make improvements for the common good, establish systems of justice, and called them to an ethical life. They even dared to speak about the consequences of failing to provide justice for the people and living in accord with the commands of Yahweh, consequences that could lead to a "failed state." They refer back to the history of the Hebrews and look to the Exodus as the most significant event in the history of the children of Israel, applying its lesson to contemporary events. They make their case in the context of discerning the will of God, and their own experience of God gave direction and urgency to their message. They were not so much seers, although that element is occasionally present in their message, as they were preachers of an inspired message about social justice.

In Isaiah's message, in his picturesque and metaphorical language, we hear about the holiness and power of God which judges the infidelity of the people who stray away from the will of God and participate in the practices of other religions. In Jeremiah, whose ministry spanned the years between 626 BCE and the fall of Jerusalem in 586 BCE, we see a strong emphasis, not just on the nation, but on the ethical life of the individual worshipper. There is a movement from the collective understanding to a more individual understanding of the religious life. There is warning in their voices as they call the people and their leaders to follow the will of God. It is this great prophetic tradition that becomes one of the foundational dimensions of Judaism, one that resurfaces again and again, and has great influence in contemporary Judaism. It carries over in very significant ways into Christianity and Islam.

Still another epoch in the Jewish narrative, related to the message of the prophets, is the continuing decline of the political life of the Jewish people. The Southern Kingdom, Judah, based in Jerusalem is overcome by the Babylonians, and the aristocracy of Judah is taken away to exile in Babylon. This is viewed by Jeremiah and other prophets as a consequence of unfaithfulness, but not as reason to forsake the heritage of the covenant with Yahweh, but a reason to return to it. Even in exile, the Jewish people **remember** and persevere as a national group and continue to honor Yahweh. The Northern Kingdom, after the Assyrian conquest, disappears, although the people remain in a loose configuration. In time (538 BCE), when another foreign power, the Persian-Medians under King Cyrus, conquers Babylon, the captivity ends and many of the people return to the challenge of restoring their way of life in Palestine. A new way of life begins and, in the middle of the fourth century BCE Nehemiah the King and Ezra the scribe help to bring some restoration and order to the Judean state. Both the Babylonian Exile and the Post-Exilic reform become a part of the memory of the Jewish people and integral to Jewish beliefs and practices.

It is here that the Biblical narrative concludes, although the Jewish people continue to struggle to find their way in the Hellenistic era, and then face the presence of the Romans in 63 BCE and the ultimate defeat by the Romans in 70 CE which results in the Diaspora. It is important to note that even before this conquest and the Diaspora, there were Jews who lived in other regions, and one of the largest of these conclaves, perhaps as many as a million people, was in Alexandria. The Jews of Alexandria achieved levels of economic success and social prominence. They did lose their capacity to speak and read the Hebrew language, and the Torah had to be translated into Greek, a translation known as the Septuagint, making these writings available to non-Jews as well. A central figure of Judaism in Alexandria was Philo (15 BCE–40 CE) who was motivated to reconcile the insights of his culture with those of the Jewish thought. In particular he attempted to show the relationship and correlation of the Hellenistic philosophy based largely on Plato with the mainstream of Jewish thought based on the documents he had of the Hebrew Bible. He introduced an allegorical interpretation of the Torah, believing he was discovering its symbolic meaning. He understood the Biblical stories as allegorical descriptions of human progress toward spiritual illumination.[4]

There are many other Biblical voices that speak in their unique ways to the challenges of the Hebrew people across the centuries and in the years of restoration. These include the wisdom tradition (Proverbs, Ecclesiastes), the landscape of the heart (Psalms), attempts to understand why the innocent suffer (Job), and those that see the only solution to be the dramatic intervention of God and provide an apocalyptic vision of the future (Daniel). The Jewish people attempt to remain true to their faith in these complex circumstances, even standing over against the actions of Antiochus IV, the Hellenistic monarch of Syria. He prohibited Jewish worship and set up a pagan alter in the Temple. This action is challenged by the military leader, Judas Maccabaeus, who fights off the Syrian forces and recaptures Jerusalem (165 BCE), an event that is remembered in Jewish life and holidays.

Jewish history, beliefs, and practices

It is beyond our scope to give a full account of the history of the Jewish people following the Roman conquest of Palestine and the resulting great Diaspora.[5] Once again, we will focus on historical eras and pivotal events that shape and give identity to these people and provide them with a religion that has come to be called Judaism.[6] We will attempt to discern from these pivotal events and historical epochs the core beliefs and practices of Judaism and the spiritual pathways that become an integral part of the religion.[7] We will focus our attention on three historical eras: The Rabbinic Age (200 BCE–500 CE); The Middle Ages and Early Modern Europe (500–1750); and the Modern Period (1750–present).[8]

We turn first to the Rabbinic Age, a time when the Jewish people begin to organize their common life following the Maccabean revolt. It is at this time that new semireligious political parties appeared to gain control and establish order. One group, an established landowning upper class was called the Sadducees. This group had many distinctive characteristics, one of which was limiting the priesthood to those who could supposedly claim Davidic ancestry. Another group, called the Pharisees challenged the dominance of the Sadducees, and the two groups differed on a range of issues including ways of interpreting the Torah. Often the differences were adjudicated in the legislative and judicial council called the *Sanhedrin*.

Both groups, however, had to deal with Roman domination and the group put in power by the Romans called the Idumeans, a people who lived in the southeast of the Dead Sea. We learn about this group during the time of Jesus, with one of their number, Herod the Great (37–4 BCE) ruling in an oppressive way. At his death, his sons assumed control of a divided kingdom, each being assigned a region. A number of overtures to relieve the oppressive policies were made by the Jewish community, and there were even military attempts to overthrow the alien government and regain freedom.[9] One group called the Essenes believed that only God could overcome the oppressive regime by sending a messiah, and they retreated to ascetic seclusion in a mountainous region near the Dead Sea to wait for the coming of the messiah or a righteous one.[10] In time, as the conflicts continued, the Romans lost patience and began a full-scale war in 66 CE, one that ended with Roman victory in 70 CE.[11] An arch commemorating this victory stands in the ruins of the Roman Forum and on it is a seven-branched candelabrum (*menorah*), one of the oldest symbols now used in Jewish synagogues and homes. It depicts soldiers carrying booty from the temple, an image that captures the pathos of this time. Later, with more Jewish resistance and Roman retaliation under Hadrian (117–138), the Jews were forbidden to practice their faith and were only allowed one day a year to visit the "wailing wall."

A more effective strategy for the preservation of the heart of Jewish life and culture was the formation of an academy for teachings of the Torah in the village of Jabneh (or Javneh) by a Pharisaic sage named Johanan ben Sakkai. It became an important training ground for leadership, scholarship, and rabbinic ordination. These Pharisaic scholars, now called rabbis, assumed leadership of the struggling Jewish community. One of their tasks was to shape the canon of the Hebrew Bible, determining which books would be included as sacred scripture. In addition, following the great loss of the temple and the rite of sacrifice in it was the emergence of the regional synagogue in which not just priests, but informed men could preside at worship, offer prayers for forgiveness and acts of penitence. The "silver lining" in the destruction of the temple was the elevation of the **synagogue led by a teaching rabbi** as a central component of Jewish life. It was during this time as well that efforts were made to codify the oral law (*Mishnah*), a document in six sections that would be used in the academies that studied the Torah and in guiding the people in the practical affairs of life.[12]

Following the decline in the teaching centers in Palestine, there was a shift of leadership to the Jewish community in Babylonia which had continued to exist since the time of the Babylonian exile. For a long time this Jewish community had looked to Palestine as the center of their faith community, but its decline gave the Jews in Babylon more autonomy. Important documents to guide the religious tradition were developed, including a collection of commentaries on the Mishnah known as the *Gemara*, and these two extensive commentaries would become known as the *Talmud*.

To the outsider, these vast documents can at times be seen as excessively detailed, even trivial, but they do underline the rabbinic reverence for the life of the mind and the importance of a keen intellect in defining God's covenant with Israel. In time, still another document would be produced, called the *Midrash* in response to the need to base beliefs, ethical teaching, rites, and the celebration of holidays on the Bible. An elaborate form of Biblical interpretation was developed by the scholarly rabbis. Two more terms might be introduced here, even at the risk of getting lost in them, *halacha* and *agada*. Halacha, meaning how the faithful Jew should walk, regulated sexual relations, business ethics, the observance of birth and death, responsibilities to the needy, the order of worship, and relations with the gentile world. It is in these areas that Jews walked in faithfulness to the covenant. Agada is more concerned with meaning of the ways that God has entered into human history to heal and free the people of God. For example, the agada explores the theological tensions that exist between God's justice and God's mercy. It was during this era that questions regarding the rise of Christianity became important, and there was care given to making sure that the Jews stressed radical monotheism and that God did not have a divine son, such as Moses, as the Christians understood Jesus. There was the strong reassertion of the Shema from Deuteronomy 6, "Hear, O Israel, the Lord our God, the Lord is One."

We turn now to a brief review of the development of Judaism in the Middle Ages and Early Modern Europe (500–1750). Babylonia continued into these centuries as the major center of Jewish life, with the rabbinic leaders (*Geonim*) having influence well beyond this region. Jews from other parts of the world would submit questions to them, and these questions and the answers have been preserved. It was here also that the Jewish religion directly encountered the spread of Islam in the seventh to the ninth century, an encounter that was initially tolerable, but became more conflicted as the two religions interacted. It was during this era that a small group of Jews, known as the Karaites, became disillusioned with the rabbinic leadership. They called for a return to scripture to deal with difficult issues, and they challenged the increased authority of the Talmud. One rabbinic sage, Sadia (882–942) responded to the more conservative Karaites, and taught a philosophical form of Judaism that attempted to harmonize the rational thought of the Greek tradition with scripture.[13] As with Philo earlier, we see in the teaching of Sadia a more "liberal" outlook, and his teaching as well as that of Philo, point to an ongoing dialogue between more conservative and liberal elements within Judaism.

In time, the leadership of the Jewish community shifted to Europe, beginning in Spain because of the Muslim conquest of Spain and their acceptance of the presence of Jews. In this period, from the ninth century to the eleventh century, the Jewish community thrived in Spain, in large measure due to the welcome they received from their Arab hosts. The Judaism in what has been called "the golden age of Judaism" was diverse. But the more liberal element that attempted to reconcile reason and revelation, and freedom and determinism, became dominant and more integrated with Arab philosophical schools that were influenced by the rational thought of Aristotle.

A shift began to occur in the twelfth century with the ongoing conflict between Islam and Christianity, and the Jews were beginning to feel caught in this crossfire. A leading Jewish scholar Maimonides (1135–1204), whose influence continues into the present, was victimized by these conflicts and forced to leave Spain, eventually ending up in Egypt. He continued the trend in Jewish thought of reconciling the biblical revelation with Neo-Aristotelian philosophy. He acknowledged that Judaism is more concerned with proper conduct than with philosophical speculation, but maintained that there is no conflict between rational thought and faithful action, and that the one provides a foundation for the other. In his *Guide for the Perplexed* he articulates thirteen principles including the oneness of God, the primacy of the Torah, and the coming of the Messiah as foundational for Jewish thought and liturgy.

Another dimension of Judaism in the Middle Ages, as an alternative to more rational ways of understanding faith, was Jewish mysticism called *Kabbalah*.[14] This tradition of Jewish mysticism maintained that the external world was only a partial reflection of an invisible higher realm. The goal of this movement was to gain direct access to this higher realm and experience personally its hidden splendor. Hints of this mystical experience are present in the Biblical witness. There is the experience of Moses and the burning bush, Isaiah's temple vision, and Jeremiah's vision of the heavenly chariot. This way is viewed as only for those who are ready, not for all. The quest is to encounter the God who is hidden in the outer garment of the Torah.

As the Jews made their exit from Spain, they immigrated to both western and eastern Europe. Those in the west were called *Ashkenazim* (a descendent of Noah), and those in the east who had left Muslim Spain and found refuge in the Ottoman Empire, Italy, and the Netherlands were called *Sephardic* (Spanish) Jews. The experience of the Jews in Europe was difficult, often filled with persecution and isolation, as they were caught in the unfortunate zealotry that caused the Crusades. This persecution continued beyond the Crusades, and it often took the form of accusing the Jews of being responsible for the death of Jesus.

A number of beliefs and practices were developed and initiated during this period. The rabbis continued to lead the Jewish community, and the practice of inviting a 13-year-old boy to read the Torah in the synagogue was instituted. The boy is called bar *mitzvah* (son of the commandment) and it is his initiation into adult life and responsibility. The experience of the Jews in Eastern Europe was no better, and many turned to piety and mysticism for comfort. One movement that grew out this experience in the seventeenth century was *Hasidism*, a movement that transformed the Kabbalah into a popular and joyous folk movement and gave the isolated Jewish communities a sense of community. One of the characteristics of Hasidism was the presence and sacredness of joy, and singing and dancing became part of celebrating God's goodness.

A third historical era that continues to inform us about the contours of contemporary Judaism is the Modern Period from 1750 to the present. We will give attention to just a few of the defining moments in this period. Leading up to this period, the Jewish community was still isolated in ghettos across Europe. But in the eighteenth century, there was a dramatic intellectual, social, and economic change in Europe. This period of enlightenment, with its questioning of traditional authority and endorsement of human reason and human progress impacted the Jewish community. It led to increased freedom and empowered them to gain full citizenship in their countries of residence. In France, in the wake of the French Revolution (1789) the Jews were formally emancipated. Napoleon offered the Jews full citizenship with the caveat that they must surrender their status as a semiautonomous people governed by Talmudic law in return for the privileges of citizenship. This freedom was welcome by Jewish leaders, but the resulting risk was the loss of the distinctive identity of the Jews as more and more Jews endorsed "liberty, equality, and fraternity" and rejected what was considered to be the intellectually untenable and socially restrictive teaching of Judaism.

One response to the threat of Jewish defection was to reform the Jewish traditional ways, both in thought and practice. A movement known as Reform Judaism, given leadership by the German rabbinic scholar, Abraham Geiger (1810–1874), offered a worship experience similar to Protestant worship, with organ playing, singing and prayers in German as well as Hebrew. He argued that what God might have required under one set of conditions may change for another setting. Men and women, in this new age, might sit together in worship, and the dietary restrictions might be changed. What was important was to honor and witness the ethical monotheism grounded in the God of love and justice.

Predictably, there was a reaction by those representing orthodoxy. They argued against these changes, fearing the potential loss of the Jewish identity. What must be conserved is the importance of living under the divine authority of the Torah, encased as it is in the traditional ways. This reaction did allow for some ways of making the tradition more attractive to enlightened Jews, but maintained the Jewish separateness was essential to maintain the Jewish presence in the world. This debate, with various types of reform and counter-reform being advocated continues into present-day Judaism.

Relief from persecution and isolation did not come in every setting. For example, it became more difficult and dangerous for Jews in Russia who continued to face persecution and even the institution of *pogroms* (massacres of Jews) under the oppressive rule of Alexander III (ruled 1881–1894). With this attack and continuing anti-Semitism in Western Europe, there was the rise of Zionism, a movement of Jewish national liberation that argued for the formation of nation state in Palestine where Jewish people could experience respect and freedom. These same movements of reform (Reform Judaism), conservatism (Conservative Judaism), orthodoxy (Orthodox Judaism), and Zionism continued in the United States as Jews migrated to a country that promised freedom.

The twentieth century brought two dramatic events into the life of Jewish people and shaped their religion and sense of identity in distinctive ways. The *Holocaust* in Germany under Hitler and the Nazi regime was horrible beyond description and annihilated one-third of the Jewish people in the world. Hitler's policy of genocide was finally overcome, but it remains firmly entrenched in the mind and soul of all Jewish people, and indeed the conscience of everyone. Jewish rabbis and theologians asked with some intensity about the "hiddenness" or "eclipse" of God.[15] Others found ways to maintain their strong belief in the God of the covenant.[16]

The other event that was to profoundly shape Jewish life was the formation of the Jewish state of Israel, a complex development with conflicting interpretations. But under the leadership of David Ben-Gurion, the first prime minister, the state became a reality and was justified by arguing that it would be a place to spiritualize power and build a nation that lived with the goal of epitomizing social justice. Since those dramatic events of 1947, the state of Israel has been a "safe haven" for Jewish settlers whose ancestors had to live with the harsh realities of the Diaspora, but also a threat to the Palestinian inhabitants of the region. Its presence remains one of the most complex political problems of our time.

Jewish beliefs, practices, and spiritual pathways

It is from the Biblical narrative, the events of Jewish history, and the formation of complex and diverse traditions that Jewish beliefs, practices, and spiritual pathways develop. It is truly an historical religion.[17] We will begin with a brief summary of the core beliefs, varied as they are among the different divisions within Judaism.[18]

1. The fundamental belief of Judaism is that there is a sovereign, personal, and transcendent God. The Hebrew people affirm that this God, Yahweh, created all, including human beings.[19] God is "Other," and not just a personified extension of nature, human experience, or the ways humans organize their affairs in empires, nations, clans, or tribes. The early Hebrews may have yielded to the cultural norm of anthropomorphism as they personified the divine, but gradually they attempted to find ways of speaking about Yahweh that went beyond local and tribal descriptions and found ways to use language that pointed beyond human patterns while attempting to preserve the belief that God is a person, not merely inanimate principle and power.

2. It was God who created all with intention and meaning. Therefore, there is the Jewish affirmation that this vast universe is not random, merely an outcome of a big bang, though it may have been started that way. The creation is called good, having inherent value, and to be cherished, honored, and sustained as

creation continues. It follows that the "stuff" of creation and its ways of being and becoming, and the ways that humans are part of creation, should be understood and respected.

3. Regardless of the origin of the universe, which is more the realm of science, divine creation implies human meaning and responsibility, and that humans are guided and held accountable for their behavior. Humans are said to be created in God's image, giving them the capacity to understand, a sense of right and wrong, and the capacity to create, to order, and to live in ways that reflect the divine image.

4. This understanding of God provided a way for the Jewish people to understand their own history. They saw God as personal and involved in the unfolding of their history, and it was an easy step to say that God has a purpose in all of history, one that humans can discern, participate in, and partner with God in realizing the divine goals for history.

5. The Jewish people, learning from their history, understand that God calls them to an ethical life, both as individuals and in the formation of the social order. It is clear from the Biblical narrative and in their other writings and traditions that individuals are to live in ways that respect others and to participate in ways of creating a social structure and laws that insure justice and lead to peace.

6. As God enters into human history to heal, redeem, and guide, so too should humans have compassion for all people, and especially those who are in need and those who suffer. Their own suffering, as individuals and as a people, should give them empathy and invite them to live in ways that relieves their own suffering and the suffering of others. Life, created by God, is sacred and to be hallowed.[20] Life is also to be lived in hope, not despair, because the God who has saved in the past will save in the present and in the future.

The question remains, given the diversity of Judaism: How does one live a Jewish life? One asks this question with the awareness that there are innumerable laws, patterns, and guidelines that provide detailed answers, but how does one sort through all of these to discern the essential spirit of living the Jewish life?[21] What are the spiritual pathways? Let me suggest the following categories:

- The first is that the Jewish life is generally lived **in the family**.[22] It is in the context of the family that one learns how to be Jewish. It is in the family that one receives the guidance of parenting, begins to understand the inherent values of being a Jew and following its ways, and is introduced to the holidays and celebrations that speak to the Biblical narrative and the history of a distinctive people. The home becomes a sanctuary, filled with love and guidance, and a pattern of life that honors the divine will and way as understood by the Jewish faith. There are symbols and ceremonies that speak to the ways of being Jewish and honoring the values inherent in being Jewish. Even daily meals are important, as are the special ones.

There is the Sabbath observance, the practice of helping others, the continual study of the Jewish thoughts and practices, and the associations that come from being a part of a larger community with a distinctive identity.

- It follows that living the Jewish life is to live **within a community** of people with shared values, common practices, and engagement with the world. The synagogue is central to the cultivation of the spiritual pathway, as one learns about the Hebrew Bible and the vast collections of scholarship and opinion represented in the Talmud and the other writings. The community is not limited to the local synagogue, but extends outward to the larger Jewish world of Judaism, regardless of one's loyalty to a particular branch of Judaism. There are the Jewish schools, ranging from daycare to the most advanced universities, and the range of supplementary formation and educational programs in summer experiences and international travel. Education is central to Jewish formation and it extends from early childhood through adulthood.
- The spiritual pathways of Judaism are filled with the **observance of holidays and celebrations**, remembering the history of a people who have distinctive identity and values. There is a calendar of holidays that include Rosh Hashanah (The New Year) and Yom Kippur (the Day of Atonement), Hanukah that remembers the victory over Antiochus IV of Syria, and Passover that recalls the Exodus to name just a few.[23] There are also the times when the pivotal events within the life cycle are honored and celebrated: birth, dedication at Bar and Bat Mitzvah, marriage, and of course death.
- There are dimensions of the spiritual pathways of Judaism that go beyond the time within the family, the community, and the range of observances. Some feel **called to the special vocation** of serving as a rabbi, a calling that involves extensive study, personal devotion, pastoral care, and the leadership of a community. There are those who seek a more mystical way, perhaps in the tradition of Kabbalah or in another pattern. There are those who feel called to a life of service and give themselves to healing, relieving suffering, and working for a more just and peaceful world.

How are we to assess this extraordinary spiritual way called Judaism, a tradition whose influence goes far beyond its size? Let's turn first to its most positive features.

1. It is a religion with a **compelling worldview**. Because of the special history of these people, recorded in the Biblical narrative and lived out since Biblical times to the present, the religion of Judaism has caught the attention of the world's greatest leaders and intellects and engaged the imagination of and influenced all "pilgrims" who seek a deep and profound spiritual pathway through life. It is a worldview that in essence has been passed on to its cousins, Christians and Muslims whose religions are the largest in the human family. The central theme of

this worldview is the way the human family interacts with the personal transcendent God.

2. It has passed on to humankind a **profound global ethic**. It is not the only one, but it may be the most influential. It is an ethic that calls humankind to the stewardship of creation, to the formation of a social order based on fairness, justice and law, and calls individuals to live lives of compassion.

3. Although not intentionally, it nevertheless became the **source and inspiration for two other great world religions**, Christianity and Islam. For a variety of theological and political reasons, these great religions have not lived in harmony, and there are deep conflicts that continue to elude solutions. It is encouraging, however, to see the ways that these faith traditions with so much in common have begun to seek reconciliation.

4. Judaism is a religion of **family and community**, giving its followers a clear sense of belonging and identity. There is a strong human need to belong and to understand one's history, traditions, and way of life, even if one is not always faithful to it.

5. Judaism is a religion of **courage and perseverance**. It is hard to imagine another religious tradition that could have survived the years of Diaspora and persecution. Continually challenged throughout history, the Jewish people (not all religious) continue to have a clear sense of identity and tradition, and the faithful Jews from the different branches of Judaism continue to live a life that honors what they understand to be the will and way of God.

Like all the great religions of humankind, Judaism continues to face the challenges of contemporary life and a *zeitgeist* that does not always encourage a spiritual way. It will continue to need to face, even overcome, the following tendencies.

1. As a minority in the major countries of the world, and surrounded by hostile neighbors as the country of Israel, there is a tendency for the followers of Judaism **to retreat into their own communities**, become ingrown, live defensively, and manifest a sectarian spirit. This certainly is not a universal norm, and it is understandable, but local and regional communities of Judaism are not always welcoming to the outsider eager to learn from and live in harmony with followers of Judaism.

2. Not unlike nearly all of the religious traditions, the various branches of Judaism **do not always respect and live in a collaborative and cooperative way** with one another. It is a strange irony that different factions within a single religion (e.g. Catholics and Protestants in Christianity, Sunni and Shia within Islam) do not learn to live with and from those within their own religious faith. The battles within can be fierce, uncompromising.

3. One of the **greatest challenges of Judaism is the conflict in Israel/Palestine**. The issues in the conflict are longstanding and incredibly difficult to resolve. It is next to impossible for either side, especially those on the extreme, to even imagine a way that the conflict can be resolved. For the people of the region, it is one that must continue to be addressed and one that the whole world watches.

4. Related to this deep conflict is the challenge of **controlling the radical elements**[24] of both sides which resort to violence and retaliation whenever there is an affront. The leaders of Judaism, given the resources of their faith tradition, must find a way to achieve a semblance of peace in the region and respect the Palestinian people.

5. Still another challenge for Judaism, and one that faces nearly all of the religions of humankind, is finding **a credible basis for belief and practice**. Increasingly, given changing worldviews and the alluring lifestyle of wealth, it is difficult to sustain loyalty and faithfulness to the fundamental beliefs and practices of Judaism. For many, the beliefs are not intellectually defensible and the ways of life, however healthy and benevolent, go against the prevailing maxim that happiness consists in the abundance of things possessed and the omnipresent gospel of consumption.

Judaism in so many ways has been the teacher of the world. We turn now to the religion that grows out of Judaism, Christianity.

Discussion questions

1. What are the fundamental differences between the religions in the category of transcendent monism and the monotheistic religions?
2. Why is history so important to Judaism?
3. What are the primary ways that Judaism teaches that humans interact with God?
4. What gives the followers of Judaism their distinctive identity?
5. What are possible ways for the people of Israel and their neighbors to achieve some form of reconciliation?

Key terms and concepts

Covenant: An agreement between two parties with each assuming some obligation, often based on trust rather than strict law. The Hebrew Bible describes covenants between God and the "children of Israel" made in the time of Abraham, Moses, and David.

1. **Exodus:** The journey of the Israelites under Moses out of Egypt to the "promised land."

2. **Diaspora:** The Jews who lived outside the land of Palestine following the Babylonian Exile and the Roman conquest of the land in 70 CE.

3. **Kabbala:** Medieval Jewish system of mysticism.

4. **Monotheism:** Belief in one God, and thus one center of revelation, meaning, and values.

5. **Talmud:** A vast, authoritative commentary on the Law composed by rabbis, completed in the sixth century CE.

6. **Torah:** The teaching or instruction of God contained in the first five books of the Hebrew Bible (Pentateuch).

Suggestions for reference and reading

Buber, Martin, *I and Thou* (New York: Charles Scribner's Sons, 1958).

Diamant, Anita with Cooper, Howard, *Living A Jewish Life: Jewish Traditions, Customs and Values* (New York: HarperResource, 1991).

Heschel, Abraham Joshua, *God in Search of Man* (Northvale, NJ, 1955).

Johnson, Paul, *A History of the Jews* (New York: Harper & Row, 1987).

Robinson, George, *Essential Judaism: A Complete Guide to Beliefs, Customs, and Rituals* (New York: Pocket Books, 2000).

Spiritual Pathways Within Christianity

9

Chapter Outline

The narrative of the New Testament 159
The story of Jesus 161
The New Testament as guide for spiritual pathways 163
Spiritual traditions of the Christian tradition 168
The contributions and challenges of Christian spirituality 172

The narrative of the New Testament

As with Judaism, the Christian narrative is rooted in history, and it is a story that is built upon the belief in a personal transcendent God who enters into human history, a belief shared with the other Abrahamic monotheistic religions, Judaism and Islam. The Christian narrative has its own distinctive features as do the other "Religions of the Book" and it is these distinctive features of the story that give us the best starting point for understanding the spiritual pathways within Christianity. Much of the story of the New Testament is common knowledge, but some review will be helpful as we attempt to understand these spiritual pathways.

The sources for the story are primarily in the New Testament, with only a few other historical documents mentioning the central character in the story who is Jesus of Nazareth. The New Testament documents are handed down to succeeding generations after a fairly complex process of development, although a much shorter one than with the Hebrew Bible. Because the Christian story is based on these documents that evolve into the New Testament, it is important to review briefly how they took shape, were collected, circulated, and became the authoritative witness to the historical foundations of the Christian faith.

The writings of the New Testament were written many years after the life of Jesus, ranging from approximately 20 to 70 or more years. The earliest of these writings come from the pen of the Apostle Paul, a first generation Christian missionary who traveled throughout the Mediterranean region proclaiming the message about Jesus. We learn a great deal about the life and mission of Paul in the material called The Acts of the Apostles, an important book of the New Testament. The epistles of Paul written to young churches focus more on the *meaning* of life, death, and resurrection of Jesus than they do on the details of the early life of Jesus. Some later documents, attributed to Paul, were circulated among these young churches as a guide for these new followers of the Christian way. One "letter" outside of the Pauline corpus and influence, called Hebrews, likely addresses a Jewish readership.

It was at least 30 years after the crucifixion of Jesus that the Gospels began to be written. These four sources of Christian faith tell us more about the birth, life, death, and a central Christian belief, the resurrection of Jesus. Another document called Revelation and some smaller epistles round out the canon of the New Testament. Revelation, variously interpreted because it is written in a literary form called apocalypse (revelation), addresses the complex political realities of these early generations of Christians, offering guidance for life in difficult times and a hope rooted in the belief that God is sovereign in history.

The Gospel of Mark is likely the first of the Gospels, and it is based on the oral tradition which had been handed down about Jesus. It was the oral tradition that became an integral part of the worship experience of the early church; it both preserved and shaped the story of Jesus. The Gospel of Luke, using other sources (Q) as well as Mark,[1] comes several years later, and then comes Matthew drawing upon Mark and Q. The Gospel of John is likely the last of the Gospels to be written and it has its own sources, distinctive style, and content. These documents should not be read as "lives of Jesus" in that they are not primarily biographies, but proclamations about the religious meaning of the Jesus event. In many ways, they might be thought of as expanded sermons that center on the worship and community needs of the early church. The Gospel writers have a point of view focused on proclaiming good news and providing guidance and comfort to the young Christian community.

New Testament scholars have been diligent about tracing the formation of the New Testament, discerning its primary religious character and attempting to read behind the religious message in order to access the essential history of the life and times of Jesus. The Christian Church has read the New Testament as authoritative in matters of faith and practice and for centuries did not fundamentally question the accounts provided in the New Testament. But it was inevitable, with the rise of critical historical scholarship in the nineteenth century, that the New Testament would be examined more closely. This historical critical study of the account of the life and meaning of Jesus has continued into the present. By reading the New Testament, guided by historical study, we can piece together the essential narrative that guides and sustains the Christian community.[2]

The story of Jesus

The Christian faith and its many spiritual pathways grow out of Judaism and the first century Jew named Jesus who was from Nazareth in the region of Galilee. Nazareth was a small village in the time of Jesus, but has now grown to a good-sized city and has a diverse population of Jews, Christians, Muslims, and a range of others with various religious beliefs and convictions. The politics of the region are complex, and there were as well during the time of Jesus. Herod Antipas, the son of Herod the Great, ruled in the region, and there was Jewish resistance to his attempt to Hellenize the culture and his policies of oppression. The Romans in 6 CE, sensing the risk of keeping Herod Antipas in charge of the region of Judea, placed this area under the direct rule of the Roman procurator. It is into the complex environment that Jesus enters the world and lives out his life.

Two of the Gospels, Matthew and Luke, contain accounts of the birth of Jesus, and place the birth in Bethlehem.[3] The time is approximately 4 BCE or earlier with the traditional dating being erroneous. The accounts, difficult to confirm with historical precision, tell the story of the holy family, Joseph and Mary, going south to Bethlehem because of a Roman census that required residents to be registered at their ancestral home. Mary is pregnant during the trip down from the region of Galilee, and Jesus is born after their arrival. It was a busy time because of a holiday, and the account in Luke has Jesus being born in a manger "because there was no place for them in the inn." (Lk. 2.7) This account has the visit of shepherds and angels, whereas Matthew records the visit of wise men that follow the star that leads them to the birthplace of Jesus. In time, perhaps following a trip to Egypt caused by a dangerous threat by

Herod (Mt. 2.13–18), the family returns to Nazareth. As Jesus matures, he likely joins his father as a carpenter. The two accounts of the birth of Jesus differ some in detail, but they live on in an extraordinary way as the Christmas story is told.

Luke records a trip to Jerusalem when Jesus is a youth, one in which he shows great insight in conversations with religious scholars in the Temple. He probably had learned Torah in the context of the family and community in Nazareth. The Gospel accounts move directly to a description of the public ministry of Jesus when he is about the age of 30.

We know very little about the specific events of the life of Jesus as he grows up, but we do know more about the context of his life. He would have been exposed to the Zealot cause for Jewish emancipation, the Essene retreat to the wilderness to seek a deeper spiritual life, the ruthlessness of imperial power, and the hope of one called a Messiah who would drive out the Romans and reestablish an independent state. It was a time of great unrest, a critical period filled with a mixture of hope and tragedy. It is unlikely that Jesus identified with any of the political factions, either in Galilee or in Jerusalem, and his teaching appears to have a pointed message for them all.

The accounts of Jesus speak about John the Baptist, a relative of Jesus, a fiery prophet who calls his hearers to repentance and to prepare for the coming Kingdom. Jesus goes to John, is baptized, and receives within himself the sense of calling to his mission.[4] Following this preparation,[5] he begins to gather disciples who travel with him, primarily in the Galilee. Jesus teaches with power and authority, performs what are recorded as miracles, heals the sick, and soon attracts large crowds. He receives all people, even those who are outcastes, and proclaims the good news of God.[6] In time, he has detractors, and as he goes to Jerusalem, there is resistance from the religious authorities who question his teaching and from the government who fear that he will cause social unrest. He is tried for treason by a Roman court, found guilty, and is crucified. His followers believe that he rose from the dead and appeared to them.[7]

This extraordinary story that has captured the imagination and hearts of so many does raise questions about the identity of Jesus. Is Jesus a radical Jewish prophet and teacher who calls his listeners to live under the reign of God, and who challenges the different governments of the region to rule with justice and care for the needs of the people? Yes, but perhaps he is more than teacher and prophet. Is he the promised Messiah, one who comes to overthrow the alien government and restore the Davidic kingdom? No doubt some of his contemporaries thought so as many have since. The Gospels indicate that the term "Son of Man" was a term that Jesus often used in reference to himself, and it may have been a reference to language taken from the book of Daniel that refers to such a messianic figure. The Pauline literature is filled with language that describes Jesus as Savior and Lord, language that has become the norm in the Christian Church. Through the early centuries, the Church struggled to find a way to express the identity of Jesus in reference to their understanding of God. These early centuries, from the third to the seventh centuries were a time of both Trinitarian and Christological controversies. There were debates and many suggestions, and ultimately, doctrines were formulated which affirm that Jesus is both human and divine, and a member of the Trinitarian Godhead, Father, Son, and Holy Spirit.[8]

What we know for sure is that Jesus "happened" to the human family. Out of his life and teaching, as difficult as it may be to describe in accurate detail, came Christianity, its beliefs, and its many spiritual pathways. Our goal is not to visit the historical complexities of Christian origins or to wander through the corridors of Christian theology and history as they developed across the centuries. These are fascinating areas of study, but beyond our present purposes. Rather, we will try to see in what ways the life, teaching, and mission of Jesus offer guidance for the formation of a spiritual center and the spiritual pathways. We will look at the life and teaching of the Apostle Paul with the same aim, and then move to a review and assessment of the many spiritual pathways which grew out of these stories of the New Testament.

The New Testament as guide for spiritual pathways

We begin our attempt to understand the range of spiritual pathways within the Christian faith by going to the heart of the teaching of Jesus found in the Gospels. As we launch this strategy, we do so in "fear and trembling" knowing that the writings of Paul came before the Gospels; that the Gospels must be read with a critical understanding of how they came to be and have been passed on to generations of Christians and other readers; and that Jesus has been understood quite differently across the centuries.[9] So with these observations clearly in mind and appropriate humility, we look to the Gospels, and to particular parts of the Gospels, as a Christian primer on spirituality, inspiring Christians and all readers to find a spiritual center and empowering them to pursue a range of spiritual pathways.

The Gospel of Mark gives a very succinct account of the heart of Jesus' mission and message. Mark describes the beginning of the ministry of Jesus in the following way: "The time is fulfilled, and the Kingdom of God has come near; repent, and believe in the good news" (Mk 1.16). Notice first of all that there is a **time concern,** and Jesus invites his listeners to focus on what is happening in their immediate present. It is a special moment because "the time is fulfilled" and the listeners of Jesus should take note. What makes the time a *kairos,* a specific and decisive moment, is that "the Kingdom of God has come near." The power and presence of God is now available and being offered to them.[10] It was a call to the contemporaries of Jesus, and is now understood as a call to contemporary Christians.

The contemporaries of Jesus would have understood the phrase in terms of their history, present circumstances, and their hope for the future. They would know that God had been there for them and their ancestors in dramatic ways, and especially in the deliverance from bondage out of Egypt. They would acknowledge the nearness, power, and presence of God in their worship and in their present circumstances, and wonder from time to time why God was not more active in their current situation of being governed by foreign rulers. But they would dare to hope that God would intervene, and therefore would listen as the prophetic rabbi Jesus said, " . . . the time is fulfilled, the Kingdom of God has come near."

Jesus catches their attention and gives them an **invitation**. It summons for them to open their lives to the nearness, power, and presence of God. But there is a condition—they will have to change the direction of their lives. The word used by Jesus, "repent," tells his listeners that their current way of life needs to be changed. He asks his hearers to examine their lives and see if their values and commitments are in accord with what they know to be the will and way of God. Implied is that there is another way to live, a spiritual way, that places God at the center, and he invites them to change directions and receive God into their lives. When you pray, Jesus advises his listeners, say "Your kingdom come. Your will be done on earth, as it is in heaven." (Mt. 6.10) This kingdom is different from the Roman Kingdom that you experience daily.

On occasion, Jesus would remind his listeners that it might be easy to miss the invitation with all of the distractions of life. God is near, but one has to be sensitive and discerning. The Kingdom of God is like a mustard seed, so small, yet able to grow into a tree in which birds can find shelter. (Mt. 13.31–32) It is like leaven in the dough, almost undetectable, but sufficient to leaven three measures of bread for a meal to feed 150 people. (Mt. 13.33) He reminds them as well that the Kingdom of God has infinite value, worth selling all that one owns for this pearl of great price. (Mt. 13.45) Therefore, one should "strive first for the Kingdom of God and his righteousness, and all these things will be given to you as well." (Mt. 6.33)

It is an invitation and also a **promise**. Jesus invites these people to "come and see, come and listen, come and change the direction of your life "and a promise, and learn what God will do for you." It is especially a promise to the poor and humble who have nothing to expect from the world and its systems. What unites those addressed in the Beatitudes (Mt. 5.3–13) and pronounced blessed and content is that they are driven to the very end of the world and its possibilities.[11] The world has no rewards for them. In many ways, it has been harsh and cruel. But God does not forsake them; in fact the opposite is the case. They are promised help in the form of God's nearness, power, and presence. Those listening, the poor, those who mourn, the humble and the meek, those who hunger and thirst for righteousness, the merciful, the pure in heart, the peacemakers, even those who are persecuted, all are invited; every category of the population is welcome.

They are promised a "blessed" life. Jesus says to them, "how happy and peaceful you can be as you open your heart to what is near and here, the power and presence of God." The word translated "blessed" is a word used in the Gospels and in Greek literature to denote the highest stage of happiness and well-being; it is to be filled with contentment and inner peace. Note that Jesus does not promise that all of life's problems will be eliminated. Stress, anxiety, problematic relationships, and financial difficulties, the loss of a loved one, and difficult political circumstances do not disappear, but there is a way to cope. Perhaps circumstances will not change, but Jesus offers a radically new way of seeing and being that comes, when, with a pure heart, we seek the power and presence of God. Our outlook is changed, and we cope with the challenges of life with a new perspective and attitude. We have a spiritual center and are offered a spiritual pathway.

As our approach to life changes and we are inwardly transformed by the power and presence of God, we are then **challenged** by Jesus to a new way a life that is an outward expression of our inner transformation. Jesus tells his listeners and followers that a whole new way of life is expected, one that asks them to love God with all of their heart, soul, mind, and strength; and to love their neighbor as they love themselves (Mk 12.30–31). He teaches that the nearness, power, and presence of God in our lives will make them humble, merciful, pure in heart, and peacemakers. Empowered by God, the believer is expected to show mercy and loving-kindness to those who live with unde-served suffering, those who never had a chance, and those who got left behind at birth. They are to show compassion for the sick and care in tangible ways for the uneducated, the unemployed, and those who are marginalized by injustice.

It was common for Jesus to insert a story to illustrate the personal transfor-mation and the need for steadfast love. He is recorded to have said, "Let me tell you a story about the man who was robbed, beaten, and left for dead on his way to Jericho. A priest came along and ignored him. The Samaritan (a person on the lower end of the caste system) picked up the beaten man, fed him, pro-vided him housing, and healed his wounds." (See Lk. 10.25–37) This is the new way for life for those near to God and who have God's power and presence. Jesus is also reported to have loved the outcast and healed a leper who cried out for help. Here, in his own behavior, Jesus demonstrates the power and pres-ence of God, as he boldly steps over the cultural norms to touch and heal the leper. (Mk 1.40–45)[12]

The Apostle Paul, the great leader of the early Christian community, also speaks about spirituality through his life and in his teaching. Again, we run the risk of oversimplification as we describe the core of the Apostle's teaching about the spiritual life, but it is a risk worth taking even if it only partially opens the door to Pauline wisdom.[13] The teaching of Paul is not a mere repeti-tion of the teaching of Jesus, in large measure because he writes about the impact of the life, death, and resurrection of Jesus. There is a different empha-sis in Paul, and some have even accused him of falsifying Christianity and becoming its real "founder." They have argued that Paul turned the ethical teaching of Jesus into a gospel of redemption, replete with current Jewish ideas and Hellenistic mythologies. And there is no doubt that as we shift from the Gospels and turn to Paul's writing that we move from the words of Jesus to the words about Jesus. Jesus is no longer a mere figure in history, belonging to his own time and a victim of circumstances, impressive though he was in his teaching and exemplary in the way he endured his fate.

Paul writes about Jesus and persuasively maintains that Jesus is the way God dealt with the world and humankind which has made all the difference for time and eternity. He understands his calling to proclaim the message that God came into the world in Jesus to save it and deliver it. (Rom. 1.1, Gal. 1.15) He begins with the premise that **humankind and the world are lost**. In what sense are humankind and the world lost? They are lost in the sense that they do not measure up to the expectations of biblical law, understood by Paul as the expression of God's will. They miss the mark. Humanity finds itself in a dark forest, having lost its way, and to be lost is to experience alienation, estrangement, meaninglessness, emptiness, disease, and to engage in all forms of self-destructive behavior. All are subject to God's law and without excuse, (Rom. 1.18, 3.20) and ironically, the law is powerless to help. (Rom. 7.7–25) The world as well is a prisoner, standing in need of redemption. (Rom. 8.19–21)

Is it hopeless? No, **there is a way provided by God**. God comes to the world and humankind in Jesus. Through the life, death, and resurrection of Jesus, we are made righteous in God's eyes. The obligations of the law are met in Jesus, and we accept what God has done for us in Jesus by faith. We are "justified by faith" as we accept the gift of God's grace. (Rom. 5.6–11) Not only are we justified, but we are transformed by this forgiveness and empowered, as we live "in Christ," to a life of faith, hope, and love. (I Cor. 13.13)

It is from this foundation, according to Paul, that we find our way into the spiritual life. What has happened in the past (the coming of Jesus) leaps forward into our time and has relevance for the way we live our lives. We have been made righteous (justified) by God's grace in Jesus, and we are now called to lead a holy (spiritual) life. The holy (sanctified) life is lived within the **community called the church**, made possible by the presence of the Holy Spirit within us, and manifested in a life of love and service.

The saving event of the life, death, and resurrection of Jesus is made a present reality within the world and in the lives of Christians within the context of the church. In Paul's view, the church is a body inaugurated by God and empowered by God's Spirit. It is the community (*ecclesia*) in which one find's a spiritual center, the spiritual life is cultivated, and people are sent out in loving service. It is in the church where people hear the good news of the gospel through proclamation, participate in worship (the language of remembrance), partake of the sacraments (know the reality of God's presence), and experience the support and inspiration of true fellowship. The church in the teaching of Paul, while seldom perfect in practice, is nevertheless the community of spiritual transformation. (I Cor. 1.2)

The saving event of God's gracious action in Jesus is concurrently made a present reality through the presence of the **Holy Spirit** within the individual believer. It is Paul's way of saying what Jesus taught about the Kingdom of God, that the presence of the Holy Spirit in our lives is the nearness, power, and presence of God in our lives. From time to time, Paul in his dealings with new and immature churches and the believers within these churches has to remind and guide them about the Holy Spirit's presence in their corporate and personal lives. He even asks the Corinthians, "Do you not know that you are God's temple and that God's Spirit dwells in you?" (I Cor. 3.16) It is the Holy Spirit who empowers the community of faith and the believers in the community of faith. Christians speak then about the "Spirit-filled" life, given guidance and order by the community and inspiring the Christian to a life of "love, joy, peace, patience, kindness, generosity, faithfulness, gentleness, and self-control." (Gal. 5.22)

According to Paul, the spiritual or sanctified life of the Christian is set apart and called to do the will and way of God in the world. Paul is clear that this **ethical life of service** is based on God's antecedent act in Christ. *Because* of what God has done, we therefore live our lives in harmony with God's intentions for the world. Most of Paul's epistles are structured with the first part laying the theological foundations and the latter part describing the consequent actions. He opens what we now know as Ch. 12 of the letter to the Romans with "I appeal to you therefore, brothers and sisters, by the mercies of God, to present your bodies as a living sacrifice, holy and acceptable to God which is your spiritual worship." (Rom. 12.1)

Paul is clear that we have "died" to the old life of self-seeking (Rom. 6.2) and that we now live empowered by the Spirit. (Rom. 8.5 ff.) He provides descriptions of this new life with admonitions comparable in many ways with those in his Jewish tradition (see, e.g. Rom. 1.29–31; 12.8–21; 13.13; I Cor. 5.10 f.; 6.9; 2 Cor. 12.20 f; Gal. 5.19–23.) What is special to note in Paul's descriptions of appropriate behavior is the way that grace makes the old life of the "flesh" unacceptable and the new life of love and service possible.

Spiritual traditions of the Christian tradition

Guided by the Hebrew Bible, the teaching of Jesus in the Gospels, the teaching of Paul in the Epistles, and the rest of the New Testament, the Christian community has developed a broad range of approaches to the spiritual life. Depending upon the historical circumstances, cultural norms, theological understanding, ecclesiastic tradition, and inspired dedication to the spiritual life, Christians have sought a spiritual center and pursued spiritual pathways. Again, the story is too long and complex for a single chapter or even a single book,[14] so we only make a beginning. Our approach will be to use many of the traditional categories of spirituality[15] and the practices within them, and on occasion reference some of the "schools" of spirituality that have developed across the centuries. The historical twists and turns are many; we will focus on six major patterns of spirituality.

One of the great patterns of spirituality within the Christian faith, often thought to be the approach to spirituality is the **mystical and contemplative tradition**. This tradition has found expression over the centuries in nearly all of the branches of Christendom, and certainly its roots are present in the Hebrew Bible and New Testament. At the heart of this tradition is the desire to be one with God, both in direct experience as in the case of mysticism, and through a variety of practices that guide one to unity with God.[16] The mystical approach is to seek a direct and unmediated loving experience of God, an experience that may be called union with God. More generally, the contemplative tradition uses the inward disciplines of prayer, meditation, ascetic practices, and study to "practice the presence of God." It is to love God with one's whole being, heart, mind, soul, and strength.

Prayer is both personal and corporate and is generally understood as a way of communication with the divine. It is often an expression of the human need for guidance, forgiveness, and empowerment. In fact, prayer may be the *sine qua non* of the religious life. Meditation, too, is central to this pattern of spirituality and helps us to center our lives, face reality, and focus our attention on what is truly important. Various ascetic practices such as fasting, forms of penance, or body positions such as kneeling serve to support meditation. The study of sacred texts, a practice that is also personal and corporate is an invaluable means of deepening the spiritual life.

Thomas Merton (1915–1968) is one of the best known modern Christians who followed the spiritual pathway of mysticism and contemplation.[17] Born in Paris, experimenting with sensual life-style in his young adult years, Merton had a conversion experience while a student at Columbia University. He joined the Roman Catholic Church, and at the age of 26, he entered Gethsemane Abbey in Kentucky as a Trappist monk. There he devoted himself to the contemplative life, wrote extensively, and in later life explored connections with spiritual leaders in the Buddhist tradition.[18] The life of Thomas Merton and his writing have had a profound influence on those seeking a contemplative spiritual pathway.

A second and closely related pattern of spirituality, based in large measure upon the practices in the contemplative tradition, is the practice of **the holy life**. In this pathway, a choice is made to cultivate the inner life by submission and obedience in response to God's call. It is to have a sense of vocation about dedicating one's life to the cause of God in the world. It is to utilize fully not only the inward disciplines of prayer, meditation, and study, but to practice the outward disciplines of simplicity and purity ("Blessed are the pure in heart, for they shall see God." Mat. 5.8). Whether in solitude or in community, one strives to live with integrity in order to give oneself to the compassionate life of service.[19] It is to sense the call of God to a life set apart for loving mission in a needy world, even if it means the sacrifice of a more normal pattern of life.[20] The life of Ignatius Loyola (1491–1556) and the Jesuit Order which he founded have become a classic paradigm for the holy life devoted to service.[21]

There are many other examples from Christian history of people who have chosen the holy life, and the lives of St. Francis of Assisi (1182–1226) and Dietrich Bonhoeffer[22] (1906–1945) come immediately to mind. I have been profoundly influenced by the model of dedicated service and the gentle, loving spirit in the life of St. Francis. I have also been challenged by the courage of Dietrich Bonhoeffer who dared to resist Hitler and the Nazi movement; events close enough to my time and life to be especially powerful. But it has been the special ministry of Mother Teresa of Calcutta (1910–1997), whose labor of love with the poor and suffering, that has spoken so profoundly to the world. She characteristically writes, "There has not been one single day that we have refused somebody, we did not have food, we did not have a bed or something, and we deal with thousands of people. We have 53,000 lepers and yet never one has been sent away because we did not have. It is always there, though we have no salaries, no income, no nothing, we receive freely and give freely. This has been the beautiful gift of God."[23]

One of the ongoing discussions within the Christian community, in the past and in the present, has been whether the spiritual life is one that is pursued out of one's own will and discipline or whether it is a life that is graced and gifted by God. Nearly all who have conscientiously sought a deeper and more profound spirituality have been inclined to follow the Apostle Paul's teaching to "... work out your own salvation with fear and trembling; for it is God who is at work in you, enabling you both to will and to work for his good pleasure" (Phil. 2.12–13). As John Wesley is often quoted as saying, "Pray like it all depends upon God, and work like it all depends upon you." A third spiritual pattern has emphasized **spiritual empowerment** and has maintained that we are graced and gifted by God for the spiritual life in order to serve the community of faith and minister to the needs of all people. Many of us who have diligently sought to serve God within the Christian tradition have had a strong belief that we cannot live the spiritual life in our own strength, but must place ourselves in the hands of God. It is God who gives us empowering *charismas* or gifts, and it is the Holy Spirit, the very power and presence of God in our lives that enables us to have a spiritual center and follow a spiritual pathway.

No less a person that Paul could say to the Corinthians, "Now there are varieties of gifts, but the same Spirit; and there are varieties of services, but the same Lord; and there are varieties of activities, but it is the same God who activates all of them in everyone. To each is given the manifestation of the Spirit for the common good" (I Cor. 12.4–7). This tradition of dependence upon God for gifts and for the strength to be a true seeker of the spiritual life has come through the Christian family in the teaching of such profound thinkers as Augustine and John Calvin because of their belief that God takes the initiative with humanity and must empower humans because of their sinful nature.[24] In a different kind of way, the same conviction is present in the charismatic movement that has emphasized an outward expression of the Spirit's presence in tongues and an inward gifting in varieties of service and ministry.

A fourth broad category that describes a way of living the spiritual life is that to be truly spiritual, one must engage in the **transformation of the world**, working to build a more just and peaceful world. This approach is based on the conviction that God loves the world and all that is in it, and asks Christians and all followers of God to be better stewards by giving of one's wealth, by caring for the good earth, and by seeking social transformation. It is to engage in making the world more just and humane. What does God require of us, asks the prophet Micah, to which he answers that we are "to act justly and to love mercy and to walk humbly with our God" (Mic. 6.8). This spiritual pathway requires vision and courage, especially as it invites us into the prophetic role and "speaking truth to power." In recent generations, we think of the prophetic ministries Dorothy Day, Martin Luther King, Jr., and Desmond Tutu.[25]

Still another pattern of Christian spirituality is rooted in the **ministry of proclamation**, or the "Evangelical Tradition" of spirituality,[26] language that might suggest an exclusively conservative movement within Christianity, but it is one that goes far beyond the American protestant, evangelical movement. This tradition believes that Word of God that comes to us in Jesus and is preserved for us in normative and life-giving ways in the New Testament must be proclaimed; it is the ministry of *kergyma*.[27] The coming of Jesus is good and joyful news (*evangelion*) for the world, and as those given a spiritual center by this good news, we live out our spiritual lives by sharing the good news with all the peoples of the world with compassion and respect.[28] We think of the worldwide ministry of Billy Graham as the model of the kerygmatic ministry, and

Dr. Graham as a truly spiritual person. But we should also keep in mind the place of those who have used their gifts as scholars to clarify the meaning of God's Word for particular times and cultures.[29]

A final pattern of the spiritual life for Christians is the **incarnational and sacramental** tradition.[30] This "stream" takes us more fully into the Orthodox branch of the larger Christian family, and places the emphasis on making the truth of the living Spirit of God a present reality.[31] God is truly incarnate coming to the human family in Jesus, taking forms in the world around us, and especially so in the religious rites of the Christian church called the sacraments. While the number and the understanding of the sacraments differ in the several ecclesiastic traditions of Christianity, there is in all of them a desire to experience the "nearness, power, and presence" of God, and it is done by discerning and discovering the presence of God in our lives, in our history, and in our world. It is not so much that we take God's love to the world as it is that we discover God's love in the world as we arrive, listen, and watch. In particular, we experience God's presence in those events in the life of the church which are set apart as sacred, and in which we experience the presence of God, or reexperience the redemptive events as in the Eucharist. For many Christians, the Eucharist, often a part of daily spiritual practice becomes the spiritual center and sustains and inspires the spiritual pathway. It is in the church that our spiritual lives are deepened and sustained through worship, celebration, and fellowship. Through holy days and participation in pilgrimage to holy sites, we experience the sacred.

The incarnational and sacramental tradition has taken a slightly different turn in the last several decades by those who have spoken about the goodness of creation. Rather than stressing the sinfulness of humankind, the emphasis has been more on "becoming" all that God intends for us to be. Matthew Fox has spoken directly about "creation spirituality"[32] and others have drawn on the thought of C. G. Jung, the Celtic tradition, and developmental psychology.[33] Holistic and integral spirituality have emerged as ways of affirming the conviction that spirituality must be about body, mind, and spirit.[34]

The contributions and challenges of Christian spirituality

As we make an attempt to summarize and assess the ways that Christian spirituality might contribute to all those who seek a more profound spiritual life and a more peaceful and just world (and the ways that Christianity might have fallen short), we do so knowing that we cannot "say it all." We can only be suggestive, hoping to provoke helpful discussions and questions. Let me suggest, then, in summary form ways that Christianity might be life-giving for all spiritual pilgrims.[35]

1. Christian spirituality brings a strong prophetic voice, urging that one part of the spiritual pathway is that the spiritual person and the community of faith should be concerned about moral and ethical issues and demonstrate tangible concern for the stewardship of the earth, doing justice, and seeking peace. The tone of the prophetic voice varies greatly depending on the ecclesiastical and theological tradition, and the time and place in history, but it has been and continues to be a dominant theme in many of the expressions of Christian spirituality. It is often in the pursuit of peace and justice that one finds common ground with those from other religious traditions.

2. Christian spirituality has also emphasized the need for a life of service, and even sacrifice. To be truly spiritual, the Christian must engage in helping others. The tradition of service was modeled by Jesus, followed by his disciples, and has been central to the Christian understanding of spirituality across the nearly 2000 years of Christian history. In serving others, it is possible to build understanding and trust and, in doing so, to find ways to cross cultures, ethnicities, and religious beliefs and practices.

3. The foundation for helping others is the conviction that we as Christians are to be compassionate and love others even as they have been loved by God in Christ. As Jesus demonstrated unselfish love for all who came into his circle of nearness, so we are to show compassion to those whom we encounter, to live "in the imitation of Christ."[36] It is the expression of unlimited love that we are able to tear down the fences of fear and extend ourselves in constructive ways in the lives of those who differ from us.

4. It follows that a true expression of Christian spirituality is to respect "the other" and all those who differ whether in religions belief, values, language, or culture. It has not always been easy for the Abrahamic religions to be accepting of other religious traditions or of each other. Believing that God loves the world, not just those in my tradition, and that all humans are created in the image of God, the true expression of Christian spirituality is to receive with joy and respect all the people of the earth.

5. Also foundational for Christian spirituality is deep gratitude that with God as our center, we flourish as human beings and those who are moving toward a clear identity, an integral view of reality, a meaningful purpose in life, and a life of inner peace and serenity. Once again, it is possible to meet those in other religious traditions in the practices of prayer, meditation, and the simple life. The Christian faith does have a center; it can change, be accommodating, and meet others at many points and places.

Those of us who "live, and move, and have our being" within the Christian community know all too well the many ways that individual Christians and the Christian church fail as they walk along their spiritual pathways. Let me again just be suggestive, not exhaustive with a list:

1. As with the other monotheistic religions that descend from Abraham, Christianity, believing that the coming of Jesus Christ is the true expression of God's Word, runs the risk of being exclusive. Is it the only way or are there other ways? There exists a large segment of Christians who do judge those who stand outside the Christian faith and find it difficult not to judge, and are often motivated to "preach" to them. It has been all too easy for Christians to say, "We are right and they are wrong." The challenge for all Christians who believe that God "spoke" in the coming of Jesus is to understand that "God so loved the *world*," not just our little group and community of faith. Christians must find a thoughtful articulation and model of God's love for the entire human family, as expressed in Jesus.

2. But there are those within the Christian faith who in fact judge other religions and say that they do not provide a valid spiritual center and life-giving spiritual pathways. It is acceptable to question and to critically assess the ways of others, but it must be done with knowledge and in fairness, always guarding against stereotypical thinking that avoids the hard work of truly understanding. Above all, the risk of demonizing the "other" must be avoided. Such an attitude is divisive and runs all the risks of intolerance, a sectarian spirit, and can become a form of xenophobia.

3. Another tendency of nearly every spiritual tradition and certainly some of the spiritual pathways within Christianity is to be overly preoccupied with one's own spiritual journey, focusing too much on seeking only positive feelings rather than the transformation of the world. Those who seek a deeper spiritual way may forget that the deeper spiritual way leads to loving our neighbor in the Christian tradition. An emotional state, often mistaken for a true spiritual way, may become an end in itself rather than the means to the end of spiritual maturity.

4. Closely tied to the self-preoccupation in some spiritual pathways is the risk of withdrawal from responsible and loving service in the world. At their best, even those who seek the spiritual life in an intentional religious community should do so with the conviction that they are there to serve the purposes of God and pray for the well-being of the world.

5. Finally, I will mention the risk of spiritual *hubris*, believing that we somehow have special access to God and have been exclusively called to carry out the will of God. We all too easily say that others are doing it in the wrong way, with the wrong theology and wrong approaches. The more constructive approach is to understand that the body of Christ is as diverse as human culture, and there are many ways

that are in keeping with the model of Jesus, the biblical witness, and the community of faith. There is the dangerous tendency to claim that the way of my group extends to political ideology as well, a viewpoint manifest in contemporary sectarian movements and in political life.[37]

There are extraordinary resources within the Christian spiritual traditions for being God's partner in building a more just and peaceful world. On this note, we turn our attention to Islam, and will look with care at the ways that spirituality is expressed in the Muslim tradition, knowing that our current global circumstances may place Christians and Muslims in conflict.

Discussion questions

1. How is the teaching of Jesus about spirituality similar and different from the teaching of the Apostle Paul about the spiritual life?
2. In what ways do the teachings of Jesus and Paul urge us to express our spirituality in being responsible in society?
3. Which of the patterns of Christian spirituality are most persuasive and appealing to you?
4. How would you describe your spiritual center and the way it takes form in a spiritual pathway?
5. What do you see as the primary strengths and weaknesses of the Christian approach to the spiritual life as you see it expressed in the world around you?

Key terms and concepts

1. **Kingdom of God:** The reign of God in the sense of the nearness, power, and presence of God.
2. **Mystical:** To seek a direct and unmediated experience of and union with God.
3. **Charismatic:** To be gifted and empowered in a special way by the Spirit of God.
4. **Evangelical:** The emphasis on the evangel or good news of the gospel; also used to describe a movement within the Christian church that is guided by a high view of Scripture and the power of proclamation.
5. **Incarnational:** The ways in which God is present on earth, and in the Christian tradition, the way God was present in the person Jesus Christ.
6. **Sacramental:** An outward and visible sign of an inward reality, as in the Eucharist or baptism.

Suggestions for reference and reading

Bonhoeffer, Dietrich, *Life Together* (New York: Harper & Bothers, 1954).

Borg, Marcus J. and Wright, N. T., *The Meaning of Jesus: Two Visions* (San Francisco: HarperSanFrancisco, 1999).

Foster, Richard J., *Streams of Living Water* (San Francisco: HarperSanFrancisco, 2001). See also the two books of readings, edited by Richard Foster and his colleagues, *Devotional Classics* (San Francisco: HarperSanFrancisco, 1990) and *Spiritual Classics* (San Francisco: HarperSanFrancisco, 2000) which contain selections from many of the great spiritual pilgrims of the Christian church, and therefore I have not listed them in suggested reading.

Fowler, James W., *Stages of Faith: The Psychology of Human Development and the Quest for Meaning* (San Francisco: Harper & Row, 1981).

Merton, Thomas, *Contemplation in a World of Action* (Garden City, NY: Image Books, 1973).

Moore, Thomas, *The Soul's Religion: Cultivating a Profoundly Spiritual Way of Life* (New York: Perennial, 2002).

Spiritual Pathways Within Islam 10

Chapter Outline

The importance of Islam in the contemporary world   177

The narrative of Islam   179

Islamic beliefs and practices   183

The history and development of Islam   190

Radical Islam   194

Summary and assessment   200

The importance of Islam in the contemporary world

We now turn to Islam, the third religion in the triad of Abrahamic monotheistic religions. Islam[1] is rooted in the belief in one personal transcendent God (called in Islam "Allah") who intervenes in the affairs of the human family. It shares this belief with Judaism and Christianity, and therefore rightly belongs in the same category of religious understanding. Even the Quran speaks about the three religions as "the Peoples of the Book" acknowledging common beliefs and practices. But it is equally true that each of these religions in their own distinctive ways have understood this core belief about one God in different ways, more in accord with the history and culture of their founding and development. It is the historical narrative that gives the distinctive character to each of these religious traditions.

The broad outlines of Judaism and Christianity are familiar in the west and these religions are generally accepted as part of the religious context. Islam, whose origins and development were more in the Arab world, is not as fully understood, and in some cases even feared because of the events of our recent history. Our goals in this chapter are to enable an increased understanding and appreciation of Islam, and in so doing, overcome some of the ignorance and misunderstandings that have led to unacceptable stereotyping and even demonizing of a religion that has provided most its over one billion followers healthy and life-giving spiritual pathways.

Islam has become one of the most important movements within the contemporary world. There are many reasons for this increased importance, reasons that need to be understood by all who have responsibility for shaping the human future. For our purposes, we might speak about the increased importance of Islam by noting that Islam is attempting **to accommodate to the modern world**. The dominant theme of contemporary Islam is *resurgence* as it struggles over issues of identity, faith, culture, and practice.[2]

As Islam engages in this accommodation to the modern world, it impacts the rest of world, in part because it is a truly global religion, one that has followers in nearly every corner of the world.[3] It also engages the rest of the world because the fundamental teaching of Islam is that **it is a total way of life**. It deals comprehensively with personal, spiritual, and social transformation. In fact, there is very little separation of the sacred and secular within Islam, and so the resurgence is not just in a segment of life that is deemed as religious practice, but a resurgence of a total worldview. As it attempts to rearticulate this worldview and then to act upon it, this action inevitably, even dramatically intersects with other worldviews in the non-Muslim world.

Most of the world has viewed the more extreme side of this endeavor as expressed in the policies and actions of al Qaeda, the network of Muslim radicals that have acted violently against those judged to be enemies of the Arab world.[4] The people of the world have experienced, observed, or been informed about the many terrorist attacks on targets around the world, and most have etched in their hearts and minds the attack on the United States on September 11, 2001. Many have been informed as well about the Taliban movement in Afghanistan that is attempting to reshape Afghanistan into the mode of a conservative Islamic state. As a result of these actions, there have been defensive measures taken by several governments and strong resistance to the "jihadist" movement within Islam in many parts of the world.

The resurgence movement within Islam should not be viewed as a statement that Islam was a dormant religion, one that was fading away because it no longer met the needs of its followers. Nor should it be viewed as exclusively a radical movement targeting the presence of "imperial forces" in the Arab world, such as the presence of the United States and its allies in Iraq and Afghanistan, or the policies and practices of what they would call the "Zionist Israeli" government against the Palestinian people. While many Arab Muslims may question the policies that led to these conditions, they have also sought to be a full partner in the global economy and world diplomacy. The Muslim accommodation to the modern world has seen an increase in emphasis on religious observances and the formation of new associations committed to nurturing spiritual practices that guide people who are attempting to follow the "straight path"[5] in secular societies. There has also been sincere attempts to reach across the religious divide to Christians, Jews, and others in an attempt to understand one another, to find common ground, and to collaborate in the building of a more livable, just, and peaceful society.[6] With the critical importance of Islam in mind, we turn to a brief study of Islam and begin with its founding and development in our effort to understand more fully and appreciate more profoundly this extraordinary global religion.

The narrative of Islam

In relation to many of the other great religions of the world, Islam is relatively young, having been founded in the early seventh century of the Common Era. But, like Christianity, it has spread well beyond its beginnings in the Arabian Peninsula; it is global in character, and there are Muslim communities in all parts of the world with concentrations in the Middle East, South Asia, and Indonesia. Remarkably, these worldwide communities have continued a common pattern of religious and social life based on the teachings of Islam. To be sure, there is diversity within Islam, divisions that occurred early in its development, and of course the diversity that comes from development over centuries in different historical circumstances and cultures.[7]

The religion had its beginning in the Arabian Peninsula, a region populated by nomadic peoples called Bedouins who traveled by caravan to different Arab cities primarily for trade. These traveling tribal Bedouins would have gone north and encountered two of the major civilizations of the time, the Byzantine

and the Persian Sassanian empires. To the south was the ancient Arab civilization in Yemen, and within the peninsula, there were several urban centers of
trade. Among the most important of these centers was Mecca where the trade
caravans came, not just to trade and to find supplies for their travels, but to
make a spiritual pilgrimage, honoring the religious traditions of their tribe.
There was in Mecca a sense of finding a shared religious, cultural, and linguistic heritage, as business was conducted with the merchants of the city.

It was in such a setting that Muhammad, the Prophet of Islam, was born in
about 570 CE.[8] The Muslim narrative, to some extent shrouded in pious legend,
has framed an account of the major events in the life of Muhammad that provide a picture of the man, his mission, and his impact on the Arab society of his
time.[9] The early years of Muhammad's life were marred by the death of both
his parents and his grandfather who had come to take care of him. His father,
Abd Allah, a member of the Hashim clan of the Quaraysh tribe died before he
was born, his mother when he was six, and his grandfather just two years later.
Muhammad was brought up by his paternal uncle, Abu-Talib, who had become
the head of the clan and would later defend Muhammad as he launched the
new religion.

As a young man, Muhammad became active in the community's commercial life, and he was trusted as a dependable and conscientious person, even
given the nickname of al-Amin (the Trustworthy). At the age of 23, Muhammad
married Khadijah, a wealthy widow 15 years his senior. It was Khadijah who
proposed after observing Muhammad as her commercial agent. The marriage
gave Muhammad some economic advantages, but it was also a marriage of
love. It was Khadijah who supported Muhammad when he first had doubts
about the validity of his religious calling, and he took no other wife while she
lived and was emotionally devastated by her death. Later Muslim tradition
honored Khadijah as the ideal woman, placing her on the level of Mary, the
mother of Jesus. There were several children in the marriage, but only one
survived him, Fatima, his daughter.

The record is not altogether clear, but evidently Muhammad was deeply
troubled during his youth and young adulthood. Prior to the time that he
began to preach publicly in Mecca, he had become alienated from the traditional religion of his clan and tribe. He became estranged from his religious
heritage in large measure because it did not address the prevailing conflicts
and injustices nor did it provide the means to reduce the lack of security for
the people that existed in his society. In time, he would speak out boldly against
what he considered to be an unenlightened religion. As a result of his exposure

to both Judaism and Christianity, Muhammad became persuaded that God had spoken in the past to inspired prophets revealing the truth about the one God, the way of life expected by God, and the judgment of those who do not follow the straight path of God.

Given his disillusionment, Muhammad began to withdraw from society to reflect, meditate, and pray. He went to a cave in Mount Hira, and it was there that he received his first revelation. The revelations would continue and ultimately, as they were recorded by his followers, would become the heart of the Quran. At this time Muhammad was 40 years old, and it was this experience that set the course for the remainder of his life. There were times when he doubted his calling and did not receive the divine communications. Then, new revelations came to him, resolving all of his doubts about their source. At first, he was reluctant to speak openly about these experiences, but in about 613 CE, he felt compelled to proclaim his message to the people.

The message about Allah was not altogether new to Muhammad's contemporaries, but some teachings were new such as his central message of radical monotheism, the themes about judgment and the future life, and his own place in the proclamation as the definitive Prophet of Allah. In regard to radical monotheism, Muhammad spoke against the worship of many gods, a form of idolatry (*shirk*) that he saw as one of the most obvious expressions of the spiritual malady of his time. Later, the Quran, reflecting the Prophet's views would very explicitly condemn the worship of many deities and polytheism. For Muhammad, nothing could take the place of God, and all of life must be organized around this central belief. God is the Creator and provides guidance for the meaning and purpose of life.

Muhammad also preached against wealth for its own sake, which he considered to be one of the primary idols of his culture, and he called on his followers to share their wealth and be generous with others in need. In addition, he attacked the idol of the tribe and kinship, but while doing so, he was careful to always honor the place of family. He said that traditions of tribe and kinship should not have control over the individual and each person's relationship with God. What matters most is the response of each person to the claims of God. He also preached against the very way of life he saw around him, a life that he considered to be a frenzied quest for fulfilling all of one's ambitions and dreams within the normal course of worldly affairs. He countered with the message that one who has faith in Allah can find peace of mind and spirit, even within the fast pace and challenges of life. The challenges and changes of time cannot take away the peace that comes from faith in and obedience to Allah; all who live with the promise of God can enjoy the world without being solely attached to it.

The first convert to the new faith was Muhammad's wife, Khadijah. The next converts were his cousin, a boy named Ali, and another close relative, Abu Bakr. Muhammad's uncle and one-time guardian, Abu-Talib, was unable to give up his traditional ways with their belief in several deities, in spite of his love for his nephew. Abu-Talib, as mentioned, defended Muhammad as his tribe turned against him. It was not long before he had many followers in Mecca, primarily from the lower classes.

Nor was it long before there was resistance to the message of Muhammad, especially from those in power and with wealth. They feared this new religion because it undermined their authority and might even threaten Mecca's trade and influence. It also went directly against the way leadership was chosen, violated tribal customs, and challenged the established *sunnah* (traditions) which included polytheism. His own tribe, the Quraysh, attempted to redirect Muhammad by inviting him into the circle of leadership, but Muhammad refused, and in time his own community turned against him.

A turning point for Muhammad come in 619 CE when his wife, Khadijah died, followed by the death of his uncle. These were deep personal losses, and coupled with the resistance from his tribe, it became difficult for Muhammad to continue his work in Mecca. He decided to leave Mecca for another city called Yathrib, later to be named Medina, an agricultural center that lacked cohesion because of tribal conflict. The people of Medina were open to a new definition of the human community and sought the help of Muhammad. He reached Medina in September of 622[10] and began his work. He had many followers that formed a supportive community (*ummah*), but their faith and commitment was not fully formed, and he had only limited political authority. His message was not totally accepted in the region as yet, and he knew that he must bring new strategy and commitment to his cause.

Gradually, as his power and influence progressed in Medina, he believed that his mission should expand, and he began to see political, economic, and military power as having a religious form and purpose. He did not want to claim this power in itself, but saw it as a means of creating **a total community embodying his religious worldview**. In time Muslims would come to believe that military, political, and economic leverages are historical forces and that history belongs to God. Muhammad began a series of attacks on the Meccan traders, and a victory in 624 was a major turning point. There were other victories, and by 628, his authority in Medina was consolidated. He attempted to negotiate peace with Mecca, but these negotiations broke down and he resorted to military action and captured Mecca in 630. He entered Mecca in triumph (known in Islam as The Final Pilgrimage), and many of his former enemies were converted to Islam. He returned to Medina, cared for his home and wives, and then died unexpectedly. The new religion was faced with the difficult task of establishing the leadership that would follow Muhammad.

At the time of his death, Muhammad had established his authority across the Arabian Peninsula, and the expansionist tendencies of the new religion were firmly in place. He had achieved enormous personal power as the prophet and leader of the new religion of Islam, a religion that had authority in the state as well as in the religious life. What was emerging was the conviction that the state's basic function was to protect and defend the faith of the people, a logical inference from the belief that all of life is under God's sovereign reign.

It was not long after his death that Muslim scholars began collecting material on his life. This material, called the *hadith*, consisted of a collection of accounts about what he did and said, transmitted by his companions and members of his family. The traditions, tested by scholars for authenticity, were passed on to succeeding generations, and they became a source of values for the ideal Muslim way of life. They were called the *Sunnah*, meaning the customs and practices of the Prophet.

Muhammad's practice of prayer and devotion to God; his role as husband and parent; his example of humility, compassion, and justice; his acts of kindness to children, orphans, the disadvantaged, and animals all served as a model for proper conduct. It is this pattern of life that has the greatest impact on the ordinary lives of Muslims.[11] Imitation of the Prophet's life represents the spiritual pathway of the faithful Muslim. He is not thought of as divine (and there is a special emphasis on this teaching), but venerated because of his godly way of life. Above all, he is honored because he is the great and final Prophet, the recipient of God's revelation, enshrined for all time in the revelation contained in the Quran.[12]

Islamic beliefs and practices

It is the Quran (meaning "recitation") that is viewed by Muslims as the final and complete revelation that God gave to Muhammad. It is truly a "holy" book, in some ways even more authoritative for Muslims than the Hebrew Bible for Jews and the New Testament for Christians. The divinely inspired revelation came to Muhammad in Arabic and it is thought that it must be read in Arabic in order to understand fully the divine message. Muslims believe that Muhammad was instrumental in both the revelations contained in the Quran and in shaping the text. The revelation came to him over a period of 22 years, often in very dramatic experiences. As Muhammad would have these experiences, often in the form of visions, he would "recite" them to his followers, some of whom would memorize what was said, and then later scribes would put it into writing. By the time of Muhammad's death, the Quran was essentially written, often memorized by faithful followers, and then recited for the people.

The Quran is divided into 114 chapters; each one is called a *surah*, and then into verses called an *aya*. After a short opening *surah*, the chapters are arranged according to length with the longest ones coming first. The chapters have titles and begin with the affirmation, "In the name of God, most Gracious, most Merciful." The Quran is meant to be recited, and the hearing helps Muslim incorporate the teachings into their lives. The topics include all aspects of belief and daily living, and the words of the Quran are recited with the goal of enabling them to live in the hearts and minds of believers as they seek to be obedient to Allah. The Quran, over time, has had an enormous influence in the Arab world. It has shaped the Arabic language and has been the starting point for the Muslim search for knowledge. In many ways, it is the heart of all Muslim scholarship.[13]

The fundamental beliefs and practices of Islam are drawn from the Quran.[14] We turn first to those beliefs that are regarded as foundational for all Muslims, regardless of historical circumstances or branches of the tradition. These beliefs demand more than merely intellectual consent, but also a commitment to action as expressed in Five Pillars of practice. The first belief is *Tawid*, **the unity or oneness of God**. The concept emphasizes the radical monotheism of Islamic teaching, stating the Allah is transcendent and absolute Reality.

> And your God is One God,
> There is no God but Him,
> the most Gracious, the most Merciful. (Surah 2.163)

This position allows for no polytheism or divisions within the Godhead. Neither can there be any hint of equality of another being with God, such as son or daughter or spouse. To suggest that there is such a being is the ultimate form of shirk or idolatry and is the only unforgivable sin a person can commit.

The belief in God goes beyond just the statement of God's unity; it affirms as well that the universe is created by and contingent upon the will of God. Every creature and inanimate object inherently "knows" its dependence and that it is to be obedient and serve its Maker. All that exists has a place in the divine plan that reaches from the beginning to the end of time.

A second foundational belief in Islam is that **God communicates with His creation** through messengers who have come to make His will known, though the great line of prophets, and through the revelation contained in the Quran. Part of this communication comes in the form of angels and other celestial beings (*jinn*) that are an integral part of the structures of existence. Celestial beings, the prophetic witness, and the Quran are closely connected, standing under God who is transcendent, even at times shrouded from the gaze of even the highest angels and the jinn. The basic function of angels is to be Allah's messengers to humans, and Gabriel has a special place as the angel of light who bestowed the revelation on Muhammad. In addition to heavenly beings, there are many prophets and messengers who have been sent by God to communicate with humankind. These include Noah, Abraham, Moses, and Jesus whose messages were sent by God, although Jews in the case of Moses and Christians in the case of Jesus misunderstood the message. God eventually spoke through Muhammad who is regarded as the "Seal of the Prophets" (*Surah* 33.40) and whose message recorded in the Quran is infallible and divinely inspired.

A third foundational belief is that **God is Creator of all that is**. He created the universe and gave order and pattern to nature with each element in balance with the others. He created the angels, the jinn, and the unseen. The function of these beings is to carry out the will of Allah, to protect and pray for forgiveness for creatures on earth, and to undertake errands on behalf of God. Those most honored among God's creation are human beings who are endowed with a greater capacity to know and respond to God. Humans are special in that they have a choice that enables them to either fulfill their potential as the most honored among God's creation or sink to the lowest level away from God by disobeying or denying Him. Even angels were asked to bow down to Adam, and one refused who became Iblis or Satan, who now attempts to lead humans away from God.

Still another foundational teaching of Islam, following from the belief in the creation of human beings by a transcendent and sovereign God is **the belief in the final judgment and the place of divine decree and predestination**. The Quran clearly teaches that human beings should create a just society, show mercy toward others, be persons of integrity in fulfilling all promises, and be obedient in following the straight path of Islam. It also teaches that God is both just and merciful, and that all creatures, humans, and jinn are accountable to God whose will reaches through eternity. The Doctrine of the Final Judgment places all human activities and institutions under the scrutiny and law of God. No deed or organization will escape divine inspection and decision, and, while no one knows the final outcome, all know that they will be judged by God who is both just and merciful.

Muslims find a certain measure of comfort in accepting and submitting to the judgment of God. They know that the eternal will of God will be done. This affirmation, however, does raise the questions inherent in the belief in divine providence and predestination. Does God both know and determine what will happen to the eternal destiny of humans? Do humans really have the freedom to determine their destiny by living in obedience to the will of God? Or has God already chosen those who will go to heaven? Is it possible that God allows even those events that are evil and harmful? There are clear teachings in the Quran that speak of God's foreknowledge and that all will ultimately conform to the will of God. But in the case of the eternal destiny of human beings, throughout the Quran there is the clear teaching that all have the opportunity to hear and respond to the message, to do good works, to worship properly, and to become Muslims. There are also teachings in the Quran that attribute some evil and suffering to evil beings. But questions remain, and the answers to these questions are sought, studied, and debated by Muslim scholars. At the end of the day, Islam shares with the other monotheistic religions all the questions of theodicy.[15]

A final foundational belief in Islam is the *ummah* or **the community of faith**.[16] The Quran regards individuals as part of a community in which all of the values and goals within Islam can be practiced and realized. The tradition teaches that this ideal community was first achieved in Medina, and that succeeding generations must work to achieve the same kind of community that encourages righteousness and forbids evil. (*Surah* 3.110) The *ummah* is the embodiment of the type of behavior expected by individuals and society, and as such serves as a model for other human societies. The model of the Muslim community in Medina becomes a turning point in Muslim history, since it marks the transition from a state in which they could not give full expression in society to their Islamic norms to one in which these norms can be fully present as the basis of the social, political, and moral order. This conviction, present today in Islamic societies, raises questions about the role of Islamic law (*shariah*) as the basis of the social order of the state. At stake are the rights of minorities and the place of democracy in less homogeneous and more secular countries, an issue to which we will return.[17]

These five beliefs lead to the foundational practices of Islam, to the heart of the spiritual pathways of the Muslim people. These practices, known as the Five Pillars of Islam, anchor human relationships with God and with others within the *ummah*. They are stated succinctly, clearly, and practically so that all can understand and apply these practices in daily life. The Pillars are regarded as the minimal acts of worship and form the direct linkage with the worldwide community (*ummah* or umma). They are viewed as interrelated parts that constitute the essence of being a devout Muslim; and they are eminently doable.

The first, called the *Shahadah*, is the act of professing one's faith or bearing witness that **there is no god but God and that Muhammad is the messenger of God**. Traditionally, a parent will whisper this affirmation and the call to prayer in the ears of the newborn, and on dying, a person says it as the last words of life. Saying the Shahadah with deep sincerity and devotion is the act by which one is truly converted and formally becomes a Muslim. It is the full acknowledgement that God is the God of all who must be worshipped and obeyed. This was fully revealed to Muhammad and is now in the divine words of the Quran.

The second Pillar or fundamental practice of Islam is *Salat*, **the five daily obligatory prayers said facing the *Ka'bah*,** the sacred cubicle in Mecca. There are other prayers which represent individual attempts to draw near to God in a personal relationship, but the practice of Salat is foundational. Muslims may pray at any time, but the traditional times for ritual prayer are dawn, noon, afternoon, sunset, and late evening. Muslims are urged to join with others, particularly for the Friday congregational ritual prayer at noon. Salat is preceded by an act of ablution in which Muslims purify themselves. The cleansing is comprehensive and facilities are provided for this cleansing in all mosques and in many public places. Where water is unavailable, sand or stone may be used for symbolic cleansing. The act of ablution links water as the symbol of purity to the idea of prayer as the means of purification of the soul. The ritual of cleansing is therefore inseparable from the ritual of prayer itself, reflecting a commitment to the total state of outer and inner purity.

The Salat generally begins with a call to prayer often done from the minarets that are part of the mosque. There is an individual trained to guide in prayer, called an imam, and as worship begins, the people are gathered behind him in straight rows, all facing in the direction of Mecca. The prayer consists of two to four parts, depending on the time, and includes the recitation from the first chapter of the Quran:

> In the name of Allah, most Gracious, most Merciful
> All praise is due to Allah, the Lord of the Worlds
> The Most Gracious, the most Merciful,
> Lord of the Day of Judgment.
> You alone we worship
> and from You alone we seek help
> Guide us on the right path,
> the path of those on whom you have bestowed grace,
> not of those with whom you have been displeased,
> nor those who have gone astray. (Surah 1.1–7)

There is a rhythmic pattern to the ritual, complete with movement and posture, thought to be based on the example of Muhammad.[18]

The third Pillar is *Zakat*, **obligatory annual alms-giving**. The purpose of this giving is primarily to help the needy, but it is also thought of as purification through sharing. The word Zakat means "purification" and suggests that the act of sharing involves making one's wealth and property pure. There is an annual "tax" that is expected to be paid by all Muslims who have an income from any source. It is calculated on the value of the person's property and may vary from 10 percent of the value of the first fruit crops and animals to 2.5 percent of the end-of-the year value of merchandise, cash, and other wealth. In some Muslim countries, the government collects and distributes the Zakat to the poor. Where this is not practiced, the Zakat is generally given to the mosque or a recognized Muslim charity in order to be distributed. The usual priorities for giving are local, and the money goes to the unemployed or the ill. It may also be given to Muslim prisoners of war, especially those who are incarcerated for their faith. The contributions are generally made during the month of Ramadan and represent an act of thanksgiving for the gift of the Quran by God through Muhammad. Through the Zakat, there is a way for those who are needy within the umma to maintain and preserve their dignity.[19] In essence, the Zakat is a key element in redressing the imbalance of wealth and poverty.

The fourth Pillar of Islam is *Ramadan*, **the month of fasting**. Even as Muslims find a pattern in the day for prayer, so too do they find patterns in the year, with the ninth month as time for specially honoring God. The fast is expected of all Muslims who are past puberty, except for those who are pregnant or ill. It extends from the time in the morning that a person is able to distinguish between white and black threads until sunset. During the day, the individual neither eats nor drinks, nor takes medication unless it is required, abstains from kissing and sexual activity, and avoids frivolity such as games and loud music. The purpose is to go through the day with a special awareness of God's closeness. Following the sunset prayer, Muslims gather in family and friendship groups for a meal. The additional purpose of the Ramadan fasting is that it enables the believer to focus on being thankful for God's generosity toward creation and humanity and to acknowledge God's grace in sending the revelation of the Quran through Muhammad. There is great festivity at the close of Ramadan with a celebration called "*Id al Fitr*," a time of celebrating, feasting, and sharing.[20]

The final Pillar of Islam is *the Hajj* **or the pilgrimage to the sacred places of Islam** in and around Mecca.[21] This obligation is for Muslims at least once in their lifetime if they are healthy enough to travel and are financially able to travel. It takes place on the last month, The Month of *Hajj*, in the Muslim year. The occasion really begins before travel, as the pilgrim prepares emotionally and spiritually for the pilgrimage. When the pilgrim arrives in the vicinity of Mecca, they are said to enter into a state called *irhan* or sacredness. This is done by putting on two seamless garments for the men, and a simple modest gown and head covering for the women. In this state, the pilgrims refrain from shaving hair, cutting nails, and wearing jewelry. More importantly, they abstain from acts of violence, hunting, and sexual relations. In this purified state, the pilgrims are ready to make a commitment to fulfill the various duties of the pilgrimage. At the heart of the pilgrimage is the visit to the sanctuary of the Ka'bah, the small structure with a black stone that is associated with Abraham and Ishmael. Tradition holds that Hager lived adjacent to the Ka'bah, and it represents the physical axis of the Muslim world, the direction to which all Muslims turn in prayer, and the symbol of human encounter with the divine.

It is important to mention another component of Islamic practice called **jihad** in that the word has now crossed over into a kind of universal language. The concept of jihad in its more basic form is thought of as the effort, endeavor, and *struggle* to sustain the spiritual or straight path of Islam. A secondary meaning of jihad is that it is a sacred struggle against unbelievers, and it is this connotation of jihad that has motivated the more radical elements of Islam. It is not viewed as one of the Five Pillars, but it has become a practice that has impacted the world.

The history and development of Islam

It is beyond the purpose of this brief chapter to give an account of the historical development of Islam, but reference to some established patterns of life,
divisions within Islam, and new modes of thought within Islam will add to
the understanding of the ways that Muslims attempt to follow the straight path
of Islam. The **established patterns of life** in Muslim society developed in
reference to the concept of ummah, the setting in which Muslims practice
their faith. There is a strong sense of community within Islam, one that gives
Muslims a feeling of belonging to God and to each other. In addition to the
ways that the umma meets for ritual observance, the Quranic and Islamic
tradition provides within the community a framework within which the daily
human interactions are defined and guided. It is within the umma that Islam
can be said to address the totality of human life and to provide guidance for
social, political, economic, and moral issues. A word that is used in the Quran
to define this comprehensive understanding of the Muslim way of life is din,
often translated as "religion." The *din* is the way that Muslims are to respond to
God's will in all the dimensions of life, to follow the straight path as individual
Muslims, but also to organize society according to the will of God.

The key concept in the ways that society is to be organized is shariah,
a word that is often translated as "law," but which has the connotation of the
total sum of duties and obligations within the umma. It was not long after
the death of Muhammad that Islam spread outside of the Arabian Peninsula
and it became necessary to find a way to organize this expansion and create
Muslim societies in the new regions where the faith had spread. Within a hun-
dred years after the death of the Prophet, the area under Muslim rule stretched
from the Atlantic to India, including most of what was under the former
Byzantine and Sassanian rule. It was a vast region, needing consolidation and
Islamization.

Following the death of Muhammad, all the territories were ruled from
Medina by the successors of Muhammad called Caliphs. The early Muslim
community believed that strong leadership was necessary to ensure the continuity, preservation, and the spread of the Islamic message. Following the first
generation of the Caliphs, honored in the tradition as model rulers, a series of
Muslim dynasties were established to rule the conquered territories. As these
Muslim rulers gained control, the people in the regions were given a choice of
converting to Islam or remaining within their own traditions. Those who did

not convert were protected under Muslim rule, but the mission to make the territories Muslim in character was consistently practiced. Islamic institutions were formed that would govern the lives of the people. A common pattern of institutions, laws, and rules were formed, based on the Quran and the Sunnah. These patterns of order became known as the shariah which essentially defined the nature of the Muslim state. At the social and personal level, it provided rules and regulations affecting economic, social, and family life. It spoke specifically to the religious duties of Muslims and to the laws governing the society. Organized systems of courts and judges became a part of the structure of the community.

In time, the notion of an ideal city, governed by the principles of shariah guided the formation of the new Muslim communities. These new cities, by definition, were cities of God, with a central place of worship. As these patterns of socialization and societal structures developed, cities were formed with the mosque in the center of city. It was not long before the mosque became the place of learning as well. Radiating from the center of the city were the streets, shops (bazaars), centers for artisans, and other commercial centers. All members of the city were provided guidance by shariah, with prohibitions about dress, diet, and social interaction. Shariah provided the "map" for the affairs of the city. Family life in the residential region of city was also controlled by the norms of shariah; for example, there were laws securing the rights of women, laws about marriage,[22] and laws that governed system of seclusion of women (*purdah*) and veiling (*hijab, burqa, or chador*)[23] which symbolized the ideal of protecting intimacy and privacy. Governance under the legal system of shariah is one of the central issues of contention in Islamic countries in that it may not have fully accounted for the non-Muslim population. The reverse situation is present today in the west, as Muslim communities exist as minorities in countries with different systems of law and order.[24]

Divisions within Islam began early following the death of Muhammad. Differences arose over the question of authority within the community. In that there were no prophets, the questions centered on how the community could continue to implement the teachings of the Quran and the ideals of the Prophet, and which person was most capable of leading such a community. Some Muslims felt that Abu Bakr, a respected early convert to Islam and father-in-law of the Prophet was best suited to this responsibility. This position prevailed, and Abu Bakr became known as Caliph, the term that is now used to designate the head of the Muslim umma. Following his death, others succeeded him, with Ali, the husband of Fatima, eventually becoming the head of the Muslim community in 656. This period including the life of the Prophet is often thought of as the "golden age" of Islam.

It was not long, however before there was conflict, with challenges to the leadership of the Ummah. A group in Syria, known as the *Kharijites*, revolted against Ali, and ultimately had him assassinated. Only a small group from this faction remains. The two largest and most important groups who had their differences are the Shia (or Shi'a, Shii, or Shiite) and the Sunni. They differed on the issues of succession, authority, and the interpretation of the Quran.

The Shia (meaning "followers") movement maintained that Ali was the one best suited to lead the ummah after the death of the Prophet. They believed that he was the one selected by Muhammad to lead in both the affairs of state and those of faith.[25] Soon, he came to represent a new order called Imamah (from the Arabic word iman meaning leader). This new institution was to continue the responsibility of spreading the Islamic message and assuring that the message would be rightly interpreted. It was through the succession of Ali and Fatima (Muhammad's daughter) that leadership would be selected with the authority for succession resting with the current imam.

The Imam was said to have divinely endowed knowledge and the capacity to provide spiritual leadership, thus claiming that the Iman is divinely inspired although not a prophet. In time, Shia thought developed the view that a true understanding of the Quran was more than merely a literal reading of the text. There was also an inner dimension in the Quranic verses that could be understood through the teachings of the Imams. This mode of interpretation influenced the development of philosophical and mystical thought in Islam, and the Imam, though constantly challenged, contributed a great deal to the developing sciences of law, philosophy, and theology. In time, there were divisions within Shia, and even charges of heresy as esoteric interpretations of the Quran were articulated.[26]

The Sunnis represent the majority of Muslims, and as implied by their name, the Sunnah has central significance for them. Conformity to past tradition and practice is the cornerstone of the Sunni understanding of Islam. These Sunnis became defined over the questions of authority and practice that had given risen to the early divisions. Sunni thought developed in reaction to the divisions, and they believed that unity could be achieved by elaborating the evolving shariah. They developed a means of resolving conflicts by appealing to consensus and the argument from analogy. In matters of disagreement, scholars should gather, discuss the issues, and arrive at a consensus position, and this process is sufficient to establish the validity of a practice in shariah. These decisions could be reached by drawing an analogy with other comparable issues already established in shariah. This would allow them to reach a resolution on issues that were not specifically addressed in the Quran. As way leads upon way, schools of thought developed regarding these practices, and four major schools of thought in Sunni law emerged.[27]

Within both the Shia and Sunni branches of Islam, a number of smaller groups developed, often driven by a particular issue or a strong desire to express a more authentic form of Islam. In many cases, these groups developed in the context of Islam's contact with other cultures and religions. The family trees are somewhat complex, but we might mention one group that grew out of the Sunni tradition and has been influential in the expression of Islam in modern day Saudi Arabia. It is the movement known as Wahhabism that grew out of the life and mission of Muhammad Ibn Abd al-Wahhab who was born in 1703. He was exposed to other religious traditions and practices within Islam that he believed were not in keeping with the Prophet's intentions. These practices related to appropriate ritual, honoring the dead, and intercessory prayer. The importance of this conservative movement is seen in the ways it has influenced the resurgence of radical Islam and leaders of radical Islam such as Osama bin Laden.[28]

The spiritual pathways of modern day Muslims fall within this broad range of teaching, traditions, branches, cultures, and customs. They accept the beliefs and practices of their particular community, and most Muslims would be less concerned with the historical shifts and theological differences than with following the "straight path" taught in the Quran and modeled by Muhammad. Some, however, have followed **new directions of thought**, wanting a faith that is more reflective, able to integrate reason and revelation and incorporate the patterns of contemporary intellectual thought. Others, while honoring ritual practice, want a faith that "moves the heart" and "touches the soul." Islam in a quite remarkable way has provided pathways for Muslims who want these dimensions within their religious life.

As the Muslim empire expanded, it came in close contact with cultures that had long-established intellectual roots. The most important of these were in the Mediterranean world, Persia, and India. Under the patronage of various rulers, academies were established in which translations were of scientific and philosophical works from Greek, Pahlavi (the language of Iran), and Sanskrit. Because of these academies, there developed within Islam an intellectual tradition that undertook a study of these sources and created a new synthesis that would incorporate, modify, and further develop this intellectual tradition. The result was that there is an extraordinary tradition of philosophical thought within Islam, going back to these early attempts to place Islamic thought in the framework of Greek philosophy in particular. It was this tradition within Islam, perhaps more than in the west that really preserved these great intellectual resources. Many of the works of these great Muslim scholars were read well beyond the Islamic world. For example, in the Middle Ages, there were many great teachers, such as Avicenna (*d*. 1061) and Averroes (*d*. 1198), who worked extensively with the thought of Plato and Aristotle. From the great changes in the Enlightenment into present, Muslim scholars have produced a broad range of credible formulations of Islamic thought.[29]

The Sufi movement has offered Muslims a more mystical tradition, ways of cultivating the inner life in search of divine love and knowledge.[30] The roots of this more devotional tradition lay in some the early Muslims' experience of the Quran and their desire to understand the nature of the Prophet's religious experience. The Sufi movement has employed vivid imagery to describe their quest for religious meaning. The poet Rumi (*d*.1273) whose *Mathnawi* is considered one of the great classics of Sufi literature began his work by citing the analogy of the flute, made out of reeds that are torn apart and long to return to unity. The central image of the flute mirrors the yearning of the soul that has been separated from God. The movement began with a simple longing to be one with God, and it developed into a system of mystical orders centering on the teachings of a leader.

Radical Islam

The movement of radical Islam, not always understood and often feared and criticized has similarities to other ideologies that advocate a fundamental change in the direction of history. Laurent Murawiec, in his recent book, *The Mind of Jihad*,[31] argues that contemporary jihad is a religious cult of violence and power. He maintains that all jihadi groups, whether Shiite (Shia) or Sunni, Arab or not, are driven by a militant ideology. He compares contemporary jihad to medieval millenarians and apocalyptics, claiming that they both share a Gnostic frame of reference; that they believe themselves to be the Elect, secretly endowed with a God-given mission that places them above the universal laws of humankind. Therefore they are justified in using the strategies of terror and violence over the West and most of the world in order to bring their eschatological dream into reality. The attack on New York and other parts of the United States on September 11, 2001 was thoroughly justified given their assumptions.

What are those assumptions? It might be well to try to list them, placing them in the context of Islamic revivalism.[32] Islamic scholar, John Esposito speaks about a more moderate form of Islamic revivalism and a more radical form that necessitates violent revolution. He lists the following beliefs as foundational for the more moderate form of Islamic revivalism:

1. Islam has a worldview that is comprehensive in scope and includes all aspects of life including social structures, legal systems, and political strategies.
2. What has happened gradually across time is the failure of Muslim societies to follow the straight path of Islam. Muslim societies have yielded to the temptation to follow Western values which are basically secular and materialistic in character.
3. What is necessary now is a return to the straight path of Islam, a comprehensive reformation that incorporates the teachings of the Quran and the inspiration of the profound changes made at the founding of Islam by Prophet Muhammad.
4. This reformation will restore God's rule and bring into society a system based on Islamic law which is the only acceptable social structure for Muslim societies.
5. The rejection of Western values and systems does not imply that Muslim society should not endorse the great advances made in science, technology, and communication. Modernization is in fact necessary for Muslim society.
6. The revival of Islam will require new strategies for implementation that should include small groups and associations dedicated to these ideals. These groups must undertake the struggle (jihad) against all forms of government that violate Islamic values and ultimately lead to corruption and social injustice.

John Esposito also proposes a list of fundamental commitments that are made by the more radical activists who maintain that a violent revolution is necessary:

1. There has been a Crusader mentality linked with neocolonialism in the West coupled with the Zionism in Israel, and together this alliance has been at war with the Islamic world.
2. It is necessary for all Muslims to commit to the formation of an Islamic system of government, based on the Quran and Islamic law.
3. Any governments even if they are in predominately Muslim countries that do not follow the Islamic law (*shariah*) are guilty of disobedience and unbelief and are no longer Muslim. They are essentially atheists and must be resisted with holy war.
4. Opposition may even be necessary against the formal religious establishment (*ulama*), and the state-support mosques and their clerics whose loyalty to the straight path is in doubt and who have yielded to the demands of the government.

5. The struggle (jihad) against all those who are unfaithful is a religious mandate. All true believers must rally to the cause and resist unbelievers of the true way. It requires unflinching obedience and total commitment. One is either the true believer or an unbeliever; there is no middle way. The holy army must march on the followers of Satan.

6. Jews and Christians are classified as unbelievers rather than "Peoples of the Book" because of their linkage with the West. For the most part, they have been co-opted by Western colonialism and Zionism. These radical jihadists see a Judeo–Christian conspiracy against true Islam. So non-Muslim minorities are at risk and subject to persecution.

The two radical Islamic movements that are most present and active in our current geopolitical environment are al Qaeda (Arabic for "the base") and the Taliban in Afghanistan. Let's look first at al Qaeda (sometimes spelled al Queda or al Qaida), a multinational organization with members from many countries and with a worldwide presence.[33] Some of the senior leaders in the organization are also active in other terrorist organizations. Osama bin Laden, from a wealthy construction family in Saudi Arabia, is viewed as the leader of al Qaeda. His fundamental strategy has been to link existing Islamic groups, to radicalize them, and then to create new radical Islamic groups in regions where none exist. The ultimate goal with this strategy is to create the comprehensive united Islamic network, which in bin Laden's view is necessary for the establishment of a government which follows the rules of the Caliphs (ruler of a community in Islam). The immediate aim for bin Laden and the organization is to overthrow nearly all Muslim governments which are viewed as corrupt, to drive Western influence from those countries, and eventually to abolish state boundaries in the formation of a pan-Islamic region.

Osama bin Laden began his path as a holy warrior in 1979, the year Soviet troops invaded Afghanistan. He joined forces with the Palestinian Muslim Brotherhood leader, Abdullah Assam, and used his extraordinary resources to build a more solid infrastructure in Afghanistan that would help liberate the land from the infidel invader. Following the removal of the Soviets in Afghanistan in the late 1980s, bin Laden returned to his native country of Saudi Arabia in order to take up the fight against what he judged to be "an infidel government." The Saudi regime strongly resisted his calls for insurrection, and quickly acted against him. In 1994, his Saudi citizenship was revoked and he was forced to leave the country. Bin Laden with his family and a large group of followers moved to Khartoum in Sudan, established a base, engaged in improving the infrastructure of Sudan, and started several companies.

In time, with Sudan listed by the United States as among the sponsors of terrorism, the government of Sudan requested that bin Laden leave the country. In May, 1996, bin Laden moved his base to Afghanistan, leaving behind several major companies that are believed to support his cause.

Al-Qaeda was founded by bin Laden in the late 1980s to bring together Arabs who fought in Afghanistan against the Soviet Union. The initial task was to help finance, recruit, transport, and train Sunni Islamic extremists for the Afghan resistance. The goals of the organization have changed over the years and the current goal is to form the pan-Islamic Caliphate throughout the world which requires the overthrow of regimes which are judged non-Islamic and eliminate Westerners and their influence from Muslim countries. The particular targets in this new Islamic World Front were (are) Jews (Israel) and Crusaders (the United States and Christians). While precise numbers are difficult to determine, it is likely that the organization has several thousand members and associates, with linkages to other Sunni Islamic extremists groups. Again, precise records are not available, but the organization has been financed by a number of sources: fronts for legitimate businesses, private donations, percentages of support from Muslim charitable organizations, and the personal wealth of the bin Laden family. Bin Laden recruited a number of associates to help him in this mission, including Dr. Ayman al-Zawahiri, leader of the Egyptian *al-Jihad*.

From his base in mountainous region between Afghanistan and Pakistan and in the pursuit of these goals, al Qaeda has engaged in a number of violent activities. The following list is illustrative, not comprehensive. The world was shocked by the violent attack on the United States on September 11, 2001. In 2002, the world witnessed the bombing of the hotel in Mombassa, Kenya, killing 15 and injuring 40 others. There was an attack of U.S. military personnel in Kuwait, and the U.S. ship, the Limburg off the coast of Yemen. In 2003 there were al Qaeda led bombings in Riyadh, Casablanca, Morocco, Jakarta, and Istanbul. Other plans for violence, such as the assassination of the Pope John Paul II during his visit to Manila in late 1994 were thwarted.

In most ways, al Qaeda expressed the religious ideology of radical Islam. It is at war with Western colonialism and Zionism. It is committed to establishing a pan-Islamic government that narrowly interprets select teachings from the Quran. It makes every effort to "religiously" follow one form of the shariah and rejects those with a different interpretation. It openly opposes the governments of more moderate Muslim countries and the religious establishment within those countries. They are motivated in this cause by their radical understanding of one narrow form of Islam and are at war with Muslims who differ from them. Their target includes Christians and Jews who, in their judgment are not "Peoples of the Book" but infidels. The movement is a dramatic illustration of a religion committed to changing the culture of the Muslim world and beyond.

The other movement that might be classified as an expression of radical Islam is the Taliban (from the language of the Pashtuns meaning "students"), also rooted in the extremist Sunni side of Islam.[34] It differs from al Qaeda in that it is based in Afghanistan and not an international network. It also carries the values of its Pashtun ethnic heritage and combines Sunni extremism with the Pashtun tribal culture. The Taliban began to exercise some influence in the 1980s as those who helped resist the Soviet invasion of Afghanistan. Their first major independent military activity occurred in October-November, 1994 when they marched from Maiwant in southern Afghanistan to capture Kandahar City and the surrounding provinces. They helped free a trade route from Pakistan to Central Asia, and soon took control over against the Mujahideen warlords of 12 of Afghanistan's 34 provinces. By September, 1996, they had captured Afghanistan's capital, Kabul, and began their rule of the country.

The Taliban has an extremely strict and in many ways tribal-bound ideology that attempts to connect a narrow interpretation of shariah with Pushtun tribal codes.[35] The Taliban exercised a harsh enforcement of their beliefs and practices, both in their governance and in the practice of their religion. The Taliban was reluctant to share power with other segments of Afghan society, would not hold elections, replaced leaders from other ethnic and Persian speaking leaders with Pasto-speaking Taliban, opposed the Shia branch of Islam, and would not tolerate debate about beliefs and practices with other Muslims.

Life under the Taliban regime was severely restricted, and shariah law was interpreted to ban several activities which had been lawful in Afghanistan. Employment and education of women was curtailed, movies, television, music, and dancing were prohibited, diets were controlled, and men were not allowed to shave. Cultural artifacts were deemed either polytheistic or heretical and many works or art were destroyed in the National Museum of Afghanistan. In March, 2001, the Taliban ordered the demolition of the two statues of Buddha carved into the cliffs of Bamiyan, an act condemned by UNESCO. There were attacks on other ethnic peoples. For example in the summer of 1998, the Taliban soldiers went north to the predominantly Hazara and Uzbek city of

Mazar-i-Sharif, the largest city in the north and began shooting everything in sight—shop keepers, cart pullers, women and children, and even animals.

The Taliban was not able to establish economic stability, not even with the continuation of opium production although it was a cornerstone of the economy. The infrastructure of the country deteriorated, and there was no running water, little electricity, few telephones, navigable roads, or energy supplies. Basic necessities like water, food, and housing were in desperately short supply. The infant mortality rate was the highest in the world, and a quarter of all children died before they reached their fifth birthday. The United Nations and NGOs made an attempt to be helpful, but were viewed with suspicion and without gratitude or even tolerance by the Taliban. While initially receiving some support from other countries of the world, including the United States, in the hope that the Taliban might bring some stability to the region, Afghanistan was essentially isolated from the rest of the world. Only three countries gave diplomatic recognition to the "Islamic Emirate of Afghanistan"— the United Arab Emirates, Pakistan, and Saudi Arabia. When Osama bin Laden moved to Afghanistan from the Sudan in 1996, there was some effort at cooperation and collaboration between Mullah Omar, the leader of the Taliban and bin Laden. Both leaders benefited from the influx of recruits from the Madrasahs in the Pakistan border region.

Following the September 11, 2001 attack, the United States delivered an ultimatum to the Taliban demanding that they meet a number of conditions:

- Deliver to the United States all the leaders of al Qaeda
- Release all imprisoned foreign nationals
- Close every terrorist training camp
- Hand over every terrorist and the supporters
- Give the United States full access to the terrorist camps for inspection.

After some stalling on the part of the Taliban, on October 7, 2001, the United States lost patience and, aided by the United Kingdom, Canada, and several NATO allies, initiated a military attack on Afghanistan, bombing the Taliban and the al Qaeda related camps. The Taliban retreated from several regions of the country and in December gave up their last stronghold. It was not long following this surrender that the Taliban began its resurgence, and the Afghan front remains one of the primary concerns of those countries with strong policies of counter-insurgency in Afghanistan. It continues to be one of the most unstable, dangerous, and strategic areas of the world.

In the Taliban movement, we observe many of the basic tenets of radical Islam, coupled as it is with Pushtun tribal codes. Although less focused on neocolonialism and Zionism, it is nevertheless persuaded that the West is pitted against the Islamic world. The Taliban is persuaded that a government based on their understanding of God's will is necessary, and the governance must enforce the Taliban interpretation of the shariah. It has no tolerance for other forms of Islam, and believes that a jihad against unbelief is a religious duty. Christians and other minority religious groups are persecuted.

Summary and assessment

Islam has a great appeal to many people around the world. It has been, if not the fastest growing religion in the world, certainly among those religions that are increasing at a remarkable rate. Its strong appeal is many-sided and speaks to the inherent quality and coherence of the religion. Among its great strengths are the following:

1. It invites those within the tradition and the pilgrim seeker into a comprehensive way of life and a coherent worldview. Islam engages the faithful follower in a total way of life, involving a logical and consistent creed, an ethical code that is comprehensive and clear, a way of practice that is direct and doable, and a community of support and commonality that gives the follower a sense of belonging to a truly worldwide religion.

2. In particular, the Five Pillars of Islam offer to the follower a very understandable spiritual pathway. The affirmation that there is one God to whom one prays on a regular basis is very understandable and inviting. It is easy to grasp the need for alms-giving for the needy, and to assume that there would be special or sacred times, such as Ramadan and the Hajj, in which one expresses worship and devotion to God.

3. The core beliefs are easy to understand and they flow together in a consistent system of thought. There is one God who has communicated with the human family through supernatural beings, prophets and particularly the Great Prophet who gave the divinely inspired Quran. This one God will judge humankind on the basis of what He has revealed, and there will be rewards and punishments from God who is fair, merciful, and compassionate.

4. There is within the community of faith the guidance and support for all the followers of Islam and especially a spirit of benevolence for those in need. One belongs to a worldwide community and will be guided and cared for within the community.

5. There are spiritual pathways within the breadth of Islam for those seeking a more intellectually credible faith, or a more personal and devotional pathway. There are

resources within this religious tradition that can meet the spiritual needs of all sincere and honest seekers. The new book by Ali A. Allawi, *The Crisis of Islamic Civilization* suggests that a credible and personally satisfying faith for modern Muslims will be found as the larger Islamic civilization finds its new configuration in the modern world.[36]

But not all are attracted to Islam for several reasons. Again, I will be illustrative rather than comprehensive.

1. As with the other great monotheistic religions, there is a strong tendency to be exclusive, believing that their tradition captures the true revelation from God and the faithful pathway expected by God. Islam is clear that Muhammad was the "Seal of the Prophets," the last in a line of those who revealed the will and way of God. This pattern of being exclusive even exists within Islam, as Sunni and Shia differ over certain issues. This position is not easy for those who stand outside of the community of faith known as Islam.

2. There is within Islam, and other religious traditions as well, a radical, even militant minority. This radical minority puts its stamp on the comprehensive worldview of Islam, and through this lens, judges those who have different views and in many cases have opposed what they believe is the way forward for human history.

3. Even within a more moderate form of Islam, the comprehensive outlook, as expressed in shariah, does not easily make room for those who are not part of the Muslim tradition. Minorities within Islamic societies are not always given equal opportunity and treated with fairness and respect.

4. There is within Islam a pattern of authority in the society and family and clearly prescribed roles for men and women. Often these patterns of authority and prescribed roles are paternalistic and discriminatory. Those within the tradition would say that women are fully respected as they follow and fulfill their God-given place within the society and the family. But what is God-given and what is a carryover from traditional paternalistic cultural patterns is not always easy to discern.[37]

5. Finally, one has to ask the pointed question about the intellectual credibility of claims and traditions which form the essence of this faith; even as one asks the same questions about other faith traditions. Many of the beliefs are "leaps of faith." It may not be easy for contemporary educated world citizens to believe that the Quran is divinely inspired and not subject to historical critical analysis. And it may not be easy to understand Muhammad, while acknowledging that he was a great prophet and leader, as "The Seal of the Prophets" bringing direct revelations from God to humanity. It may be even harder to believe in angels and jinns, who share in the divine engagement with human history.

We see in this great monotheistic religion a comprehensive worldview, asking its followers to pursue spiritual pathways that lead to social and personal transformation. We turn now to exploring the ways that these several religious traditions that we have discussed (those which see the divine within nature and culture, those that see the divine as beyond, yet within all, and those that believe there is one transcendent, personal God) can teach contemporary spiritual pilgrims who seek to find authentic and life-giving spiritual pathways.

Discussion questions

1. Is it possible to be a "true believer" in one's religion and yet accept the spiritual pathways and beliefs of others as valid and life-giving?
2. Why is it especially hard for the Abrahamic monotheistic religions to be accepting of the religious beliefs and practices of others?
3. In what ways are the beliefs and practices of the majority of Muslims different from the radical minority (Jihadists) of Muslims?
4. Why do you think that Islam is the fastest (or one of the fastest) growing religions in the world?
5. What are some ways that Muslims, and those of other religions, might find common ground with those outside of their tradition and collaborate with them in a variety of causes?

Key terms and concepts

1. **Hadith:** An account of the sayings and actions attributed to the Prophet Muhammad.
2. **Hajj:** The annual pilgrimage to Mecca.
3. **Iman:** The leader in the Muslim congregation who leads in congregational prayers.
4. **Jihad:** To struggle in the ways of faith; to defend and protect the faith.
5. **Jinn:** The hidden ones or spirits that can be used by God.
6. **Ramadan:** The ninth month in the Islamic calendar in which one fasts.
7. **Salat:** The ritual prayers performed five times per day.
8. **Shahadah:** To witness that there is one God and that Muhammad is the Messenger of God.
9. **Shariah:** The law within Islam.
10. **Shirk:** Making others or something equal to God.
11. **Sufi:** The mystics of Islam.
12. **Sunnah:** The example, actions and sayings of Muhammad as contained in the *hadiths*.
13. **Ummah:** The Muslim community.

Suggestions for reference and reading

Ali A. Allawi, *The Crisis of Islamic Civilization* (New Haven: Yale University Press, 2009).

Esposito, John L., *Islam: The Straight Path* (New York: Oxford University Press, 2005). See as well Dr. Esposito's *What Everyone Needs to Know About Islam* (New York: Oxford University Press, 2002) and *The Future of Islam* (New York: Oxford University Press, 2010).

Murawiec, Laurent, *The Mind of Jihad* (New York: Cambridge University Press, 2008).

Nasr, Sayyed Hossein, *The Heart of Islam: Enduring Values for Humanity* (San Francisco: HarpersSanFrancisco, 2002).

Phillips, Kevin, *American Theocracy: The Peril and Politics of Radical Religion, Oil, and Barrowed Money in the 21st Century* (New York: Viking, 2006).

Ramadan, Tariq, *In the Footsteps of the Prophet: Lessons from the Life of Muhammad* (New York: Oxford University Press, 2007).

Riedel, Bruce, *The Search for Al Qaeda: Its Leadership, Ideology, and Future* (Washington, D.C.: Brookings Institution Press, 2008).

The Quran (several translations and editions are available).

Wagner, Walter H., *Opening the Quran: Introducing Islam's Holy Book* (Notre Dame, IN: Notre Dame University Press, 2008).

Part V
The Common Elements of Life-Giving Spiritualities

This concluding chapter addresses the ways that our time and place in history invite us to find a changed or new spiritual pathway that accounts for the rapid changes of our time and yet honors the spiritual traditions of the ages.

In this new ecological age of developing global community and interfaith dialogue, the world religions face what is perhaps the greatest challenge that they have ever encountered. Each is inspired by a unique vision of the divine and has a distinct cultural identity. At the same time, each perceives the divine as the source of unity and peace. The challenge is to preserve their religious and cultural uniqueness without letting it operate as a cause of a narrow and divisive sectarianism that contradicts the vision of divine unity and peace. It is a question whether the healing light of religious vision will overcome the social and ideological issues that underlie much of the conflict between religions.

p. 169 Steven C. Rockefeller, *Spirit and Nature*.[1]

Finding a Spiritual Pathway

Chapter Outline

A time of choice   207

Insights and practices for all   211

The dimensions of a spiritual pathway for contemporary pilgrims   214

A time of choice

We spoke in Chapter 1 about living "East of Eden." For many, the new world has thrust them out of a secure place that was safe and comfortable. We suggested that we live in a time of rapid and fundamental change when both our ways of understanding our world and the world itself are shifting. In such times many are seeking a spiritual pathway that will anchor and guide them. As the map changes and the familiar landmarks disappear, vast numbers of people from many cultures and religious traditions may need a changed or new pathway in order to arrive at the destination of a true spiritual home, one filled with purposeful living and inner peace. The human family is looking at the global compass, hoping to find true north.

We spoke as well in Chapter 1 of this new pathway needing to have several characteristics if we are to arrive at our true destination and avoid as many false paths and wrong turns as possible. Our list could be quite long, and we acknowledge that everyone's list will vary some, depending on their religious tradition, place in life, and unique culture. So we suggested just a basic starting point, knowing that pilgrims from every corner will need to lay out their true path. Regardless of its many twists and turns, we maintained that a new pathway should be simple in the sense, pure and undivided. Our new pathway must have integrity, being a genuinely sincere and whole-hearted effort. Going in several directions at once and being pulled, often unknowingly, in different directions by influences and forces that we have not chosen will not lead us home. True hearts must directly and honestly seek a clear destination. "Blessed are the pure in heart, for they will see God." (Mt. 5.8)

We said that our pathway should be open and thoughtful, facing squarely the realities of our time and place, and then finding a way that is authentic, realistic, and intellectually credible. The market places of religion have a broad range of goods, many of them marked down and on sale, and they are staffed by excellent sales people. Most of these religious ways are offered by people with sincerity and integrity, and those who commit to them often find a true and life-giving home. We should listen and learn, but be discerning about the credibility of the claims and the promises. Often more is promised than delivered. And we should be aware that nearly anyone, given the right people making an attractive offer, can believe almost anything, even commit to a way that has no credibility whatsoever and may even be harmful.

We also suggested that our way should be in dialogue and transition, eager to listen and learn in order to incorporate the best insights from those with wisdom and who have been touched by the divine. There are those, whose positions are thoughtfully and carefully expressed and followed, who can teach and mentor us. It is important to study these positions and learn from those who are less into persuasion and more into assisting us find our way. We are in transition, and as those on the move, we need to be open to views that may "connect the dots" for us given where we are on our spiritual pathway.

We stressed as well that our new spiritual way should give our lives meaning and purpose by having a strong ethical lodestar. We noted that our lives should be filled with love and compassion. Any pathway that does not lead to improving the welfare of all and caring for the good earth is not viable. A true spiritual way not only helps us find a sense of peace and tranquility, but nudges us out into the world to love our neighbor and to find ways to help build a more just, humane, and peaceful society and world.

Many other characteristics might be listed, but with at least these in mind, let's turn to the range of options which our new world offers:[2]

1. **Stay put:** For the majority of people in the world, their current patterns of religious expression or lack of it will remain largely unchanged. It may be a factor of age, a busy and demanding life, or a relatively protected and isolated environment, or simply the serenity that comes from current beliefs and practices that allow them

to remain in their current place. Of course, there is always some change, but for many, the world goes by and life goes on as it has in the past. Staying put is acceptable and can bring a measure of peace. But not all will be able to remain at rest in current spiritual or customary ways, given the nature of our changing world. The obvious risks of this option are that it may too easily allow us to become passive about our spiritual life, and it may not pull us forward into a responsible engagement with our new and emerging world.

2. **Recover, reclaim, and recommit:** A second option for us is to try to find the original path that we claim to follow, believing that it was given by God. Whether it is the teaching and life of Moses or Buddha, Muhammad or Jesus, this option is to find the original and true way and reclaim it. This is a noble and worthy endeavor, involving a careful study of the founding documents (scripture), serious historical inquiry, a thoughtful and relevant restatement, and great care about the risk of imposing one's current worldview full of presuppositions onto the material. There is a dramatic resurgence of these movements in an effort to find what the original founder did and what the authoritative literature surrounding the founder truly says. There is so much to learn from this quest, and many of the more conservative movements in different religions have gone this route in the sincere hope of recovering the true spiritual way that "puts life together" and gives a clear direction. But the risks are many and include the following:

   - It may be that the recovery is more elusive than expected, and that what is found is just an earlier interpretation rather than the original source. In the case of conservative Christianity, it is often a return to an earlier orthodoxy, often based on a view of the Bible as inerrant and inspired. It may be that a better approach is a careful return to the first century, a review of how the New Testament developed, and then to follow with a conscious and intentional hermeneutical position that enables the first century truth to come forward into the present for guidance.

   - It may be that one's contemporary "sunglasses" shade the material in a way that makes it fit one's current culture and its biased positions. It is all too easy to claim that this interpretation is based on the divinely inspired Scripture that describes the original, and with this inherent authority, affirm it as the only correct position. But scripture, inerrant and inspired or not, is read in many different ways.

   - It may inadvertently lead to a merely secure position to hold and provide the comfort of believing that it is the *true one*, not so much because it was accurately recovered but simply because it provides a place to stand. Many seek this comfort, which is not altogether misguided, but religious faith must be both credible and efficacious.

   - A risk for one who holds this view is that it can easily be a place from which to judge others who hold different views. We do not easily say "God bless" to those with a different pathway.

But the option of recover, reclaim, and recommit, despite the risks, is still an extremely valid option and perhaps the most attractive option for many people. No less a spiritual mentor than the current Dalai Lama counsels this pathway. Our way may have some limitations, as all religious traditions do. But these limitations can be changed or merely accepted as the way it happened or is happening, and we must learn some patience and acquiescence about these realities. Within one's own faith tradition, there are usually great resources for spiritual growth, and plenty of room to rethink, alter one's views and ways, and pursue the best expressions of the tradition. To some extent, this is the position I have chosen as a Protestant Christian in the Presbyterian and Reformed tradition. It is possible to hear John Calvin speak about God's sovereign love and turn down the volume as he speaks about election and predestination. It is possible to follow the Reformed Church family in its profound and deep commitments to social justice, the environment, and world peace and move on from our Dutch cousins who at an earlier time propped up apartheid in South Africa. There is within American Christianity a movement known as "The Emerging Church" that is helpful to those who want to "stay home and remodel." So I recommit, think, and move freely, following my conscience and expressing grace toward those who differ.

1. **Thoughtful incorporation:** I hint in the previous paragraph about my practice of incorporation, while remaining loyal to the tradition that has given me a life-giving spiritual pathway. It is possible to turn to the Hindu tradition and incorporate the great insights of yoga and the healing of meditation without any violation of one's own faith. It is possible to follow the Noble Eightfold Path of Buddhism and become a better human being. Right mindfulness is to walk in the light of the Spirit of God. It is possible to reach across to Muslim brothers and sisters and engage in dialogue about interreligious understanding and collaboration. I can learn from the indigenous people of the world about my interdependence with all the earth. Given my Scottish heritage, I can incorporate Celtic insights about creation spirituality, yet remain loyal to the truths of the Scottish Reformation. In this current pattern of eclectic incorporation,[3] there is a growing tendency to separate "being religious' from "being spiritual" and to think of religious ways as dated, full of traditions, customs, and liturgies that no longer have meaning. This point of view does have the ring of truth about it for whole generations, but it is also the case that "religious" practices find their way back into these groups. It is not uncommon for antiliturgical movements simply to substitute informal and occasionally sloppy liturgy in their worship services. The spiritual way in most cases needs the sustaining support of the tradition and the community.

2. **Change:** There may come a time when there is deep-seated disillusionment about one's religious tradition and a growing conviction that its beliefs and practices no longer have any meaning or power. It may also be possible that one may have been deeply hurt by its teachings, perhaps based on fear and legalism, and even violated by some of its immoral leaders. In these cases, a clear change may be the best, and getting some assistance form a trusted person who has your interest at heart may help with the healing and transition. I know many who have made this transition and who have found a pathway that is for them redemptive and healing, intellectual credible, and spiritually fulfilling.[4] Often this new pathway is eclectic, drawing upon the best insights and practices from several religious traditions and the social sciences.

3. **Seek a secular way:** I encounter many who have either never accepted or given up on religion, believing that its beliefs are intellectually indefensible and its spiritual practices are unnecessary and at times even harmful.[5] Most of these thoughtful and honest people believe that it is entirely possible to have a good and meaningful life and to be a thoroughly responsible person who is compassionate and caring about both one's neighbor and the world. Their way may not always be called a spiritual pathway, but many would say that they are spiritual in their intentions and practices, although not religious.

Insights and practices for all

Regardless of the choice of a spiritual or secular way, it is still important to keep in mind the ways that may be life-giving or the ways that it might be life-denying. A review of our study of the selective and representative spiritual pathways of the human family may guide us as we take stock of our current situation.[6] We may discover that our best move is to recover and recommit to the great teachings and insights from our inherited religious faith. Or we may see that what we need to do for greater satisfaction in our spiritual walk is to learn more and deepen the spiritual resources that are within our tradition, and perhaps incorporate other views and practices that easily harmonize with our tradition. Or perhaps we need to make a basic shift, as for example, moving from the Christian family in its fundamentalist expression, to an eclectic "spiritual" pathway that has less to do with customs and norms of a church body and more to do with life-giving practices. Or we may opt to be free of all religious belief and practice, viewing it as fundamentally superstitious but still incorporating the life-giving insights from the great wisdom teachers of the ages.

But regardless of our direction, we can and should learn from others. Let's review, and then take with us, or perhaps leave behind us, lessons from the spiritual pathways of the world's religions. We will only provide an example or two from these religious expressions that we have discussed, but perhaps they will be suggestive. What did we learn from the indigenous wisdom traditions and what might we incorporate into our lives that came from the first people who pondered the mysteries of the world and the complexities of life and who understood the divine as interwoven with nature? We learned much, and have more to learn from these wise people. In particular, given the urgency surrounding the condition of our environment and global warming, we learned from them that humans are an integral part of nature, not its master (though maybe its steward), and that nature must be honored and respected. Less able to articulate the dangers of global warming, they nevertheless understood that their welfare was tied to the care of Mother Earth. So regardless of our spiritual pathway, we know that our way forward will be green.

What might we learn from those classical religious traditions that see the divine as tangled in the web of culture and politics? Perhaps we can say right upfront that the emperor is not divine, nor is the politician, the political position held, nor the particular configuration of the political structure. But we can learn that the divine way is about social transformation, and that a true spiritual pathway leads us directly into ways of caring for the earth, relieving human suffering, and building a more just and humane world. Religion, politics, and culture are interwoven, and to find ways to make sure that this mix is healthy and serves the welfare of the people is part of our spiritual responsibility.

We turned next to the expression of the "nature/culture religions" in contemporary times and looked at two movements. We can certainly affirm Wicca in its endeavor to care for the earth and support of women's rights, but we might question the wisdom and validity of using magic or casting spells. We can learn from the Shinto religion of Japan how intimately one's religious faith is tied to one's natural surroundings and culture. As a thoughtful follower of the Shinto way would advise, our task is to discern the universal ethical norms and spiritual guidance that are inherent in the natural and cultural framework of our religious beliefs and practices.

The religions of transcendent monism have much to give all the spiritual pilgrims of the world. In so many ways, they offer what has been called "perennial philosophy," a wisdom of the ages that reappears in the thought of successive sages of humankind.[7] This is certainly the case with Hinduism. Behind the layers of superstition and polytheism in popular Hinduism, there is a comprehensive worldview that gives its followers a frame of reference to understand the world, meaning to life, guidance for living, and a sense of arriving at ultimate peace in nirvana. It has clear ethical guidance, an array of practices that may be used by all to deepen spirituality and improve health, and it remains one of the few religions of the world that is open to the teachings and practices of other religions.

Buddhism, too, has many of the same qualities. It is less speculative in character and focuses on a way of life that leads to inner peace. It too has different traditions linked to the local culture and a variety of practices that reflect regional and popular customs. But, beyond these, there are many of the practices of Buddhism, such as meditation, that calm the spirit and are easily adopted by those of other religious traditions. Buddhism is also fundamentally ethical in character, believing that a truly spiritual person will be a compassionate person, committed to relieving the suffering of others and showing compassion in the form of both personal and social transformation.

Each in their own way, the great religions of China, Confucianism and Taoism, have taught spiritual pathways that have been positive for their followers and have insights that can teach those who stand outside of these traditions. We learn from Confucianism that respect and civility should be the norm for all human interaction and be infused into the practice of government. Taoism, as we reflect on finding the natural order and way, can be our teacher. We need to continually search for those pathways that match with nature's ways, and as we do, we will find pathways that help us to have integrity and to live congruently with our deepest values.

As we turn to the Abrahamic monotheistic religions, we come to the one over-arching belief in a personal and sovereign God who is engaged with all of reality, human history, and even individual persons. Other religious traditions have a form of monotheism as well, but these three are clear in their invitation to the whole human family to a life that is centered on the will and way of God (Allah). It may be based on Torah, or the Gospels, or the Quran, but beyond the words of scripture is the belief in the connection with the one true God. This belief is ours to accept or reject as the foundation of our spiritual pathway.

In addition, the adherents of these faith traditions, as others do as well, have the gift of living in societies that have already incorporated the beliefs, insights, and values of these religious traditions into their cultures, and for the most part these incorporations have been positive. These are present for us in our spiritual pathways. For example, we learn from all three of the traditions about ways to order society, and in particular we have learned and continue to learn from Judaism about the role of law in the preservation of the rights of all.

While all three of the religions speak about justice, the Jewish tradition has pointedly spoken about protection of those who have little or no voice. Few traditions have spoken with such eloquence and passion about the centrality of justice in the management of human affairs.

In the case of Christianity, we discover in a very focused way that love brings a healing and redemptive side to justice and that together, an ethic of justice and love is an integral part of the ideal spiritual pathway. If we add the emphasis within Islam that one's spiritual pathway is about the totality of life, not just a part of life that we call religious, then, taken together, we begin to understand what is expected in a commitment to a spiritual pathway within these traditions. Each of these religions speaks of justice, love, and commitment, and we learn that the way of faith involves the commitment of all of life.

The dimensions of a spiritual pathway for contemporary pilgrims

What are the ideal components for a spiritual pathway? Is it possible to isolate a few essentials and say that they must be a part of the spiritual pathways of contemporary pilgrims? Though there is much in common, I think that it is not possible to find a universal list of beliefs and practices, given the rich variety and the passionate levels of commitment which people have for their own way. Neither should we, given the richness of the many religious traditions of the human family. A better direction is to suggest patterns of belief and practice that are truly life-giving, patterns that are possible in most of the great religious traditions of the human family and which will be given specificity within them.[8] Let me at least point in a direction by returning to the four major characteristics of a religion: Creed, Code, Cult, and Community.

Articulating a creed for a universal religion, although it has certainly been tried, is very difficult, given the ways in which patterns of belief are inevitably framed in the language of a time, place, and culture. The Tower of Babel is with us. Further, human language does not fully or accurately describe reality, but only gives a lens through which to peer at it. When it comes to articulating what we believe about the divine, we move to a realm that is not a description of observations by the senses or their scientific extensions. So we speak about the divine in terms of what we know in "our hearts" and experience, and what we have learned from those whose experience is deeper and whose words are wiser and more profound than ours. For example, in the Abrahamic monotheistic religions, we speak from the narrative about Moses, Jesus, and Muhammad using the "authoritative and normative" literature that passes on the narrative.

The better part of wisdom as we articulate our creed is to accept and affirm the following:

1. Accept the words of our creeds as approximations of the divine, words that point to a reality that is greater than formulations and beyond the limitations of our minds and language. The images, symbols, and metaphors that fill our creeds put us in touch with the divine, but do not contain or capture the divine. Another way of making this point is to say that God (the divine) "condescends" to be heard and known within the limitations of our historical era, our culture bound language, and our limited understanding. We are met more than halfway. Even "true believers" use the language of *via analogia* or *via negativa* and metaphor when speaking about God as did the founders and prophets of the religion they follow.

2. The articulation of one's faith should be done in a way that is as intellectually credible as possible, taking into account the best historical scholarship and the currents of contemporary thought while remaining true to the foundation of the religion. This is no small task, and, alas, the work of critical historical scholarship and theology is never done. Nor will all be persuaded by such work, in that beliefs will differ, and not all will find any religious affirmation acceptable. But honest, disciplined, and thoughtful we must be.

3. The creedal statement must be more than propositions strung together in logical order. It must be consistent, but it will never be heard and followed if it is only a set of intellectual propositions. Our statements, as our Muslim sisters and brothers teach us so well, must be about all of life. We remind those who say yes to the creedal statements that they are also saying "yes" with head, heart, and hand; with body, mind, and spirit.[9] As we are told by Jesus quoting Torah: "You shall love the Lord your God with all your heart, and with all your soul, and with all your mind." (Mt. 22.37)

Articulating a universal code is also difficult, although there are some values held in common though expressed in different ways in the teachings of the world's religions. Words and concepts such as altruism, compassion, and love occur with great frequency in the ethical codes of most of the world's religions.[10] In addition, most of the world's religions have statements about the ordering of human affairs and the ways humans relate to nature. Justice and a nascent ecology are often present. Again, we might suggest that an ethical code, evolving and adapting to new understandings, and the changing world should include statements about the following:

1. It should call on its followers to show love, respect, and compassion in all human relationships.[11]
2. It should call on its followers to engage in improving the welfare of people near and far, reducing all forms of human suffering, and creating a more just and peaceful society and world.
3. It should call on its followers to be responsible in practices that are sensitive to the environment, exhibit ecological understanding and sensitivity, and demonstrate intelligent care for the earth, the mother of us all.

With some care, I use the word "cult" in that it means a system used by a community for worship and ritual. I do not use it in this instance as a reference to an exclusive group of persons sharing esoteric belief. It is the way that we worship, celebrate, and honor the divine. It is next to impossible to generalize norms for worship and ritual in that each religious tradition has developed these across the centuries in accord with their beliefs and culture. Again, we merely point to ways that will encourage the health and well-being of the participants. Let me suggest as a very sketchy minimum the following guidelines:[12]

1. The worship and liturgy should be an act of remembrance, expressed in profound and imaginative ways using appropriate and colorful language filled with image, symbol, and metaphor. In most cases, as we gather for worship, sing, pray, listen to homilies and sermons, and say the litanies, we are transported back to our roots and models of behavior and then empowered and inspired to go forward into lives of meaning and responsibility.
2. The experience of celebration should transform our motivation for living the spiritual life, enabling us to leave behind those enticing tugs for power, prestige, wealth, and exploitation for personal pleasure and gain.
3. The experience of worship should cultivate emotional wisdom: how to develop inner peace and serenity, increase our understanding of how to live with integrity, control our negative emotions, reduce our fear, and cultivate love and gratitude.
4. It should teach us how to leave worship with a better idea of how we might contribute to "loving our neighbor" in doing good deeds that improve the life of others and changing social structures that provide fairness under the law and access to health, education, and meaningful work for those around us.
5. Our worship and liturgy should "take us into the presence" of the divine, whether in symbol as is done in the Christian Eucharist, or in spirit as we celebrate in song, or in prayer and meditation as we begin to see the sacred in all that is around and inside of us.

I mention our final "c" for community. In the experience of community, the religions of the world find a great deal of common ground. As we speak about community, we note once again that not all communities, just as not all religious practices are healthy and life-giving. Some in fact are damaging to the spirit and harmful to the participants. What it does provide is a sense of belonging, but this alone, while very important to all of us, does not insure that it will lead to a healthy and responsible life. Gangs provide a sense of belonging. At the very least, the healthy religious community has the following dimensions:

1. It provides a place in which one can feel accepted and affirmed as a human being of worth, with a contribution to make to the common good. It can be our second home, with a larger family of those that notice, receive, and delight in us, and appreciate what we do for the good of all.
2. It is the place that one goes for guidance in life, for directions on how to face the day and the week, and how to be a better wife, husband, parent, child, student, boss or employee. It is where we learn how to live the good life.
3. It is the place one goes for comfort and solace, for understanding and for strength and wisdom in times of anxiety, stress, and suffering. It is the place that provides the needed support in times of trouble.
4. And, of course, it is the place where we see the divine on the faces and in the actions of sisters and brothers. From this association, we begin to flourish, get inspired, and move into the challenges of life with vision, energy, and courage.

The human family, in all of its many shades and tones, variety beyond measure, follows spiritual pathways that vary accordingly. Our way must be good for us, and our responsibility is to affirm the ways of others and assist all who seek to find life-giving ways for them. In particular, we are reminded again and again from the great spiritual classics of the human family that we are called to be peacemakers. The Hebrew Bible captures this great truth when it says, "The whole of the Torah is for the purpose of promoting peace." And it was Jesus who said, "Blessed are the peacemakers, for they will be called the children of God." President Baruch Obama quoted these passages and others in his historic speech in Cairo on June 4, 2009, and concluded, "The people of the world can live together in peace. We know that is God's vision. Now that must be our work here on earth."

Discussion questions

1. Do you think it is important, given the extraordinary changes that are occurring in our world, to reframe and change your spiritual pathway?

2. What do you think are the essential qualities of a healthy and life-giving spirituality?
3. What "beliefs and practices" would you want to borrow from religious traditions other than your own and incorporate into your spiritual pathway?
4. What are the differences or are there any between being religious and being spiritual?
5. How would you state in a few sentences your creed? Code? Cult (worship practices)? Community?

Key terms and concepts

1. **Creed:** A statement of core beliefs.
2. **Code:** A statement of ethical values and practices.
3. **Cult:** A system used by a community for worship and liturgy.
4. *Via Analogia* **or** *Via Negativa*: Ways of speaking about God by analogy, for example, God is like a father; or by defining God in the negative, for example, God does not change.
5. **Hermeneutics:** An approach or pattern of interpretation that allows events and literature of the past to speak in the present.

Suggestions for reference and reading

Chopra, Deepak, *How to Know God: The Soul's Journey into the Mystery of Mysteries* (New York: Three Rivers Press, 2000).

Foster, Richard J., *Streams of Living Water* (San Francisco: HarperSanFrancisco, 2001).

Heschel, Abrahm Joshua, *God in Search of Man: A Philosophy of Judaism* (Northvale, NJ, London: Jason Aronson Inc., 1987).

Neusner, Jacob and Chilton, Bruce, eds., *Altruism in World Religions* (Washington, D.C.: Georgetown University Press, 2005).

Tolle, Eckhart, *A New Earth: Awakening to Your Life's Purpose* (New York: A Plume Book, 2006).

Walsh, Roger, *Essential Spirituality: The 7 Central Practices to Awaken Heart and Mind* (New York: John Wiley & Sons, Inc., 1999).

Wilbur, Ken, *Integral Spirituality: A Startling New Role for Religion in the Modern and Postmodern World* (Boston: Integral Books, 2006).

Notes

Chapter 1

1. His Holiness the Dalai Lama, *The Spirit of Peace: Teachings on Love, Compassion, and Everyday Life* (London: Thorsons, an Imprint of HarperCollins, 2002).

2. Steinbeck, John, *East of Eden* (New York: Penguin Books, 2002, first published in 1952).

3. See Grenz, Stanley J., *A Primer on Postmodernism* (Grand Rapids, MI: William B. Eerdmans Publishing Company, 1996).

4. See Wilbur, Ken, *Eye to Eye: The Quest for a New Paradigm* (Boston: Shambhala, 2001) for a thoughtful response in this postmodern moment.

5. See Stiglitz, Joseph, *Globalization and Its Discontents* (New York: W. W. Norton & Company, 2003).

6. See Eck, Diana L., *A New Religious America: How a "Christian Country" Has Become the World's Most Religiously Diverse Nation* (San Francisco: HarperSanFrancisco, 2001).

7. See Huntington, Samuel P., *The Clash of Civilizations and the Remaking of the World Order* (New York: A Touchstone Book, 1997).

8. See Thomas Friedman, *Hot, Flat, and Crowded* (New York: Farrar, Straus and Giroux, 2008).

9. See, for example, Brown, Lester B., *Plan B 2.0: Rescuing a Planet Under Stress and a Civilization in Trouble* (New York: W. W. Norton & Company, 2006); and Diamond, Jarod, *Collapse: How Societies Choose to Fail or Succeed* (New York: Viking, 2005).

10. See Berry, Thomas, *The Dream of the Earth* (San Francisco: Sierra Club Books, 1988).

11. Gore, Al, *An Inconvenient Truth: The Planetary Emergency of Global Warming and What We Can Do about It* (New York: Rodale, 2006).

12. See McFague, Sallie, *The Body of God: An Ecological Theology* (Minneapolis, MN: Fortress Press, 1993) and *Models of God: Theology for an Ecological, Nuclear Age* (Philadelphia: Fortress Press, 1987) pp. 3–28.

13. Sacks, Jonathan, *The Dignity of Difference*, p. 29.

14. Sachs, Jeffrey D., *The End of Poverty: Economic Possibilities for Our Time* (New York: The Penguin Press, 2005); and *Common Wealth: Economics for a Crowed World* (New York: The Penguin Press, 2008).

15. See Borg, Marcus J., *The Heart of Christianity: Rediscovering A Life of Faith* (San Francisco: HarperSanFrancisco, 2003) for a "progressive" point of view about the new spirituality.

16. The works of Jack Miles, *God: A Biography* (New York: Vintage Books, 1995) and *Christ: A Crisis in the Life of God* (New York: Vintage Books, 2002) offer a thoughtful effort reinterpreting the Christian faith for our time.

17. Post, Stephen G., *Unlimited Love: Altruism, Compassion and Service* (Radnor, PA: Templeton Foundation Press, 2003), pp. 133–155. See also the work upon which Stephen Post partly bases his

understanding of love, Sorokin, Pitirim A., *The Ways and Powers of Love* (Philadelphia: Templeton Foundation Press, reprinted in 2002) pp. 15–35.

18. See as well the definition of altruism in Neusner, Jacob & Chilton, Bruce, eds., *Altruism in World Religions* (Washington, D.C.: Georgetown University Press, 2005) pp. ix–xiii.

19. See Kimball, Charles, *When Religion Becomes Evil* (San Francisco: HarperSanFrancisco, 2002).

20. Kessler, Gary E., *Ways of Being Religious* (Mountain View, CA: Mayfield Publishing Company, 2000) p. 3.

21. Kessler, Gary E., *Ways of Being Religious*, pp. 4–6.

22. For example, Smith, Huston, *The World's Religions: Our Great Wisdom Traditions* (San Francisco: HarperSanFrancisco, 1991) and a well illustrated volume by John Bowker, *World Religions* (London, New York: DK Publishing, Inc., 1997, 2003). See as well, the new *Atlas of World Religions* published by Hammond (New York: 2009).

23. See a discussion of this issue in reference to current foreign policy in Suskind, Ron, *The One Percent Doctrine: Deep Inside America's Pursuit of Its Enemies Since 9/11* (New York: Simon & Schuster, 2006).

24. Otto, Rudolf, *The Idea of the Holy* (London: Pelican Books, 1959, first published in 1917).

25. See Hitchcock, Susan Tyler with Esposito, John L., *Geography of Religion: Where God Lives, Where Pilgrims Walk* (Washington, D.C.: National Geographic, 2005).

26. Doniger, Wendy, Consulting Editor, *Encyclopedia of World Religions* (Springfield, MA: Merriam-Webster, Incorporated, 1999), p. 915.

27. See Hitchcock, Susan Tyler with Esposito, John L., *Geography of Religion.*

28. See Eliade, Mircea, *The Quest: History and Meaning in Religion* (Chicago, IL: The University of Chicago Press, 1969) and *A History of Ideas*, tr. by Willard R. Trask, 3 vols (Chicago, IL: The University of Chicago Press, 1978–1985).

29. McGrath, Alister E., *Christian Spirituality* (Malden, MA: Blackwell Publishers, 1999), p. 2.

30. See Shils, Edward, *Tradition* (Chicago, IL: University of Chicago Press: 1981).

31. Hiebert, Paul, G., *Cultural Anthropology* (Grand Rapids, MI: Baker Book House, 1983, Second Edition), p. 25. See also two classical studies of culture. Powys, John Cowper, *The Meaning of Culture* (New York: W. W. Norton & Company, Inc., 1929) and Wissler, Clark, *Man and Culture* (New York: Thomas Y.Crowell Company Publishers, 1923). There are also many contemporary studies of the meaning of culture such as Phillip Smith's *Cultural Theory: An Introduction* (Malden, MA: 2004).

32. See, e.g., the classic work of Max Weber, *Religion and the Spirit of Capitalism* (New York: Charles Scribner's Sons, 1958) and H. Richard Niebuhr, *Christ and Culture* (New York: Harper & Brothers, 1951).

33. Roman, Sanaya, *Spiritual Growth: Being Your Higher Self* (Tiburon, CA: H J Kramer Inc, 1987).

34. See Fowler, James W., *Stages of Faith* (San Francisco: Harper & Row, Publishers, 1981).

35. *The Missing Dimension of Statecraft*; See as well Benazir Bhutto's book, published just before her tragic assassination, *Reconciliation: Islam, Democracy, and the West* (New York: HarperCollins Publishers, 2008).

Chapter 2

1. Quoted by Brown, Dee, *Bury My Heart at Wounded Knee: An Indian History of the American West* (New York: Bantam Books, 1970).

2. See Eliade, Mircea, *A History of Religious Ideas* (Chicago, IL: University of Chicago Press, 1978), vol. 1, pp. 3–28. Other classic works such as James G. Frazer's *The Golden Bough: The Roots of Religion and Folklore* (New York: Avenel Books, 1980, first published in 1890) though dated, are still very informative. Nearly every study of ancient religions has an approach and assumptions that influence outcomes, and across the years, these approaches and assumptions change, but basic to them all is some kind of evolutionary development.

3. For a recent introductory essay on the beginnings of religious belief and practice, see the chapter by John L. Esposito entitled "Origins" in *The Geography of Religion*, pp. 17–69. The volume is beautifully illustrated.

4. Carmody, Denise L. and John T., *Ways to the Center: An Introduction to World Religions* (Belmont, CA: Wadsworth Publishing Co., 1984 second edition), p. 23.

5. See the account in Eliade, *A History of Religious Ideas*, Vol. 1. It is a fascinating story, one that we will refer to in the next chapter.

6. *The National Geographic*, Journal of the National Geographical Society, Tampa, FL, May, 2008, Vol. 213, No. 5, p. 25.

7. See Partridge, Christopher, ed., *New Religions: A Guide for New Religious Movements, Sects and Alternative Spiritualities* (New York: Oxford University Press, 2004).

8. See Kauffmann, Stuart A., *Reinventing the Sacred: A New View of Science, Reason, and Religion* (New York: Basic Books, 2008), for a rigorous scientific argument for belief in the divine based on evolution. A new study, done by Robert Wright also suggests ways of framing a new religious outlook based on the thesis that the evolution of our traditional ideas about God or gods point to a credible transcendent point of view, and that a modern, scientific worldview leaves room for a point of view that may contain room for what may be called divine.

9. Kessler, Gary E., *Studying Religion: An Introduction Through Cases* (New York: McGraw Hill, 2003) pp. 53–152. I am informed by Kessler in this section on sacred power. A new study entitled *The Evolution of God* by Robert Wright (New York: Little, Brown and Company, 2009) confirms this trend.

10. Myth, in this sense, is a sacred story capturing profound sacred truths, not the popular sense of a false story.

11. Kessler, Gary, *Studying Religion*, p. 87.

12. Kessler, Gary, *Studying Religion*, pp. 112–114.

13. Bowker, *World Religions*, p. 200.

14. Without the detail, I am keenly and painfully aware of running the risks of oversimplification and distortion, but I want to keep the focus on the "spirit" or "soul" of these religious expressions.

15. Yates, Kyle M., General Editor, *The Religious World: Communities of Faith* (New York: Macmillan Publishers, 1980, second edition), p. 33.

16. It was my privilege to visit the Masai tribe in East Africa and learn about their customs and culture.

17. Nielsen, Jr., Niels C., Hein, Norvin, Reynolds, Frank E., Karff, Samuel, Cochran, Alice C., McLean, Paul, *Religions of the World* (New York: St. Martin's Press, 1983), pp. 30–32.

18. We will use the generic term "Native Americans" and include within this term the indigenous people of the Americas such as Alaska Natives, and to a more limited degree, the indigenous peoples of Central and South America. Our focus will be on North America. I feel privileged to have lived in Alaska for five years and to have been given the opportunity to learn about the Indian and Eskimo cultures.

19. Yates, Kyle M. Jr., General Editor, *The Religious World*, p. 13. I will borrow some from this volume as this section is developed.

20. Ibid., p.13.

21. Some have argued that this challenge is at the core of the unrest in the Muslim world.

22. See, for example, Don Miguel Ruiz's small volume *The Four Agreements: A Practical Guide to Personal Freedom*, San Rafael, CA: Amber-Allen Publishing, 1997 in which Ruiz translates classic Toltec wisdom into contemporary relevance.

23. There is still a lingering stereotypical understanding of many native people, often expressed in discriminatory ways.

Chapter 3

1. See Karen Armstrong's book *The Great Transformation: The Beginning of Our Religious Traditions,* (New York: Anchor Books, 2007) for a thoughtful discussion of the origins of religion.

2. See Nielsen, et. al., *Religions of the World*, pp. 34–38 for a description of the 4 cosmologies.

3. Frankfort, Henri, *Kingship and the Gods* (Chicago, IL: University of Chicago Press, 1978) pp. 15–214, quoted by Denise L. Carmody & John T. Carmody in *Ways to the Center: An Introduction to World Religions.*

4. Several hymns, attributed to Akhenaton, reflect this tendency.

5. Ellwood, Robert S. Jr., *Many Peoples, Many Faiths: An Introduction to the Religious Life of Humankind,* (Englewood Cliffs, NJ: Prentice Hall, 1982), p. 220.

6. Thought somewhat dated, the foundational work of Jane Harrison, *Prolegomena to the Study of Greek Religion* (New York: Meridian Books, 1955, first published by Cambridge University Press in 1903) is essential reading.

7. Hutchinson, James, *Paths of Faith* (New York: McGraw-Hill Book Company, 1981), p. 45.

8. We will follow Gilbert Murray, in his classic work *Five Stages of Greek Religion* (New York: Doubleday Anchor, 1955, first published in with an additional chapter in 1925). James Hutchinson in *Paths of Faith* provides a good summary of Murray's position, pp. 46–54.

9. David Gemmell gives us a graphic and insightful picture of these events in his trilogy of novels about Troy, *Troy: The Fall of Kings,* 2007 with his spouse Stella Gemmell; *Troy: Shield of Thunder,* 2006; and *Troy: Lord of the Silver Bow,* 2005, all published by Bantam Press.

10. See Mircea Eliade, *A History of Religious Ideas*, vol. 1, pp. 247–253.

11. Jupiter is the Latin name, and each of the gods and goddesses had Latin names as they became a comparable pantheon in Roman religion.

Chapter 4

1. See Morris Berman's book, *The Reenchantment of the World* for a thoughtful and philosophical treatment of this theme.

2. Ibid. pp. 147–186.

3. For a further full account of this trend in western intellectual history, see Karen Armstrong's *A History of God* (New York: Ballantine Books, 1993) pp. 346–376.

4. Quoted by Armstrong, *A History of God*, p. 354, from Karl Marx's *The Communist Manifesto*.

5. See Nietzsche, Friedrich, *Thus Spoke Zarathustra* (New York: Penguin Books, 1961).

6. Freud, Sigmund, *The Future of an Illusion*, tr. by James Strachey (New York: W. W. Norton & Company, 1961).

7. James, William, *The Varieties of Religious Experience* (London and New York: Routledge, 2002, first published in 1902).

8. Ibid. p. 264.

9. John Bowker in *World Religions: The Great Faiths Explored & Explained* maintains that there are nearly 100 million adherents of the native religious traditions.

10. Dukas, Helen & Hoffman, Banesh (eds), *Albert Einstein: The Human Side* (Princeton: Princeton University Press, 1981) p. 43.

11. Einstein, Albert, *The World As I See It* (New York: Citadel Press, 1956, 1984, first published in 1949) pp. 26–37.

12. Kauffman, Stuart A., *Reinventing the Sacred: A New View of Science, Reason, and Religion*.

13. See Robert Wright's *The Evolution of God* (New York: Little, Brown and Company, 2009).

14. See Brian Swimme's book *The Hidden Heart of the Cosmos: Humanity and the New Story* (Maryknoll, NY: Orbis Books, 2003). See as well the book by Thomas Berry, *The Dream of the Earth*.

15. See Lovelock, James, *The Ages of Gaia: A Biography of Our Living Earth* (New York: Norton); *Gaia: A New Look at Life on Earth* (New York: Oxford University Press, 1987); and *The Revenge of Gaia: Why the Earth is Fighting Back and How We can Still Save Humanity* (New York: Basic Books, 2006).

16. See the article by Christopher Partridge in *New Religions: A Guide*, pp. 295–297. I borrow from the article and from "Wicca" in the Wikipedia Free Encyclopedia as well as many other sources.

17. Pearson, Joanne, Roberts, Richard H., and Samuel, Geoffrey, *Nature Religion Today: Paganism in the Modern World* (Edinburgh: Edinburgh University Press, 1998), p. 6.

18. Farrar, Janet and Farrar, Stewart, *A Witches' Bible: The Complete Witches Handbook* (London: Phoenix Publishing Co. 1981) pp. 181–182.

19. Adler, Margot, *Drawing Down the Moon: Witches, Druids, Goddess-Worshipers and Other Pages in America Today* (Boston: Beacon Press, 1979), p. 25.

20. Valiente, Doreen, *The ABC of Witchcraft Past and Present* (London: Phoenix Publishing Co., 1988), p. 264.

21. Farrar, Janet and Farrar, Stewart, *Eight Sabbats for Witches* (London: Robert Hale Publishing, 1992).

22. Crowley, Vivianne, *Wicca: The Old Religion in the New Age* (London: The Aquarian Press, 1989), p. 23.

23. Starhawk, *The Earth Path: Grounding Your Spirit in the Rhythms of Nature* (SanFrancisco: HarperSanFrancisco, 2004).

24. Starhawk, *The Earth Path*, p. 184.

25. Kessler, Gary E., *Shinto Ways of Being Religious* (New York: McGraw –Hill, 2005), p. 4.

26. Hutchison, John A., *Paths of Faith*, pp. 238–239.

27. Ibid., pp. 239–240.

28. Holtom, *The National Faith of Japan: A Study in Modern Shinto* (New York: Dutton, 1938), p. 106.

29. Bocking, Brian, *A Popular Dictionary of Shinto* (Richmond, VA: Curzon, 1995), p. viii.

30. Markham, Ian, the introductory article in Gary E. Kessler's *Shinto Ways of Being Religious*, pp. 3–9.

31. Hardacre, Helen, *Shinto and the State* (Princeton: Princeton University Press, 1989), p. 10.

32. Earhart, H. Byron, *Japanese Religion: Unity and Diversity* (Belmont, CA: Dickenson Publishing Co., 1969) p. 76.

33. See Ian Markham's essay in Kessler's *Shinto Ways of Being Religious*, p. 8.

34. Brocking, *A Popular Dictionary of Shinto*, p. 186.

35. Reader, Ian, *Religion in Contemporary Japan* (Basingstoke, UK: Macmillan Press, 1991), p. 236.

36. See Crowley's *Wicca: The Old Religion in the New Age*.

Chapter 5

1. Mitchell, Stephan, tr., *Bhagavad Gita: A New Translation* (New York: Three Rivers Press, 2000) pp. 16–19.

2. See Diana L. Eck, *A New Religious America*.

3. See Feuerstein, Georg, *The Deeper Dimension of Yoga: Theory and Practice* (Boston: Shambhala, 2003) for an excellent introduction to yoga. See as well Eliade, Mircea, *Yoga: Immortality and Freedom* (New York: The Bollingen Foundation, 1958).

4. An excellent treatment of the development of the religious traditions of Asia is *The Religious Traditions of Asia* edited by Joseph M. Kitagawa in the larger series, *The Encyclopedia of Religion*, edited by Mircea Eliade (New York: Macmillan Publishing Company, 1987, 1988).

5. Nielsen, Niels, Jr. et. al., *Religions of the World*, p. 91.

6. Ibid., p. 92.

7. Ibid., p. 95.

8. Three introductory books on Hinduism focusing on the religion's basic elements and the questions that arise are helpful introductions: *Vasudha, Narayanan, Hinduism: Origins, Beliefs, Practices, Holy Texts, Sacred Places* (New York: Oxford University Press, 2004; and Renard, John, *101 Questions and*

Answers on Hinduism (New York: Gramercy Books, 1999). See as well the book by David R. Kinsley, *Hinduism: A Cultural Perspective* (Englewood Cliffs, NJ: Prentice-Hall, 1982).

9. Hinduism is often described as having three spiritual pathways (*margas*), the Way of Action, the Way of Knowledge, and the Way of Devotion. Our category of right living and social order is akin to the Way of Action.

10. I am again indebted to the thoughtful description of this pathway in Nielsen, Niels, Jr. et. al., *Religions of the World*, pp. 136–152.

11. See Hans Torwesten's book, *Vedanta: The Heart of Hinduism* (New York: Grove Press, 1991), and Brian Hodgkinson, *The Essence of Vedanta* (Edison, NJ: Chartwell Books, 2006).

12. Many in the West have turned to this pathway as a means of finding peace and meaning in their lives. See, for example, the account of Ram Dass, *Paths to God: Living the Bhagavad Gita* (New York: Random House, 2004).

13. The pathway of Tantra has created a great deal of popular appeal because of its attention to the erotic in human life. It is often misunderstood. See Georg Feuerstein's excellent study, *Tantra: The Path of Ecstasy* (Boston: Shambhala Publications, 1998).

14. Mitchell, Stephen, tr., *The Bhagavad Gita*.

15. For a profound personal reflection on living in both East and West, see Diana Eck, *Encountering God: A Spiritual Journey from Bozeman to Banaras* (Boston: Beacon Press, 1993).

16. For example, The Society for Believers in Brahman, and The Aryan Society.

17. Among them are Ramakrishna Paramahamsa (1836–1886), Sarvapalli Radhakrishnan (1888–1975), Sri Aurobindo (1872–1950), and Rabindranath Tagore (1861–1941).

18. An excellent biography is Stanley Wolpert's *Gandhi's Passion: The Life and Legacy of Mahatma Gandhi* (New York: Oxford University Press, 2002).

Chapter 6

1. See John Bowker, *World Religions*, p. 210.

2. The name "Buddhism" came into use about 300 years ago.

3. Scholars disagree the precise dates of the life of Buddha.

4. For a good introduction to the life and teachings of Buddha, see Armstrong, Karen, *Buddha* (New York: Penguin Books, 2004). In addition, for access to the founding and guiding scriptures of Buddhism, turn to Goddard, Dwight, *A Buddhist Bible* (Boston: Beacon Press, 1994). See as well the more popular biographical work of Deepak Chopra, *Buddha: A Story of Enlightenment* (San Francisco: HarperSanFrancisco, 2007).

5. See the article in Gary Kessler's *Eastern Ways of Being Religious* (Mountain View, CA: Mayfield Publishing Company, 2000), p. 100.

6. Frequently, Buddhism is understood to have two major branches, Mahayana and Theravada, but others suggest that Tibetan Buddhism is really a third stream.

7. Zen Buddhism received a great deal of attention in the 1960s and 1970s in the West, and continues to be of interest to people everywhere. Two books, widely read at the time, were Watts, Alan W.,

The Way of Zen (New York: Vintage Books, 1957) and Suzuki, D. T., edited by Barrett, William, *Zen Buddhism* (Garden City, NY: Doubleday Anchor Book, 1956).

8. There is a relatively new tr. of the *Lotus Sutra* by Burton Watson (New York: Columbia University Press, 1993). For a sampling of the teaching of Nichiren Buddhism, see *The Quotable Nichiren: Words for Daily Living* (Santa Monica, CA: World Tribune Press, 2003).

9. Smith, *The World's Religions*, pp. 122–127. Smith mentions 8 fundamental differences on p.136.

10. Smith, *The World's Religions*, pp. 94–99.

11. Thich Nhat Hanh, a Vietnamese Buddhist monk, now living in a Buddhist community in France, provides an insightful and richly nuanced introduction to Buddhism in *The Heart of Buddhism: Transforming Suffering into Peace, Joy, and Liberation* (New York: Broadway Books, 1998).

12. See Antony Fernando with Leonard Swindler, *Buddhism Made Plain* (Maryknoll, NY: Orbis Books, 1985). For obvious reasons, I am a bit reluctant to include a reference to "dummies and idiot's" books, but the one on Buddhism by Jonathan Landaw and Stephan Bodian, *Buddhism for Dummies* (Hoboken, NJ: Wiley Publishing, Inc., 2003) is a very thoughtful and helpful, though popular, introduction. See pages 62–70 on the Four Noble Truths.

13. See Thich Nhat Hanh, *The Heart of Buddha's Teaching*, p. 57.

14. Das, Lama Surya, *Awakening the Buddha Within: Tibetan Wisdom for the Western World* (New York: Broadway Books, 1997), pp. 97–129.

15. Here we encounter one of the more difficult to understand assertions in Buddhism, that of the no- or non-self (*anatta*). It has been interpreted in two primary ways: (1) that we have no eternal soul, no atman, no solid self; and (2) that we have no true self or authentic identity. I lean toward the view that what is meant is that we must overcome our false self (false consciousness), become congruent and centered in order to see reality. Otherwise we will view the world through the lenses of our needs.

16. There is a difference of interpretation on this injunction to right livelihood between Mahayana and Theravada traditions, with the Mahayana, as the "large vehicle" maintaining that lay people may be liberated, whereas the Theravada traditions says that it is very difficult, if not impossible, for the lay person to be liberated.

17. See Mipham, Sakyong, *Turning the Mind Into an Ally* (New York: Riverhead Books, 2003). See also Thich Nhat Hanh, tr. by Annabel Laity, *The Blooming of a Lotus: Guided Meditations for Achieving the Miracle of Mindfulness* (Boston: Beacon Press, 1993).

18. See Chodron, Pema, edited by Berliner, Helen, *No Time to Lose: A Timely Guide to the Way of the Bodhisattva* (Boston: Shambhala Publications, 2005)

19. Das, Lama Surya, *Awakening to the Sacred: Creating a Spiritual Life from Scratch* (New York: Broadway Books, 1999), p. 96.

20. Buddhism puts less emphasis on a distinctive self that is eternal in its own right, and speaks rather of nonself, the belief that we are interconnected and a part of everything. We are impermanent. See Thich Nhat Hanh, *The Heart of the Buddha's Teaching*, pp. 133–136.

21. Thich Nhat Hanh, *The Heart of the Buddha's Teaching*, p. 136.

22. Ibid., pp. 121–254.

23. Mipham, *Turning the Mind into an Ally*.

24. Landaw and Bodian, *Buddhism for Dummies*, pp. 149–150.

25. See His Holiness the Dalai Lama with Howard C. Cutler, M. D., *The Art of Happiness* (New York: Riverhead Books, 1998). pp. 37–51.

26. In his book, His Holiness the Dalai Lama, edited by David Kittelstrom, *The Compassionate Life* (Boston: Wisdom Publications, 2003) places the emphasis on compassion as the appropriate ethical expression of Buddhist spirituality.

27. Robert Thurman, the noted American interpreter of Buddhism, in his book *Inner Revolution: Life, Liberty, and the Pursuit of Happiness* (New York: Riverhead Books, 1998) underlines this point, pp. 261–288.

28. His Holiness the Dalai Lama, *Freedom in Exile: The Autobiography of the Dalai Lama* (New York: Harper Perennial, 1990).

29. His Holiness the Dalai Lama, *Ethics for the New Millennium* (New York: Riverhead Books, 1999).

30. See Chondron, Pema, edited by Berliner, Helen, *No Time to Lose*, p. 129.

31. His Holiness the Dalai Lama, *Ethics for the New Millennium*, pp. 63–77.

32. Thich Nhat Hanh in his *Teachings on Love* (Berkeley, CA: Parallax Press, 1998) suggests a way to cultivate a life of love. He does the same for those who want to create a more peaceful world in *Creating True Peace* (New York: Free Press, 2003).

33. Dalai Lama, *The Compassionate Life*, pp. 20–23.

34. See the Dalai Lama, *The Good Heart: A Buddhist Perspective on the Teachings of Jesus* (Boston: Wisdom Publications, 1998) and Thich Nhat Hanh, *Living Buddha, Living Christ* (New York: Riverhead Books, 1995).

35. Landaw and Bodian, *Buddhism for Dummies*, pp. 326–329 for a glossary of Buddhist terms.

Chapter 7

1. Bowker, *World Religions*, p. 210.

2. Bush, Richard C., et. al., *The Religious World: Communities of Faith*, pp. 172–177.

3. Ancient Chinese society was patriarchal in character.

4. Nielsen, Niels, Jr. et. al., *Religions of the World*, p. 258.

5. It is in following the path of nature that we encounter the Doctrine of the Mean (*chung yung*), often attributed to Confucius. This doctrine suggests that we are not merely to pursue the middle course, but primarily to be in harmony with the universe. See Ch'u Chai and Winberg Chai, *Confucianism* (Woodbury, NY: Barron's Educational Series, Inc. 1973), p. 90.

6. I am indebted to Professor Julia Ching of the University of Toronto and her book *Chinese Religions* (Maryknoll, NY: Orbis Books, 1993) for guidance in this section. Professor Ching has also contributed to the essays about Confucianism in Gary Kessler's *Eastern Ways of Being Religious*.

7. Neo-Confucian thought was based on a smaller set of books, called the Four Books, and it included the *Analects*, the *Book of Mencius*, the *Great Learning* (taken from the *Book of Rites*), and the *Doctrine of the Mean* also taken from the *Book of Rites*.

8. See Huston Smith, *The World's Religions*, p. 172.

9. I follow Huston Smith's outline of the five qualities for an ideal society.

10. See Julia Ching in *Eastern Ways of Being Religious,* p. 167.

11. Julia Ching in *Eastern Ways of Being Religious,* p. 171.

12. Lao Tzu, tr. by Charles Muller, *Tao Te Ching* (New York: Barnes and Noble Classic, 1997), p. 2.

13. Again, I follow the summary given by Huston Smith in *The World's Religions,* pp. 198–206.

14. Ibid., pp. 199–206.

15. See Pamela Ball, *The Essence of Tao* (Edison, NJ: Chartwell Books, 2004), chapters 6 through chapter 9 suggest practices and include exercise (yoga) and meditation.

16. See Pamela Bell, *The Essence of the Tao,* pp. 111–126.

17. Benjamin Hoff, *The Tao of Pooh* (New York: Penguin Press, 1982).

18. Fritjof Capra's *The Tao of Physics* (New York: Bantam Books, 1984).

Chapter 8

1. Feiler, Bruce, *Abraham: A Journey to the Heart of Three Faiths* (New York: William Morrow, An Imprint of HarperCollins Publishers, Inc., 2002).

2. Smart, Ninian, *The Religious Experience of Mankind,* Third Edition (New York: Charles Scribner's Sons, 1984), p. 288. I am indebted to Ninian Smart for this section. A modern and acclaimed Jewish scholar, Martin Buber provides us with a study of Moses in his book, *Moses* (Oxford, UK: East & West Library, 1946).

3. Exodus 3. 1–14.

4. See Niels C. Niesen, Jr. et. al., *Religions of the World,* pp. 434–435.

5. There are many accounts (libraries) of the history of the Jewish people. One that has been helpful to me is Paul Johnson's *A History of the Jews* (New York: Harper and Row Publishers, 1987).

6. *A New Handbook of World Religions* edited by John R. Hinnels (Oxford, UK: Blackwell Press, 1997) p. 17 records the world Jewish population at 14,420,000.

7. Jewish scholar, Jacob Neusner, suggests four epochs of Jewish history: The first age of diversity (586 BCE–70 CE; The age of definition (70–640); The age of cogency (640–1800); and The second age of diversity (1800–present). Neusner's essay is in *The Four Periods in the History of Judaism* in Gary E. Kessler's *Western Ways of Being Religious,* (Mountain View, CA: Mayfield Publishing Co. 2000), pp. 41–49.

8. I follow the account and categories in Niels C. Nielsen, Jr., et. al., *Religions of the World.*

9. A group called the *Zealots* led the resistance.

10. The rituals and structure of this community came to light in the discovery of the Dead Sea Scrolls.

11. The Jewish historian, Josephus, is a good source of information about this period in his writings called *The Jewish War.*

12. For a helpful discussion of this era of Jewish life, see Karen Armstrong's *The Bible: A Biography* (New York: Grove Press, 2007) pp. 79–101.

13. His writing includes *The Book of Beliefs and Opinions* which is described by Paul Johnson, *A History of the Jews* (New York: Harper & Row Publishers, 1987), pp. 161 and 191 and Max L. Margolis and

Alexander Marx, *A History of the Jewish People* (Philadelphia: The Jewish Publication Society of America, 1927), pp. 264–272.

14. A good introduction to Kabbalah is David Aaron's *Endless Light: The Ancient Path of Kabbalah to Love, Spiritual Growth, and Personal Power* (New York: Berkley Books, 1997). See also the book in the series *The Classics of Western Spirituality* tr. by Daniel Chanan Matt, and attributed to Moses de Leon (1250–1305, *Zohar: The Book of Enlightenment* (New York: Paulist Press, 1983). This spiritual pathway is complex and elusive.

15. Martin Buber spoke with this language, and Elie Wiesel gave personal testimony to his suffering in the Holocaust in his book *Night* (New York: Hill and Wang, 2006, a new translation from the French by Marion Wiesel).

16. See Abraham Joshua Heschel, *God in Search of Man: A Philosophy of Judaism* (Northvale, NJ: Jason Aronson Inc., 1955) and *Man Is Not Alone: A Philosophy of Religion* (New York: Farrar, Straus and Giroux, 1951).

17. An excellent introduction to Jewish beliefs and practices is George Robinson's *Essential Judaism: A Complete Guide to Beliefs, Customs, and Rituals* (New York: Pocket Books, 2000). Another introduction, a bit more popular in tone, is Shmuley Boteach, *Judaism for Everyone: Renewing Your Life Through the Vibrant Lessons of the Jewish Faith* (New York: Basic Books, 2002).

18. There are many excellent theological works that articulate the many and varied beliefs of Judaism. One quite philosophical and influential book is Franz Rosensweig's *The Star of Redemption* (Boston: Beacon Press, 1972). It was translated from an earlier edition by William W. Hallo.

19. See the influential work of Martin Buber, *I and Thou* (New York: Charles Scribner's Sons, 1958).

20. See Huston Smith, *The World's Religions,* pp. 299–303.

21. I have been helped with this question by Anita Diamant and Howard Cooper's book, *Living the Jewish Life* (New York: HarperResource, 1991).

22. For those without family, the larger community of the synagogue becomes family.

23. Others include Sukkot and Simchat Torah, Tu B'Shvat, Purim, Shavuot, and Tisha B'Av as historical holidays, and those added more recently include Holocaust Remembrance Day and Israel Independence Day.

24. Called by CNN "Warriors of God."

Chapter 9

1. New Testament scholars speak about another document called Q (German word *Quelle* meaning "source") which contains sayings of Jesus, not accounts of his life, and this material is used in Luke and Matthew, not Mark.

2. There is great diversity in the understanding the documents of the New Testament and how accurate they are in providing direct historical descriptions of the life and teaching of Jesus. There are those within the Christian community that believe in their full accuracy and others that believe that they must be understood in the framework of critical historical scholarship.

3. Some scholars doubt the historical accuracy of the birth accounts of Jesus and would prefer to call them "legends" that attempt to see Jesus in a supernatural framework. A more traditional view with

excellent scholarship is Raymond E. Brown's *The Birth of the Messiah: Commentary on the Infancy Narratives in the Gospels of Matthew and Luke* (New York: Doubleday, 1977)

4. Mt. 3.16–17.

5. Mt., in 4.1–11 records the "temptations of Jesus" in the wilderness as part of his preparation for his life work.

6. Mk 1.14–15.

7. There are many accounts of the resurrection. Paul provides a summary in I Cor. 15.3–8.

8. There orthodox tradition became creedal at the Council of Nicea in 325 CE, and then again at the Council of Chalcedon in 451 CE.

9. There are many books that trace this story, and many which focus on recent scholarship about Jesus. See Pelikan, Jaroslav, *Jesus Through the Centuries: His Place in the History of Culture* (New Haven, CT: Yale University Press, 1999). See Borg, Marcus J., *Jesus: Uncovering the Life, Teachings, and Relevance of a Religious Revolutionary* (San Francisco: HarperSanFrancisco, 2006 for a contemporary interpretation if Jesus.

10. There is an extensive and impressive array of scholarship on the meaning of "the Kingdom of God." I have chosen to interpret the term as the "reign" of God, and because "reign" has connotations of a monarch, I often speak of the term as the "nearness, power, and presence" of God. For our purposes, I am also interpreting the Kingdom of God in terms of its personal application for spiritual formation.

11. Bornkamm, Gunther, *Jesus of Nazareth* (New York: Harper & Row, Publishers, 1960), pp. 64–95.

12. A thoughtful introduction to the place of Jesus in the nurture of the spiritual life may be found in Placher, William C., *Jesus the Savior: The Meaning of Jesus Christ for the Christian Faith* (Louisville, KY: Westminster John Knox Press, 2001). See as well the "progressive-conservative" dialogue between Marcus J. Bork and N. T. Wright in *The Meaning of Jesus* (San Francisco: HarperSanFrancisco, 1999).

13. As with Jesus, there are "libraries full of books" about Paul. We will not review this literature and the many issues about the interpretation of the Apostle Paul's teaching and influence. Our goal is rather to see in what ways the core of his teaching provides guidance in spiritual formation. A recent book by John Dominic Crossan and Jonathan L. Reed, *In Search of Paul: How Jesus's Apostle Opposed Rome's Empire with God's Kingdom* (San Francisco: HarperSanFrancisco, 2004) is especially helpful.

14. See the first three volumes of the encyclopedic history of spirituality that deal with Christian spirituality, Cousins, Ewert, General Editor, *Worldly Spirituality* with the first volume on *Christian Spirituality: Origins from the Twelfth Century,* edited by McGinn, Bernard, Meyendorff, John, and Leclercq, Jean, (New York: Crossroad, 1985); see also the series entitled *The Classics of Western Spirituality,* Farina, John, Editor in Chief, which has published several volumes.; and there is the introductory book edited by Jones, Cheslyn, Wainwright, Geoffrey, and Yarnold, Edward, *The Study of Spirituality* (New York: Oxford University Press, 1986*).* See as well the work of Smith, Huston, *The Soul of Christianity: Restoring the Great Tradition* (San Francisco: HarperSanFrancisco, 2005) and Borg, Marcus J., *The Heart of Christianity: Rediscovering a Life of Faith* for two recent attempts to describe the pathways of Christian spirituality.

15. Foster, Richard J., *Streams of Living Water* (San Francisco: HarperSanFrancisco, 1998), pp. 3–22.

16. See Evelyn Underhill's class work *Mysticism* (New York: New American Library, 1955) and Johnston, William, ed., *The Cloud of Unknowing* (New York: Image Books, 1973). See as well the classic work *Meister Eckhart: A Modern Translation* (New York: Harper & Row, 1941).

17. See Thomas Merton's book, *Contemplative Prayer* (New York: Image Books, 1971).

18. See Mott, Michael, *The Seven Mountains of Thomas Merton* (Boston: Houghton Mifflin Company, 1984) for an excellent biography of Thomas Merton.

19. The Quaker tradition is expressive of these values. See Steer, Douglas V. ed., *Quaker Spirituality: Selected Writings* (New York: Paulist Press, 1984).

20. See Benedictine Monks of St. Meinrad, *The Holy Rule of St. Benedict* (St. Meinrad, IN: Grail Press, 1956).

21. See Corbishley, T., *The Spiritual Exercises* (London: Burns & Oates, 1963).

22. Bonhoeffer, Dietrich, tr. by Doberstein, John W., *Life Together: A Discussion of Christian Fellowship* (New York: Harper & Brothers, 1954).

23. *Life in the Spirit: Reflections, Meditations, Prayers* (San Francisco: Harper & Row, Publishers, 1983), p. 26. Only in 2007 did we learn about Mother Teresa's personal struggle of not sensing the immediate presence of God in her life.

24. See the classic study of "call" to the holy life in Law, William, *A Serious Call to a Devout & Holy Life* (New York: E. P. Dutton & Co., 1906).

25. The emphasis on the "the social gospel" in the early twentieth century and emergence of liberation theologies in recent decades may be seen as an expression of spiritual pathways that seek to transform oppressive social structures.

26. Foster, Richard J., *Streams of Living Water*, pp. 185–233.

27. See I Cor. 15.1–ll, Rom. 1.1–4, and Acts 2. 22–24.

28. A widely circulated book in the last few years in the evangelical tradition is Rick Warren's *The Purpose Driven Life* (Grand Rapids, MI: Zondervan, 2002).

29. The list is quite long, but on it should be people of different genders and the many branches of the Christian family. Many contemporary feminist theologians have enriched and guided the whole of Christendom. On the American scene, I think particularly of Sally McFague and Rosemary Radford Reuther.

30. Foster, Richard J., *Streams of Living Water*, pp. 235–274.

31. See Maloney, George A., S.J., ed., *Pilgrims of the Heart: A Treasury of Eastern Christian Spirituality* (San Francisco: Harper & Row, Publishers, 1983).

32. Fox, Mathew, *Creation Spirituality: Liberating Gifts for the Peoples of the Earth* (San Francisco: HarperSanFranciso, 1991).

33. Fowler, James W., *The Stages of Faith: The Psychology of Human Development and the Quest for Meaning* (San Francisco: Harper & Row, 1981).

34. Wilbur, Ken, *Integral Spirituality: A Startling Role for Religion in the Modern and Postmodern World* (Boston: Integral Books, 2006). We will speak more about these patterns of spirituality in the final chapter.

35. Note: I write these observations as an "insider" and therefore have both an insider's knowledge and bias.

36. Thomas A' Kempis, *The Imitation of Christ* (New York: Books, Inc., no date given). His dates are 1379–1471.

37. Wallis, Jim, *God's Politics* (San Francisco: HarperSanFrancisco, 2005).

Chapter 10

1. Islam means submission, but it also contains the root word for peace. So we might say that Islam teaches the spiritual way of submission that leads to peace.

2. Esposito, John L., *Islam: The Straight Path,* Revised Third Addition (New York: Oxford University Press) pp. 159–159. See also Allawi, Ali A., *The Crisis of Islamic Civilization* (New Haven, CT: Yale University Press, 2009).

3. John Bowker in *World Religions: The Great Faiths Explored and Explained* lists the number of Muslims of the world as 1,033,453,000.

4. See Bruce Riedel's *The Search of al Qaeda: Its Leadership, Ideology, and Future* for a thoughtful and thorough account of the al Qaeda movement.

5. The term, "straight path" comes directly from the opening page of the Quran. It is occasionally translated "right path."

6. One good example of interreligious cooperation is expressed in the work of Ranya Idliby, Suzanne Oliver, and Priscilla Warner in *The Faith Club: A Muslim, A Christian, A Jew—Three Women Search for Understanding* (New York: Free Press, 2006).

7. For a good introduction to Islam, written by a keen observer although not an "insider," see Karen Armstrong's *Islam: A Short History* (New York: The Modern Library, 2002).

8. One helpful account of the life of Muhammad is Karen Armstrong's *Muhammad: Prophet for Our Time* (New York: HarperOne, 2006).

9. See the account of the major events of the life of Muhammad, written by the scholarly "insider" Tariq Ramadan, *In the Footsteps of the Prophet: Lessons from the Life of Muhammad* (New York: Oxford University Press, 2007).

10. The Muslim calendar begins on the first day of the lunar year in which Muhammad immigrated to Medina. This event is called the *Hijrah*.

11. Bush, Richard C., et. al., *The Religious World: Communities of Faith*, pp. 316–317.

12. Tariq Ramadan makes this point very strongly in his book, *In the Footsteps of the Prophet*.

13. I have been helped in my understanding of the Quran by Walter H. Wagner's book, *Opening the Qur'an: Introducing Islam's Holy Book* (Notre Dame, IN: University of Notre Dame Press, 2008).

14. A very helpful book about the teachings of Islam written by a Muslim scholar is Sayyed Hossein Nasr's *The Heart of Islam: Enduring Values for Humanity* (San Francisco, CA: HarperSanFrancisco, 2002). For those wanting basic questions to be answered, see John L. Esposito's *What Everyone Needs to Know about Islam* (New York: Oxford University Press, 2002).

15. See Wagner, *Opening the Quran*, pp. 90–91.

16. There are other lists of foundational beliefs for Islam that differ from this list. This list of five here does not represent an authoritative creedal statement such as the Five Pillars of practice.

17. See Seyyed Hossein Nasr in *The Heart of Islam*, pp. 113–156.

18. For a more detailed description of the pattern of worship, see Richard C. Bush, et. al., *The Religious World: Communities of Faith*, pp. 324–325.

19. Wagner, Walter, *Opening the Quran*, p. 82.

20. There are many other holidays and festivals during the year.

21. For a vivid account of the experience of the pilgrimage is in the book by Asra Q. Nomani, *Standing Alone: An American Woman's Struggle for the Soul of Islam* (San Francisco: HarperSanFrancisco) pp. 115–145.

22. One of these laws prohibited men from having more than four wives.

23. These customs continue in many Muslim countries today.

24. There have been recent incidents and conflicts in both France and the United Kingdom.

25. We observe the role of the senior Iman, called the Ayatollah, in the leadership of Iran.

26. Two major groups were formed, differing on succession and interpretation: *Ithna Ashariyya* and *Ismailiyya*.

27. See Seyyed Hossein Nasr, *The Heart of Islam* for a thoughtful treatment of the various schools of law within Sunni Islam, pp. 115–156.

28. Schwarz, Stephen, *The Two Faces of Islam: The House of Sa'ud From Tradition to Terror* (New York: Doubleday, 2002) pp. 66–91.

29. The works of Tariq Ramadan and Seyyed Hossein Nasr are examples.

30. I have been helped by the collection selected and translated by Carl W. Ernst, *Teaching of Sufism* (Boston: Shambhala, 1999) and John Baldock's *The Essence of Sufism* (Edison, NJ: Chartwell Books, 2004).

31. Published by Cambridge University Press, 2008.

32. See Esposito, John L., *Islam: The Straight Path*, pp. 165–166. I am using some of his language, his categories, and lists and remain grateful for his knowledge and insight.

33. I have used several sources for the information about al Qaeda, including extensive searching of websites such as Middle East Facts, and scouring current magazines and newspapers. There are daily reports.

34. Once again, I have found the most recent information about the Taliban in various websites including the Wikipedia free encyclopedia, currents magazines, and daily newspapers. Hardly a day goes by when there isn't an article about the Taliban.

35. For a fictional account of this era, see Khaled Hosseini's *The Kite Runner* (New York: Riverhead Books, 2003).

36. Published by Yale University Press, New Haven, 2009.

37. See the writings of Asra Q. Nomani who raises these questions in *Standing Alone: An American Woman's Struggle for the Soul of Islam*. See as well Irsha Manj's *The Trouble with Islam Today: A Muslim's Call for Reform in Her Faith* (New York: St. Martin's Griffin, 2005).

Chapter 11

1. Published by Boston: Beacon Press, 1992.

2. There are a number of excellent books that describe the wide range of new spiritual ways that are available to the honest searcher. Earlier I referred to the helpful volume edited by Christopher Partridege, *New Religions: A Guide.* One other book that I will mention is edited by Laurence Brown, Bernard C. Farr, and R. Joseph Hoffmann, *Modern Spiritualities: An Inquiry* (New York: Prometheus Books, 1977).

3. There are many authors who describe a spiritual pathway that is thoughtfully eclectic, drawing upon ancient wisdom and current insight. Eckhart Tolle's writings, including *A New Earth: Awakening to Your Life's Purpose* (New York: A Plume Book, 2006) which was recommended by Oprah Winfrey is a good example. So too is Gary Zukavs *The Seat of the Soul* (New York: Simon and Schuster, 1989). Deepak Chopra's *How to Know God: The Soul's Journey into the Mystery of Mysteries* (New York: Three Rivers Press, 2000) is a thoughtful contribution from a Hindu perspective. This genre is widespread.

4. The works of Ken Wilbur, rooted in both the social sciences and classic religious wisdom, are attractive to many because of the level of scholarship, the seriousness with which he asks his readers to engage with the changing world, and the way he frames an outlook that is future oriented. See, for example, Wilber, Ken, *Integral Spirituality: A Startling New Role for Religion in the Modern and Postmodern World.*

5. There are several books, written by well-educated and thoughtful people who argue this point of view. See Christopher Hitchens, *God Is Not Great: How Religion Poisons Everything* (New York: Twelve, 2007).

6. Gary Kessler's *Ways of Being Religious* provides an excellent summary of the world's religions with readings as I mentioned in Chapter 1.

7. Huston Smith in his *Forgotten Truth: The Primordial Tradition* (New York: Harper & Row, 1976) prefers "primordial" over perennial in that it means from the beginning or always with us.

8. See Chapter One for a description of "life-giving," p. 13. There are also a number of wise and thoughtful people who have written about this strategy. In particular, the book by Roger Walsh, *Essential Spirituality: The 7 Central Practices to Awaken the Heart and Mind, Exercises from the World's Religions to Cultivate Kindness, Love, Joy, Peace, Vision, Wisdom, and Generosity* (New York: John Wiley & Sons, 1999) is especially helpful.

9. See Wilber, Ken, *Integral Spirituality.* Ken Wilber has made an extraordinary attempt to provide an integrated and comprehensive worldview that has a spiritual core.

10. See the work of Jacob Neusner and Bruce Chilton, eds., *Altruism in World Religions*

11. See Chapter One for a list of qualities expected in the practice of love and compassion, pp. 11–12.

12. In these suggestions, I learn from Roger Walsh in *Essential Spirituality.*

Index

Abel 3, 33, 142
Abraham 82, 137, 139, 140, 141, 142, 143, 144, 157, 159, 173, 174, 185, 189
Abrahamic 41, 137, 140, 159, 173, 177, 202, 213, 215
Abu Bakr 182, 191
accents 85, 88, 92, 95, 96
accommodate 42, 95, 178
accommodation 15, 38, 178, 179
Acropolis 48
advaita 139
Aeschylus 51, 55
Afghanistan 16, 178, 179, 196, 197, 198, 199
afterlife 24, 26, 46, 47, 48, 54, 71, 120
agape 8
agriculture 24, 30, 43, 44, 45, 46, 57, 85, 87
ahimsa 91, 96
al Qaeda 178, 196, 197
al Qaida *see* al Qaeda
Alaska 31, 35, 222n. 18
Ali 182, 192
Allah 140, 177, 181, 184, 185, 188, 213
Analects 122, 123, 124, 125, 227n. 7
ancestor 29, 120, 137
ancestors 24, 26, 29, 30, 31, 32, 39, 76, 120, 121, 122, 126, 153, 164
angel 185
angels 161, 185, 201
anger 26, 39, 113
animism 26, 65, 83
apocalyptic 147
Apollo 48, 49, 50
Arab 141, 150, 178, 179, 180, 184, 194, 197
Arabian Peninsula 140, 179, 183, 190
Arabic 184, 192, 196
archeological 70, 120
archeology 48
arhat 104, 105, 111
Aristotle 52, 53, 150, 194
Arjuna 94, 95

artifacts 28, 32, 48, 101, 198
Aryan 84, 85, 86, 87, 88, 89
ascetic 92, 102, 103, 106, 148, 169
Ashkenazim 151
Athens 48, 51, 56
atman 86, 90, 91, 111, 139, 226n. 15
Aton 46, 47
Augustine 171
Australia 10, 28, 62
authentic 11, 15, 41, 109, 112, 134, 193, 202, 208, 226n. 15
awakening 103, 105, 109, 111
awe 24, 37, 62, 63, 71
aya 184

Baals 144
Banaras 97, 99
Bar 151
Bat Mitzvah 151
beauty 50, 62, 65, 66, 70, 74, 75, 108, 128, 130, 134
Being 14, 29, 92, 99, 139, 140, 148, 174, 184
beings 6, 13, 18, 25, 26, 29, 33, 37, 50, 51, 60, 64, 88, 89, 90, 91, 97, 98, 104, 106, 121, 122, 134, 135, 139, 173, 185, 186
belief(s) 5, 7, 10, 11, 12, 13, 14, 15, 17, 18, 24, 25, 26, 31, 32, 33, 34, 35, 36, 37, 39, 42, 45, 46, 47, 48, 53, 54, 55, 57, 60, 61, 63, 64, 66, 67, 68, 74, 81, 82, 83, 85, 87, 88, 89, 92, 94, 96, 98, 99, 101, 104, 106, 110, 113, 116, 119, 120, 121, 122, 126, 130, 133, 137, 139, 140, 141, 143, 144, 146, 147, 149, 151, 153, 157, 158, 159, 160, 161, 163, 170, 171, 173, 177, 181, 182, 183, 184, 185, 186, 187, 192, 195, 198, 200, 201, 202, 208, 211, 212, 213, 214, 215, 216, 218, 221n. 3, 226n. 20, 229n. 17, 233n. 16
Bible 11, 137, 141, 142, 143, 147, 148, 149, 155, 157, 158, 159, 168, 169, 183, 209, 217
blessed 165, 208

bliss 103, 111
Bodhi 103
bodhisattva 104, 110, 111, 113, 115
body 27, 45, 47, 83, 86, 91, 97, 109, 110, 112, 129, 169, 172, 174, 215
Book of Changes 121, 124
Brahman 89, 90, 91, 92, 94, 95, 96, 99, 139, 225n. 16
Brahmin 88, 95, 99, 102
branches 15, 48, 101, 104, 115, 156, 169, 184, 193, 225n. 6, 231n. 29
breath 14
bridge(s) 1, 11, 82
British 63, 84, 95
Buddha 101, 102, 104, 105, 106, 107, 109, 110, 111, 112, 115, 116, 122, 196, 209, 225n. 3
Buddhism 13, 14, 15, 71, 73, 76, 79, 83, 100, 101, 104, 105, 106, 107, 109, 110, 111, 114, 115, 116, 122, 127, 133, 140, 210, 213, 225n. 6, 226n. 15
burial 35, 44, 120
Byzantine 179, 190

Caliph 191
Caliphate 197
Canaan 144
canon 104, 142, 148, 160
caste 74, 87, 88, 98, 102
center 36, 52
centered 36, 46, 47, 90, 102, 108, 112, 115, 191, 213, 226
ceremony 34, 43, 72, 86, 130
change 6, 9, 15, 30, 44, 47, 49, 61, 63, 70, 71, 75, 84, 90, 95, 119, 122, 131, 134, 145, 151, 152, 181, 194, 195, 205, 207, 209, 211
chien ai 124
China 5, 25, 44, 62, 67, 76, 82, 83, 84, 104, 119, 120, 122, 126, 129, 130, 133, 134, 213
Chinese 6, 68, 71, 79, 115, 118, 119, 120, 121, 122, 123, 126, 127, 133, 134, 135
Christian 11, 14, 15, 18, 36, 72, 111, 141, 144, 149, 155, 159, 160, 161, 163, 164, 166, 167, 168, 169, 170, 171, 172, 173, 174, 175, 179, 183, 185, 196, 197, 198, 200, 210, 211, 216, 219n. 16, 229n. 2

Christianity 9, 13, 15, 31, 52, 133, 140, 141, 142, 144, 146, 149, 150, 156, 157, 159, 163, 166, 171, 172, 173, 174, 177, 178, 179, 181, 209, 210, 214
chun tzu 125, 126
church 4, 160, 161, 163, 167, 169, 172, 174, 210
Circle of Life 67
city 93, 161, 180, 182, 191, 198, 199
city-state 24, 43, 44, 49, 52, 54, 56, 118
civilization 44, 48, 49, 84, 85, 120, 179, 180, 201
commitment 14, 67, 82, 96, 114, 135, 182, 184, 187, 189, 195, 210, 214
community 4, 8, 9, 11, 13, 14, 15, 16, 17, 24, 30, 31, 33, 42, 43, 63, 64, 68, 96, 97, 101, 105, 111, 113, 114, 126, 148, 149, 150, 151, 155, 156, 160, 161, 162, 166, 167, 168, 170, 173, 174, 175, 180, 182, 186, 187, 190, 191, 192, 193, 196, 200, 201, 210, 214, 216, 217, 26n. 11, 229n. 2, 229n. 22
compassion 7, 8, 9, 10, 17, 65, 74, 95, 96, 97, 100, 101, 103, 104, 107, 108, 109, 111, 112, 113, 114, 154, 156, 166, 170, 171, 173, 183, 208, 213, 215, 216
Comte, Auguste 60
Confucian 83, 122, 124, 126, 133, 134
Confucianism 13, 44, 67, 73, 76, 79, 83, 84, 118, 119, 121, 122, 126, 127, 128, 130, 133, 134, 140, 213
Confucius 120, 122, 123, 124, 125, 126, 127, 227n. 5
consciousness 6, 14, 25, 60, 83, 90, 91, 103, 110, 119
conservative 134, 150, 171, 178, 193, 209
Conservative Judaism 152
construct 107, 115
constructs 8
contemplative 169
context 7, 8, 11, 14, 15, 23, 35, 38, 43, 53, 56, 66, 67, 73, 83, 84, 87, 88, 100, 101, 111, 115, 119, 120, 131, 137, 141, 145, 154, 162, 167, 178, 193, 195
core 17, 64, 85, 101, 106, 109, 111, 114, 137, 147, 153, 166, 177, 200, 230n. 13
cosmology 84, 86
cosmos 6, 26, 27, 32, 75

coven 64, 65, 66
covenant 141, 143, 144, 145, 146, 149, 153
covens 63
crave 107
craving 106, 107
creed 14, 42, 64, 96, 200, 214, 215
creeds 24, 31, 43, 82, 215
Crete 48, 49
critical 4, 6, 13, 60, 94, 141, 161, 162, 163,
     179, 201, 215
crucifixion 160
cult 47, 52, 64, 82, 96, 97, 101, 194,
     214, 216
cultic 10, 14, 24, 31, 42, 51, 84, 102, 115,
     145
cultivate 12, 16, 65, 97, 108, 127, 128,
     129, 169, 216
cultivation 105, 106, 112, 113, 129, 155
cultural 4, 5, 7, 14, 18, 48, 55, 67, 76,
     126, 128, 153, 166, 168, 180, 198, 201,
     205, 212
culture 4, 5, 8, 9, 15, 16, 17, 24, 25, 27, 28,
     30, 31, 32, 35, 36, 37, 38, 41, 42, 43, 44,
     45, 48, 52, 53, 54, 55, 57, 59, 64, 65, 67,
     68, 69, 70, 71, 74, 75, 76, 82, 83, 85, 96,
     98, 101, 110, 115, 116, 119, 124, 126,
     127, 129, 132, 133, 134, 135, 140, 147,
     148, 161, 172, 173, 174, 177, 178, 179,
     181, 193, 198, 202, 207, 209, 212, 213,
     214, 215, 216, 222n. 16, 222n. 18
cycle 24, 30, 34, 54, 67, 90, 92, 96, 105,
     107, 110, 132, 155
cyclical 24, 45

Dalai Lama 14, 17, 105, 113, 115, 210,
     219n. 1
Daniel 142, 147, 163
Darwin, Charles 60
David 144, 145, 148, 162
Dead Sea 148
death 23, 24, 27, 34, 35, 45, 47, 53, 54, 60,
     65, 67, 69, 90, 103, 105, 110, 111, 119,
     120, 123, 129, 131, 149, 155, 160, 166,
     167, 180, 182, 183, 184, 190, 191, 192
deconstruction 4
deities 50, 70, 84, 92, 181, 182
deity 29, 46, 49, 60, 69, 70, 96, 123
demon(ic) 94, 101, 115

destiny 24, 50, 51, 52, 62, 110, 186
devotion 92, 93, 97, 105, 121, 155, 183,
     187, 194, 200, 225n. 9
dharma 87, 88, 102, 106, 107, 111
Diaspora 146, 147, 153, 156
diet 91, 97, 129, 141, 191, 198
din 190
Dionysus 48
discipline 14, 16, 17, 27, 36, 37, 48, 74, 83,
     91, 92, 95, 97, 99, 104, 105, 106, 109,
     110, 112, 113, 114, 129, 169, 170, 215
distortion 37, 61, 221n. 14
divination 39, 121
divine 7, 8, 13, 16, 17, 18, 21, 25, 26, 27,
     28, 29, 30, 32, 35, 36, 37, 38, 41, 42, 43,
     44, 46, 47, 48, 50, 52, 54, 55, 56, 57, 62,
     63, 64, 65, 66, 67, 68, 69, 72, 73, 75, 89,
     90, 91, 92, 93, 96, 97, 98, 105, 106, 118,
     121, 135, 139, 149, 152, 153, 154, 163,
     169, 181, 183, 184, 185, 186, 187, 189,
     194, 201, 202, 205, 208, 212, 214, 215,
     216, 217, 221n. 8
divinely 183, 185, 192, 200, 201, 209
document 149, 159, 160, 209, 229n. 1,
     229n. 2
dreamtime 28
dynasty 44, 120

ecology 215
Eden 3, 4, 5, 8, 59, 60, 69
Egypt 26, 44, 45, 46, 47, 48, 49, 53, 54,
     55, 56, 120, 141, 142, 143, 150, 161,
     164, 197
Eightfold Path 114, 210
Einstein, Albert 62, 74
Elohim 141, 142
El-Shaddai 141
enlightenment 28, 37, 42, 43, 60, 100,
     101, 102, 168, 103, 105, 106, 107, 108,
     109, 110, 111, 151, 194
epistemological 4
equanimity 104, 108, 111, 113, 114
Eskimo 31, 33, 222n. 18
Esposito, John 195
essence 16, 26, 66, 86, 89, 90, 92, 96, 105,
     155, 187, 188, 201
Essene 162
Essenes 148

eternal 45, 53, 86, 111, 115, 118, 119, 127, 186, 226n. 15, 226n. 20
ethic(al) 8, 14, 17, 18, 26, 30, 34, 37, 42, 43, 51, 53, 55, 64, 65, 73, 87, 97, 98, 102, 106, 112, 113, 114, 120, 123, 126, 131, 133, 134, 135, 143, 145, 146, 149, 152, 154, 168, 173, 200, 208, 212, 213, 215
ethnocentric 56
Eucharist 172, 216
Euripides 51
evangelical 171, 231n. 28
evolution 60, 62, 66, 68, 115, 142, 221n. 8
exile 142, 146, 149, 158
Exodus 142, 144, 145, 155
Ezra 142, 146

fast(ing) 34, 103, 169, 188, 189
fatalism 56
fate 24, 47, 50, 51, 52, 166
Fatima 180, 192
fear 10, 18, 24, 27, 42, 53, 62, 90, 91, 110, 115, 119
fecundity 24
fertility 43, 67, 71, 84, 85, 93, 120, 121, 144
Feuerbach, Ludwig 60
filial piety 125
Five Pillars of Islam 14, 187, 200
Four Noble Truths 14, 106
Four Passing Sights 103
Freud, Sigmund 60
fundamentalism 7

Gaia 63
Galilee 161 162
Ganges River 102
Gautama, Siddhartha 101, 102
Gemara 149
Genesis 14, 60, 68, 142
God(s) 7, 8, 11, 12, 14, 26, 27, 29, 30, 31, 33, 34, 37, 42, 44, 45, 46, 47, 48, 49, 50, 51, 52, 53, 54, 55, 56, 60, 62, 64, 65, 66, 68, 79, 81, 85, 86, 87, 89, 92, 93, 95, 96, 97, 98, 101, 102, 110, 111, 115, 119, 121, 129, 135, 139, 140, 141, 142, 143, 144, 145, 146, 147, 148, 149, 150, 151, 152, 153, 154, 156, 158, 159, 160, 162, 163, 164, 165, 166, 167, 168, 169, 170, 171, 172, 173, 174, 175, 177, 181, 182, 183, 184, 185, 186, 187, 188, 189, 190, 191, 194, 195, 200, 201, 202, 208, 209, 210, 213, 215, 217, 221n. 8, 223n. 11, 230n. 10, 231n. 23
Goddess(es) 26, 30, 45, 49, 50, 63, 64, 65, 66, 70, 71, 93, 101, 115, 119, 140, 144, 223n. 11
gospel 157, 160, 161, 162, 163, 164, 165, 166, 167, 168, 213, 231n. 25
Greece 26, 44, 48, 49, 50, 51, 52, 53, 54, 55
Greek 48, 49, 51, 52, 54, 55, 56, 63, 64, 74, 146, 150, 165, 193, 194
guru 14, 97

hadith 183
Hagar 141
Hajj 189, 200
Hanukah 155
harmony 16, 30, 37, 41, 79, 86, 112, 121, 122, 126, 127, 131, 134, 135, 156, 168, 227n. 5
Harry Potter 63, 64, 74
Hasidism 151
Hellenistic 146, 147, 166
Herod 148, 161, 162
hieroglyphics 44
Higher Power 16, 123
Hindu(ism) 13, 76, 79, 81, 83, 84, 85, 86, 87, 88, 89, 90, 91, 92, 93, 94, 95, 96, 98, 100, 101, 103, 111, 114, 140, 210, 212, 225n. 9
history 8, 9, 30, 31, 36, 43, 44, 45, 46, 47, 48, 51, 54, 60, 63, 66, 70, 71, 81, 83, 84, 85, 96, 118, 123, 127, 134, 140, 141, 142, 144, 145, 147, 149, 153, 154, 155, 159, 161, 163, 164, 166, 170, 172, 173, 177, 178, 182, 186, 190, 194, 201, 205, 213, 228n. 5, 228n. 7, 230n. 14
holiness 15, 146
holy 14, 68, 71, 95, 97, 161, 163, 167, 168, 169, 170, 171, 172, 183, 195, 196
Holy Spirit 163, 167, 168, 170
Homer 49, 50, 53
hsiao 125
hubris 51, 174

ideological 7, 10, 205
Iliad 49
iman 192, 233n. 25

immortal(ity) 44, 90, 93, 96
incarnation 65, 94, 102, 110, 115, 172
India 5, 6, 13, 82, 83, 84, 85, 87, 88, 93,
     94, 95, 96, 100, 102, 103, 104, 118, 139,
     190, 193, 222n. 18
Indra 86, 92
Indus Valley 85
Iraq 5, 179
Isaiah 142, 146, 151
Ishmael 141, 189
Islam(ic) 5, 11, 12, 13, 14, 15, 31, 52,
     73, 133, 140, 141, 142, 144, 146,
     150, 156, 159, 175, 177, 178, 179,
     180, 183, 184, 185, 186, 187, 188,
     189, 190, 191, 192, 193, 194, 195,
     196, 197, 198, 199, 200, 201, 214,
     232n. 1, 232n. 16
Israel(ites) 13, 143, 144, 145, 149, 153,
     156, 157, 179, 195, 197, 229n. 23

Jainism 83
James, William 61
Japan 62, 67, 68, 69, 70, 71, 72, 73, 75, 76,
     82, 83, 84, 104, 105, 111, 140, 212
Jen 125, 126
Jeremiah 142, 146, 151
Jerusalem 145, 146, 147, 162
Jesus Christ 11, 16, 106, 122, 123, 142,
     144, 148, 149, 151, 159, 160, 161, 162,
     163, 164, 165, 166, 167, 168, 171, 172,
     173, 174, 175, 180, 185, 209, 215, 217,
     229n. 2, 229n. 3, 230n. 12
Jews 146, 148, 149, 150, 151, 152, 156,
     158, 161, 179, 183, 185, 196, 197, 198
jihad(ist) 178, 189, 194, 195, 196, 200
jinn 185, 186, 201
John the Baptist 160, 162
Joseph 161
Judaism 13, 14, 52, 73, 84, 135, 140, 142,
     143, 145, 146, 147, 149, 150, 151, 152,
     153, 154, 155, 156, 157, 159, 161, 177,
     178, 181, 213

Kabbalah 14, 150, 151, 155
Kabul 198
karma 65, 88, 89, 90, 95, 96, 102, 107,
     110, 115
Kauffman, Stuart 62, 74
kerygmatic 171

Khadijah 180, 182
Kingdom of God 164, 165, 167, 230n. 10
knowledge 4, 18, 42, 43, 51, 62, 64, 88, 89,
     90, 91, 106, 129, 159, 174, 184, 225n. 9,
     232n. 35
Krishna 93, 94, 95

Lao Tzu 127
li 126, 136
liberation 25, 28, 90, 92, 93, 95, 96, 102,
     103, 107, 110, 111, 119, 129
life 3, 5, 6, 10, 12, 14, 15, 16, 17, 18, 23, 24,
     25, 26, 27, 28, 29, 30, 32, 33, 34, 35, 36,
     37, 38, 41, 42, 43, 45, 46, 47, 48, 49, 50,
     51, 53, 54, 55, 60, 67, 70, 71, 72, 76, 79,
     81, 83, 84, 85, 86, 87, 88, 89, 90, 91, 92,
     93, 94, 95, 96, 97, 100, 101, 102, 103,
     106, 107, 108, 109, 110, 111, 112, 113,
     114, 115, 118, 119, 120, 122, 123, 125,
     126, 127, 128, 129, 130, 131, 132, 133,
     134, 135, 137, 140, 141, 144, 145, 146,
     147, 148, 149, 151, 152, 153, 154, 155,
     156, 157, 160, 161, 162, 163, 164, 165,
     166, 167, 168, 169, 170, 171, 172, 173,
     178, 179, 180, 181, 183, 187, 190, 191,
     193, 194, 198, 200, 207, 209, 211, 212,
     213, 214, 215, 217
life-denying 9, 10, 18, 32, 45, 55, 56, 61,
     74, 98, 211
life-giving 7, 10, 11, 17, 35, 36, 42, 54, 61,
     66, 74, 103, 137, 171, 173, 178, 208,
     211, 217
Lord 47, 94, 163, 171, 215
love 6, 7, 8, 9, 10, 16, 50, 72, 75, 106, 111,
     114, 124, 125, 152, 154, 165, 166, 167,
     168, 169, 171, 172, 173, 174, 180, 194,
     208, 210, 214, 215, 216, 227n. 32
Loyola, Ignatius 14, 170
Luke 160, 161, 162, 229n. 1

magic(al) 42, 59, 63, 64, 65, 74, 89, 129,
     130, 212
Mahayana 15, 104, 105, 106, 113, 226n. 16
Maimonides 150
mana 29, 141
martyrs 26
Marx, karl 60
Mary 161 180
Matthew 160, 161

maya 91, 139

meaning(s) 4, 12, 13, 27, 30, 41, 53, 60, 62, 63, 69, 81, 87, 89, 90, 98, 110, 118, 127, 128, 135, 139, 147, 229, 232, 238, 239, 246, 252, 253, 149, 153, 154, 160, 161, 172, 181, 183, 189, 192, 194, 198, 208, 210, 211

Medina 182, 183, 186, 190, 232n. 10

meditation 27, 37, 66, 67, 83, 85, 89, 90, 91, 92, 95, 97, 105, 109, 110, 111, 112, 113, 114, 129, 130, 169, 170, 173, 210, 213, 216

Memphis 44, 45, 46

Mencius 123

Merton, Thomas 169

Middle East 5, 28, 43, 144, 179

Midrash 149

militant 5, 7, 194, 201

miracle 42, 59, 71, 162

Mishnah 149

mission 28, 123, 160, 162, 163, 164, 170, 180, 182, 191, 193, 194, 197

missionary 31, 160

Mo Tzu 124

moira 50, 51

moksha 90, 93, 96

monastic 91, 105, 113, 115

monism 41, 74, 76, 81, 82, 90, 133, 139, 212

monotheism 55, 82, 92, 94, 141, 144, 149, 152, 158, 181, 184

Moses 27, 45, 142, 143, 144, 145, 149, 151, 185, 209, 215

Mother Earth 24, 33, 212

Mother Teresa 17, 170

Mount Olympus 50

Muhammad 11, 180, 181, 182, 183, 184, 185, 187, 188, 189, 190, 191, 192, 193, 195, 201, 209, 215

Mujahideen 198

multicultural 5, 7, 8

mystical 14, 52, 89, 90, 130, 151, 155, 169, 192, 194

myth 24, 26, 27, 32, 38, 43, 45, 46, 47, 48, 50, 51, 59, 68, 69, 70, 102, 221n. 10

natural law 122

nature 6, 18, 24, 25, 26, 27, 29, 30, 31, 32, 34, 35, 36, 41, 43, 45, 47, 55, 57, 61, 62, 64, 65, 66, 67, 68, 69, 70, 71, 72, 74, 75, 82, 84, 118, 132

Nazareth 161, 162

Nehemiah 146

nemesis 51

Neo-Confucianism 126, 134

New Testament 14, 143, 159, 160, 161, 163, 168, 169, 171, 183, 209, 229n. 1

Nichiren Buddhism 71, 105

Nietzsche, Friedrich 60

Nile 44, 45, 46, 47, 48, 54

Nirvana 103, 104, 107, 110, 111, 140, 213

Odyssey 49

om 92

omnipresent 35, 37, 49, 83, 157

order 3, 17, 29, 30, 31, 37, 45, 47, 50, 51, 52, 55, 75, 83, 84, 85, 87, 88, 89, 96, 98, 103, 105, 119, 124, 127, 130, 131, 132, 134, 135, 139, 146, 148, 154, 156, 186, 187, 191, 192, 194, 225n. 9

origin 24, 26, 29, 32, 51, 55, 60, 62, 83, 87, 140, 154, 163, 178

Orthodox Judaism 152

Osiris 46, 47, 48

pagan 66, 147

Pakistan 6, 85, 197, 198, 199

Palestine 141, 144, 146, 147, 149, 152, 157, 158

Pali 101, 102, 104

pantheism 139

pantheon 26, 29, 33, 46, 47, 49, 50, 52, 53, 54, 65, 68, 69, 86

path 7, 14, 94, 106, 107, 109, 128, 179, 181, 186, 189, 190, 193, 195, 196, 207, 209

peace 7, 8, 10, 11, 16, 17, 25, 31, 37, 38, 41, 45, 46, 71, 83, 84, 85, 90, 94, 100, 102, 109, 110, 112, 113, 114, 119, 121, 126, 131, 134, 154, 157, 165, 173, 181, 183, 205, 207, 208, 209, 210, 213, 216, 217, 232n. 1

Pentateuch 142

Peoples of the Book 177, 196, 198

perennial philosophy 212

pharaoh 44, 45, 46, 47, 48, 55, 56, 143

Pharisees 148

philosophy 48, 51, 52, 101, 123, 124, 147, 150, 192, 194, 212
Plato 51, 52, 53
Plotinus 52
pluralistic 4, 5, 7
pneuma 14
polytheism 181, 182, 184, 212
Poseidon 49, 50, 54
postfoundationalism 4
postmodern 4, 7, 35, 43
power 7, 16, 25, 26, 27, 28, 29, 30, 33, 38, 43, 44, 46, 48, 50, 53, 65, 68, 70, 71, 72, 85, 86, 89, 92, 93, 118, 120, 121, 122, 128, 146, 162, 164, 165, 166, 167, 171
predestination 185, 186, 210
prehistoric 24, 142
pre-modern 4, 5
prophet(ic) 11, 85, 141, 145, 146, 162, 171, 173, 180, 181, 183, 185, 190, 191, 192, 193, 194, 195, 200, 201
Protestant 9, 152, 156, 171, 210
providence 186
Pure Land Buddhism 105
purity 8, 71, 91, 97, 107, 109, 115, 129, 170, 187
pyramids 44, 46, 48, 55

quantum 62
quest 3, 7, 10, 11, 15, 16, 34, 38, 41, 44, 53, 61, 79, 81, 85, 89, 100, 106, 113, 115, 118, 119, 122, 129, 134, 135, 151, 181, 209
Quran 11, 177, 181, 183, 184, 185, 186, 187, 188, 189, 190, 191, 192, 193, 194, 195, 197, 200, 201, 213, 232n. 5

rabbi 149, 155, 164
radical 60, 121, 149, 157, 162, 178, 179, 181, 184, 189, 193, 194, 195, 196, 197, 198, 200, 201
Rama 93, 94
Ramadan 188, 189, 200
rational 37, 48, 51, 53, 55, 59, 83, 88, 150
Realists 123, 124
redemption 166, 167
redemptive 9, 27, 61, 172, 211, 214
reductionism 4, 43
reform 47, 96, 140, 146, 152

Reform Judaism 152
reformation 142, 195, 210
reincarnation 66, 102, 110, 115
relativism 4
religion 1, 4, 5, 7, 11, 12, 13, 14, 15, 16, 17, 18, 24, 25, 26, 27, 28, 29, 30, 31, 32, 33, 34, 36, 38, 41, 42, 43, 44, 45, 46, 47, 48, 49, 50, 51, 52, 53, 54, 55, 59, 60, 61, 62, 63, 64, 65, 67, 68, 71, 72, 74, 75, 79, 81, 82, 83, 84, 85, 86, 93, 94, 95, 96, 98, 100, 101, 106, 110, 114, 115, 116, 118, 119, 120, 121, 122, 126, 129, 133, 134, 135, 137, 139, 140, 141, 142, 143, 145, 146, 147, 150, 152, 153, 155, 156, 157, 159, 173, 174, 177, 178, 179, 180, 182, 183, 186
Republic 51
resurgence 1, 25, 59, 178, 179, 193, 199, 209
resurrection 11, 160, 166, 167, 230n. 7
revelation 150, 160, 181, 183, 184, 185, 189, 193, 201
Roman 142, 146, 147, 148, 161, 162, 164
Rome 44
Rosh Hashanah 155
ruach 14
Rumi 194

sacramental 172
Sadducees 148
sage 87, 89, 92, 95, 125, 148, 150, 212
St. Francis 170
Salat 187
samadhi 91, 92, 109
samanas 102
samsara 88, 90, 105, 107, 110, 115
Samson 144
Sangha 14, 105, 111
Sanhedrin 148
Sankara 90
Sanskrit 86, 87, 94, 101, 193
Sarah 141
Satan 185, 196
Saudi Arabia 193, 196, 199
Savior 38, 106, 163
science 38, 48, 61, 62, 132, 134, 154, 195, 211

scripture 4, 7, 8, 36, 71, 83, 89, 97, 101, 102, 148, 150, 209, 213, 225n. 4
Seal of the Prophets 185, 201
sectarian 10, 38, 42, 115, 156, 174, 175, 205
Sephardic 151
Septuagint 147
serenity 10, 16, 37, 41, 71, 81, 84, 89, 97, 101, 112, 114, 116, 119, 134, 135, 173, 208, 216
sexuality 24, 65
Shahadah 187
shaman 27, 33, 73
shariah 187, 190, 191, 192, 193, 195, 197, 198, 200, 201
Shinto 26, 62, 67, 68, 69, 70, 71, 72, 73, 74, 75, 76, 83, 84, 140, 212
shirk 181, 184
Shiva 92, 93, 94, 140
Sikhism 84, 140
simplistic 4, 7
Sinai 143, 144
slavery 45, 143
Socrates 51, 53
solidarity 6, 75
Solomon 142, 145
Son of God 21
Sophocles 51, 55
soul 26, 32, 36, 44, 90, 91, 95, 96, 101, 102, 110, 115, 126, 128, 135, 139, 153, 165, 169, 187, 194, 215, 221n. 14, 226n. 15
sovereign 42, 68, 140, 153, 160, 185, 210, 213
spirit 12, 14, 26, 27, 28, 29, 30, 31, 33, 34, 42, 68, 73, 90, 95, 101, 109, 111, 115, 120, 121, 122, 126, 127, 135, 163, 167, 168, 170, 171, 172, 181
spirituality 1, 7, 9, 10, 11, 14, 15, 16, 17, 35, 36, 38, 42, 62, 64, 109, 112, 114, 115, 118, 163, 166, 168, 169, 170, 171, 172, 173, 175, 210, 213
Starhawk 64, 66, 74
stereotype 12, 63, 75
story 14, 26, 28, 29, 33, 35, 37, 44, 45, 47, 49, 50, 51, 68, 69, 70, 71, 82, 83, 94, 95, 102, 139, 140, 141, 142, 143, 144, 145, 159, 160, 161, 162, 166, 168

Sudan 196, 197, 199
Sufi 14, 194
sunnah 182, 183, 191, 192
Sunni 15, 156, 192, 193, 194, 197, 198, 201
superhuman 13, 25, 33
Surah 184, 185, 186, 188
survival 6, 23, 24, 27, 48, 122
sutra 87
sweat lodge 34
synagogue 148, 149, 151, 155

Taliban 16, 178, 196, 198, 199, 200, 233n. 34
Talmud 149, 150, 151, 155
Tantra 225n. 13
Tao(ism) 68, 74, 76, 79, 83, 105, 119, 121, 122, 127, 128, 129, 130, 131, 132, 133, 134, 135, 140, 213
Tao Te Ching 127, 128, 130, 131
te 125, 126, 128, 129
temple 47, 97, 144, 145, 147, 148, 151, 162
terrorism 7, 12, 13, 197
Thebes 45, 46
theological 4, 96, 106, 149, 156, 168, 173, 193
theology 123, 163, 174, 192, 215
Theravada 15, 104, 105, 113, 225n. 6, 226n. 16
Thich Nhat Hanh 111, 113, 226n. 11, 227n. 32
tolerance 199, 200
Torah 142, 146, 147, 148, 149, 150, 151, 152, 162, 213, 215, 217
Tower of Babel 142, 214
tradition 8–17, 21, 25–33, 35–7, 38, 42, 43, 44, 51, 53–6, 62, 64, 67, 68, 71–3, 75, 76, 79, 82, 83, 85, 86, 89, 92, 93, 94, 97, 98, 104–6, 110–15, 124, 129, 133, 134, 135, 139, 140, 141, 142, 146, 147, 149, 150, 152, 153, 154, 156, 157, 160, 243, 244, 252, 264, 266, 267, 268, 168, 169, 170, 171, 172, 173, 174, 175, 177, 180, 181, 183, 186, 189, 190, 192, 193, 194, 201, 202, 205, 207, 210–14, 216, 226n. 16, 230n. 8, 231n. 18
transition 8, 27, 62, 186, 208, 211
Trinitarian 163
Trinity 11

Tripitaka 83, 102
truth 4–8, 14, 36, 38, 43, 53, 61, 70, 75,
   91, 106, 107, 108, 116, 181, 217

ulama 195
United States 5, 12, 33, 66, 152, 178, 179,
   195, 197, 199
unity 16, 27, 34, 44, 90, 96, 106, 121, 139,
   169, 184, 185, 192, 194
Upanishads 89, 90, 94

Vajrayana Buddhism 105
Varuna 86, 92
Vedanta 90, 91
Vedas 83, 86, 88, 89, 92, 93, 102
via analogia 215
via negativa 4, 215
violence 12, 13, 32, 38, 157, 189, 194, 197
virtue 104, 113, 120
Vishnu 92, 93, 94, 140
vision quest 34

Wahhabism 193
witchcraft 61, 63, 64, 66, 67, 74, 75

Wi-Wei 136
worldview 4, 11, 12, 14, 32, 34, 35, 37, 42,
   45, 46, 54, 65, 73, 76, 98, 100, 155, 156,
   157, 178, 182, 195, 200, 201, 209, 212,
   221n. 8
worship 18, 30, 36, 37, 42, 47, 48, 71, 72,
   73, 82, 85, 86, 87, 92, 93, 96, 97, 116,
   121, 144, 145, 147, 148, 152, 160, 164,
   167, 168, 172, 181, 186, 187, 191, 200,
   210, 216

Yahweh 140, 141, 142, 143, 144, 145,
   146, 153
yin and yang 126, 131, 132
yoga 27, 83, 85, 91, 95, 97, 103,
   129, 210

Zakat 188
zealotry 10, 137, 151
zeitgeist 4, 156
Zen 71, 105, 112
Zeus 48, 49, 50, 54
Zionism 152, 195, 196, 197, 200
Zoroaster 140

CPSIA information can be obtained
at www.ICGtesting.com
Printed in the USA
LVHW010145271222
735859LV00005B/250